Humility and Love:
The Foundation of Orthodox Christian Life

Humility and Love:
The Foundation of Orthodox Christian Life

Saint Sofian of Antim Monastery

Translated by Grig and Ioan Gheorghiu

HOLY CROSS
ORTHODOX PRESS
Brookline, Massachusetts

Published by Holy Cross Orthodox Press
Hellenic College, Inc.
50 Goddard Avenue
Brookline, MA 02445

ISBN: 978-1-960613-15-8 (print)
978-1-960613-17-2 (epub)
978-1-960613-18-9 (audio)

Publisher's Cataloging-in-Publication
(Provided by Cassidy Cataloguing Services, Inc.)
Names: Boghiu, Sofian, 1912-2002, author. | Gheorghiu, Grig, translator. | Gheorghiu, Ioan, translator.
Title: Humility and love : the foundation of Orthodox Christian life / Saint Sofian of Antim Monastery ; translated by Grig and Ioan Gheorghiu.
Other titles: Smerenia şi dragostea, însemnele trăirii ortodoxe. English
Description: [First English edition from the fourth Romanian edition]. | Brookline, Massachusetts : Holy Cross Orthodox Press, [2026] | Translation of: Smerenia şi dragostea, însemnele trăirii ortodoxe (Iasi, Romania : Doxologia Press, 2023).
Identifiers: ISBN: 9781960613158 (paper) | 9781960613172 (epub) | 9781960613189 (audio)
Subjects: LCSH: Orthodox Eastern Church--Doctrines. | Biserica Ortodoxă Română--Doctrines. | Christian life--Orthodox Eastern authors. | Spirituality--Orthodox Eastern Church. | Spiritual life--Orthodox Eastern Church. | Humility--Religious aspects--Orthodox Eastern Church. | Love--Religious aspects--Orthodox Eastern Church. | BISAC: RELIGION / Christianity / Orthodox. | RELIGION / Christian Theology / General.
Classification: LCC: BX320.3 .B6413 2026 | DDC: 281.9--dc23

Born in 1912 in Bessarabia, the future Elder Sofian Boghiu entered monastic life at a young age and went on to become one of the most beloved spiritual fathers of modern Romania. A gifted iconographer, theologian, confessor, and abbot of Antim Monastery in Bucharest, he united deep spiritual wisdom with extraordinary artistic talent, painting and restoring churches throughout Romania and the Middle East. Closely associated with the renowned "Burning Bush" spiritual movement at Antim Monastery, Father Sofian became a guiding presence for generations of Orthodox Christians through his humility, gentleness, and unwavering faith.

In 1958, during the Communist persecution of the Church, he was arrested and sentenced to sixteen years of hard labor for his participation in the "Burning Bush" movement. After more than six years of imprisonment in some of Romania's harshest prisons, he returned to Antim Monastery, where he continued to receive and spiritually guide countless faithful, eventually becoming known as "the Apostle of Bucharest" until his repose in 2002. Revered during his lifetime for his holiness and discernment, Elder Sofian was officially canonized by the Romanian Orthodox Church in 2024 under the title "Venerable Confessor Sofian of Antim Monastery," with the feast day of September 16.

Table of Contents

Foreword 1

Preface 5

Biographical Highlights 9

"Who Do You Say That I Am?" 13

"Let Us Live In Light So That We Can Pass Into Light When We Leave This Life!" 15

The Value of the Soul 17

The Spiritual Portrait of a Vladika 23

Humility Means Life 25

On the Unexpected Hour of Death 50

Words at the Beginning of Lent 55

Encouragement for Prayer 58

Humility: Gateway to the Kingdom 84

Love For Enemies 88

Thoughts on the Sunday of Orthodoxy 93

Icons: Living Signs of Divine Blessings 97

Transformation 102

Spiritual Blindness 113

Discernment 119

"May God Grant that the Entire Country Be a Burning Bush of Prayer!" 154

Thirty Testimonies on Love 161

The Monk Before the Final Judgment 171

"Jesus Christ has Risen for the Joy of the Entire World!" 182

Christ has Ascended! This means that heaven is open to humankind! 185

The Presence of the Holy Spirit in Our Life 187
Letters 190
Prayer to the Lord Jesus Christ, Who Was Transfigured on Mount Tabor 196
Prayer to Saint John the Baptist 197
Testimonials about Father Sofian 198
Photo Section 231

Foreword

All of Elder Sofian's Life was a Light that he Shared with Others![1]

— METROPOLITAN TEOFAN OF MOLDAVIA AND BUKOVINA —

Elder Sofian was an image of love, gentleness, and humility *par excellence*! I could compare him to a candle that consumed itself in order to illuminate others. All of his life was a light that he shared with others. There are three principal aspects through which one can say that Father spread light around himself.

First, he was one of the greatest painters that the Romanian Orthodox Church had. The thousands of hours spent on scaffolding painting churches—in the country or in the Near East—represented his first love, which he served with such dignity and from which he did not distance himself until the final years of his life, when his trembling hand no longer allowed him to paint.

The icon of St. Anthim the Iberian, who was canonized in 1992, was one of the last icons painted by Elder Sofian. We see how, already 82 years old, Elder Sofian still painted so beautifully—not only the icon of St. Anthim but also that of the Romanian saints is painted by him. The church of Dealu Monastery, the church of Radu Vodă, and many other churches bear witness to how close to God Elder Sofian felt when, brush in hand, he sought to paint the face of Christ the Savior, of the Mother of God, and of the saints whom he always loved so much.

Second, the Elder burned and mystically gave off light like a candle, since he served the Holy and Divine Liturgy so often. Maybe you remember how each morning at Antim Monastery you would see him discretely approaching the church, with a group of faithful always waiting to ask him for money, a word of guidance, or to hear their confession. I remember that in the final period of his life, on account of bodily illnesses, he served less frequently, but he would come to the Divine Liturgy and sit next to Fr. Adrian in the Holy Altar. He would take his epitrachelion and sit there, on a chair, while the Hours were being read at the chant

1 Romanian publisher: This *Foreword* represents the transcript of a conference held by Metropolitan Teofan in Bucharest in 2003.

stand. At the beginning of the Divine Liturgy, when the curtain would be drawn and the faithful would see him, there would be a kind of "Ah!" in the church, a kind of discovery, of relief that they saw Elder Sofian there, seated in the Holy Altar. He would not speak, he would not serve, but this was sufficient for the faithful—Father was there!

Lastly, he burned like a candle in the confessional chair. Only God knows how many hundreds and thousands of confessions this man heard! He allocated so many hours a day to these personal relationships with the faithful in Holy Confession! Again, only God knows how many sins this man was burdened with throughout his life. I know one thing: if confession was the heavy cross that he carried his entire life, his dedication to hearing the confessions of the faithful was what damaged his health beyond repair. You will remember how he would stay up late at night, there, on the left side of the Holy Altar, and huge numbers of Christians would come for confession. All the faithful longed to draw closer to Father so that no one would go ahead of them [in line]; they would come so close, two or three meters away, that the Elder would bend over with his ear as close as possible to the mouth of the one confessing, so that no one would hear the penitent's confession. And then, sitting like this, bent over on one side for entire hours, with his back bent, finally, he was beset with that pain that he was not able to heal for the rest of his life. Despite all the treatments he had later on, not much could be done.

We should also recall his years of suffering in prison, where he was imprisoned for taking part in the phenomenon called the "Burning Bush." We should recall his love for Basarabia, the land that offered him to the entire world, and from which he never felt separated. What great joy he had when he would meet monks from Dobrușa, the monastery where he took his monastic vows!

I remember how, in '95-'96, I went with the Elder to Basarabia. We went from Bucharest to Tiraspol in order to find Ilie Ilașcu there, in prison. I remember how happy Elder Sofian was when we entered the Basarabian territory, and how much he felt at home even up to where Ilie Ilașcu was. I cannot forget how he was brimming with joy when he returned to his native land, after a rather long absence. This pilgrimage had the goal of transmitting a message of encouragement from Patriarch Teoctist to brother Ilie Ilașcu. And who could have been more suited to pass on this message, face to face, than Elder Sofian?

And a final word: I mentioned confession. I too would like to give a personal testimony about Elder Sofian in regards to the confessional chair; because I aso had the joy, from the moment I came to Bucharest, in the '90s, up to the hour of his death, even after I left for Craiova, to have him as a spiritual father. This is on the one hand. On the other hand, Patriarch Teoctist assigned us as co-leaders, so to speak, of Antim Monastery until October 2000 when I left for Craiova. Elder Sofian was more involved in liturgical problems, while I was more occupied with the administrative demands of the monastery. You know that, sometimes, when there are two people with responsibilities in the same place, temptations can appear. I want to give this testimony: with Elder Sofian, I never felt a different approach in the administration of Antim Monasteries needs from the economic, human, or spiritual point of view.

And what else can I testify now, a year and a half since my last confession [with him]? When you were confessing, you had the feeling that you were unburdening your soul without holding anything back. You felt that Father lifted all the weight from your soul. He would give you a few instructions, there, at the end, that were very important, but it was almost as if this was not the essential thing. The most important thing was that you felt how he listened to you, you felt how he participated in your pain, you felt how he lifted all the weight that you had on your shoulders and heart. At the moment you got up from the ground, you felt like a totally new person. You felt that you were going home with much power in your soul, that you could begin your life again, that you could carry your cross more easily, as mine was then, as vicar bishop, and later, as Metropolitan of Oltenia. Even when I left for the city of Craiova, I would come to Bucharest quite often and would do all that I could to go to confession with Father. I would return to Craiova each time with much more strength and much more courage, because Father's words would resound in my mind and heart: "Don't give up, Father! Keep going, God is with you! How many difficulties I went through as well..." I gave this personal testimony not for the sake of testimonies. I am certain that, alongside other aspects of the relationship the majority of you had with Elder Sofian, this state of spiritual fulfillment, of perfect peace after a conversation with Father, after he had listened to the fire of your heart, is a defining spiritual state for all those who had the blessing from God to confess to him.

Elder Sofian was born in heaven. That is what the fathers before us would say: "He was born in heaven," he did not die. And we are saddened. We too, those from Antim Monastery, and the members of ASCOR[2] who had him as a spiritual father, and the church painters, and Basarabia. On one hand, we are all saddened, but, in the end, we all rejoice. What Elder Sofian did for us in this earthly world is of immense importance! But what Elder Sofian does there, above, before the Throne of the All-Holy Trinity, both for the bishops that he had as spiritual sons, and for the members of ASCOR, for Basarabians, and for painters, means much more. Because his passing beyond means an increase in the relationship with all those whom he knew, and, I say with certainty, it also means the formation of a relationship with all those who did not know him physically, but begin to discover him now, through spiritual books, recordings, and testimonies left behind. I wish you all well! Remain with God and with Elder Sofian!

2 ASCOR is the Romanian acronym for "Association of Romanian Orthodox Christian Students"

Preface[3]

PROFESSOR VIRGIL CÂNDEA († 2007)

Our separation from Elder Sofian—see, two years have passed since then—gave his disciples and all who had the privilege of enjoying his instructions and the grace that he spread, the occasion for more profound reflections in regard to his providential presence in the spiritual life of Romanians in the twentieth century.

We can give several answers to the question concerning the chief meaning of our meetings with Elder Sofian. Father Archimandrite is part of the uninterrupted line of great Elders of the Romanian Orthodox Church. Displaced to the other side of the Prut [River] in free Romania, in his flight from the occupied area of Moldavia, Elder Sofian brought with him, to the monastic communities in which he spent time, a tradition of monastic life carefully preserved after the occupation of 1812. It was the tradition of Blessed Paisius of Neamț. Elder Sofian was—through teaching and experience—a *paisian*. Coming to Romania, alongside other Basarabian monks, he received refuge and a place of inner fulfillment in the lavras of the same paisian tradition: Căldărușani and Cernica Monasteries. Through his presence and that of his monastic brothers who enjoyed the same shelter, he continued, in these communities in the country of Romanian the spirit of spiritual fulfillment that Blessed Paisius and his beloved disciple Gheorghe [of Cernica] worked for and spread. In these two communities, the Elder encountered and consolidated the teachings of the great Elders of old, from the Holy Hierarch Calinic [of Cernica] to Blessed Antipas Dinescu and his disciples. Strengthened in his work by the teachings of the Philokalic Fathers (renewed by Fr. Stăniloae and the living example of a hesychast of our times who had come right from the inferno of Soviet totalitarianism[4]) and with a spiritual life intensified by his own trials in the Communist prisons, Elder Sofian was, at the same time, the living connection between the best tradition of Romanian monasticism and that of our times. We must also not forget the importance of Father's

3 The preface was composed in 2004 for the third Romanian edition of the book.

4 Namely, Fr. Ioann Kulighin.

connection to the most notable intellectual current of Romanian Orthodoxy in the years immediately following the Second World War: the "Burning Bush" spiritual movement.

Elder Sofian's spiritual perfection called him, in the midst of the most difficult age of spiritual and social life for the Romanian society, to an obedience that few priests would have accepted and fulfilled in such a God-pleasing manner. He was the Abbot of Antim and Plumbuita Monasteries. In Holy Hierarch Anthimos the Iberian's establishment, he took on a mission that surpassed monastic life: that of a guide and spiritual teacher to the faithful of Bucharest, the country's capital being a realm of many Christians who preserved the faith, seekers of true perfection, yet, at the same time, an area assaulted by temptations and heresies, more than any other city in Romania. *Elder Sofian was, par excellence, the Romanian spiritual father of the modern age.* There, at Antim, during the Communist takeover, Father fulfilled the great desire of its holy founder, following and adding to the tradition established by Saint Anthim regarding almsgiving, community life, the ordinances of Orthodox monasticism, and exemplary liturgical practices that were kept at Antim Monastery with more attention and beauty than in any other place in all of Romania. Future reflections and inspired thoughts of those who knew Elder Sofian, who listened to him and lived his teachings, will doubtlessly be added in time, recounting other important actions of his, other accomplishments and characteristics of his personality.

A collection of spiritual teachings contemporary to us—which is proof that Christian thought and life are not only possible, but also alive and active in this epoch which Blessed Paisius, Abbot of Neamț Monastery, named, even three centuries ago, "the terrible times we live in"—the present book is, fittingly, a document of Romanian religious life from the end of the second millennium and the start of the third. It is fitting for the full understanding of these teachings, spoken by Archimandrite Sofian for the souls of young people, to be internalized through references to his spiritual lineage, to his discipleship in the renowned sites of our monastic tradition beyond and on the other side of the Prut, through the testimonies about the Elders of one mind and life with him, from Cernica, Antim, or Plumbuita Monasteries, such as Ioann the Stranger [Kulighin], Daniil (Sandu Tudor), Petroniu [Tanase], Benedict Ghiuș, Felix Dubneac, Damian Stogu, and others.

In the years immediately following the Second World War, especially until the intensification of the Communist persecutions (but also after), there were holy places with an intense liturgical life in Bucharest, with clergy of great valor; there were experienced spiritual fathers who together fulfilled their providential mission of strengthening and guiding the faithful of our Church.

The course of the spiritual life in a Christian community often resembles the opening that a river enters to flow underground, only to spring again to the surface downstream.

The tradition of unceasing prayer and seekers of the path of perfection seemed to have entered a period of drought in our country during the 19th century, following the blossoming of philokalic teachings and monastic life in the golden years of hesychastic renewal under the guidance of Blessed Paisius and his disciples. But the crystal clear, life-giving waters of Tradition were again brought to the light, pure and powerful, during the years in between the two World Wars. They caused the field of Romanian faith to bear fruit when the awakening zeal of Fr. Dumitru Stăniloae and the spiritual fathers of the Carpathian hermitages opened a new well for those thirsty for the water springing up into eternal life, from which he who drinks "shall never thirst again" (John 4:14). In aquifers, during those four decades of official suspicion and repression towards any manifestation of mysticism, these sources of living water were preserved pure through the sacramental relationship between spiritual fathers and their spiritual children, again showing the regenerative power of the Romanian Orthodox Church, which was humiliated, wronged, but undefeated.

The resources of Truth and experience that strengthened Romanian Christianity during its years of trial could be seen, after December 1989, when faced with the ridiculousness of Christian denominations from abroad which sent useless and absurd missions into a country in which the divine Word had been preached two thousand years before by the Holy Apostle Andrew, thus establishing one of the most ancient and powerful Churches. It was seen, similarly, in the increased request and dissemination of spiritual books—banned by the atheistic censure for a long time—of these sources of teaching and Christian living upon which the Romanian culture itself was founded five centuries earlier. It was especially seen in the return to the divine Word of those who may have still been ignorant of His power, as were the young students of this country—not only theologians, but also from all the branches of knowledge, eager for a stable foundation and correct orientation for their life—seekers of the Light that casts out the darkness and confusion of the "terrible times we live in."

The present book, having now reached a third, improved edition, is the fruit of an obedience entrusted by Elder Sofian to a disciple of his, a former president of the ASCOR of Bucharest, in the 1990s, who in the meantime became a hieromonk. The providential purpose of the meeting between Fr. Sofian's skillful guidance and the thirst for truth of the young people in ASCOR is shown in the testimony which ends this volume. In the name of those of one mind and heart with him who entrusted him with the difficult problems of those first years of the Association, with assured intentions and with a disciple's obedience, Tudor (now Fr. Teofan) Popescu asked for answers and solutions from Fr. Sofian, the skilled teacher and image of spiritual life from St. Antim's Monastery, whose words wove the strand of the Paisian tradition with the experience of the "Burning Bush" group of prayer and Christian reflection. These words are not only addressed to young people in monasteries or the world, but also to anyone who is starting out on his spiritual ascent, because, in this area, most of us are barely at the beginning of the road, regardless of age.

Reading these beautiful teachings collected between the covers of this work of the soul, let us remain grateful to Elder Sofian for his teachings, knowing that we can show our gratitude to him especially by fulfilling what he told us with wisdom and love.

Biographical Highlights

Elder Sofian Boghiu (1912-2002)

- **October 7, 1912**—Sergei (Sofian) Boghiu is born in Basarabia, in the village of Cuconeştii-Vechi, on the shore of the Prut River in Bălţi County, to a pious family of peasants with six children.
- **1922-1926**—Attends primary school in his native village.
- **Fall of 1926**—At age fourteen, he enters the Rughi Skete in Soroca county as a novice.
- **1928-1932**—Attends the School of Ecclesial chanters at the Monastery of Dobruşa, Soroca.
- **1932-1940**—He is a student at the Monastic Seminary of Cernica Monastery. From the fifth to the eighth grade, he is the librarian for the Monastery's Seminary. His school colleagues include Father Teoctist Arăpaşu (the future Patriarch of the Romanian Orthodox Church), Gherasim Cristea (the future Bishop of Râmnic), and Grigorie Băbuş (the future director of the Library of the Holy Synod).
- **December 25, 1937**—He receives the monastic tonsure at Dobruşa Monastery, changing his name from Sergei to Sofian.
- **August 6, 1939**—He is ordained a deacon in the cathedral of the town of Bălţi by Metropolitan Tit Simedrea, the Metropolitan of Hotin at the time.
- **June 28-19, 1940**—Shortly before Basarabia is completely occupied by the Soviet Union, Father Sofian, along with a significant part of Dobruşa Monastery's inhabitants, take refuge in Romania and settle at Căldăruşani Monastery, close to Bucharest.
- **Fall 1940**—He enrolls as a student in the Academy of Fine Arts in Bucharest, in the Decorative Art section, and receives a scholarship while residing in the student housing at Antim Monastery. He is assigned to the position of deacon—chanter at the monastery.
- **1941**—He enrolls in the School of Theology in Bucharest.

- **1941-1950**—He holds the position of treasurer and secretary at Antim Monastery. During this time, Elder Sofian was very involved with the work of restoration of the monastery, when the church's old, timber-framed towers were replaced with towers made of reinforced concrete and brick.
- **April 11, 1945**—He is ordained a priest at Antim Monastery in Bucharest on the Sunday of St. John of the Ladder. In the same year, he graduates from the Academy of Fine Art.
- **October 1946**—He defends his thesis at the School of Theology, with a work titled "The Image of the Savior in Iconography."
- **1945-1950**—He participates in the meetings of the "Burning Bush" group at Antim Monastery.
- **Holy and Great Friday, 1947**—He is elevated to the rank of spiritual father.
- **June 15, 1950**—He is named abbot of Antim Monastery.
- **1950**—He is appointed as a technical advisor to the Commission of Ecclesiastical Painting.
- **1950-1951**—He participates in the restoration of the paintings in the church of Antim Monastery, as well as repainting the chapel of Antim Monastery.
- **November 12, 1951**—He is elevated to the rank of archimandrite.
- **1954-1958**—He is abbot of Plumbuita Monastery in Bucharest.
- **June 14, 1958**—He is arrested[5] and then sentenced to 16 years of hard labor, under the accusation of "conspiring against the social order" through the hostile, mystical activity of the "Burning Bush" organization. He will be imprisoned at Jilava, Aiud, Galați, and Salcia-Ostrov.
- **July 29, 1964**—After six years and forty-five days of imprisonment, he is freed following the general amnesty decree.

5 See the *Appendix* at the end of the book for the arrest warrant issued for Elder Sofian.

- **1964-1967**—He is a member of Plumbuita Monastery. He works as a painter for the Biblical Institute's Workshop of Ecclesiastical Painting. During this time, alongside the painter Olga Greceanu, he restores and repaints the exterior, ornamental decoration of the Holy Synod's Palace.

- **1967**—He returns to Antim Monastery, where he will reside until the end of his life. Until 1998, when severe health problems no longer allow him, the Archimandrite patiently forms hundreds of disciples in his confessional chair, rightly being called "the Apostle of Bucharest."

- **During the '70s, '80s, and beginning of the '90s**—He travels repeatedly to Syria and Lebanon to paint various churches.

- **September 14, 2002**—During the Divine Liturgy for the Feast of the Elevation of the Holy Cross, after great suffering, Elder Sofian falls asleep in the Lord. He is then buried at Căldărușani Monastery.

  During his life, he painted, alone or with others, many churches in Romania: Antim, Radu-Vodă, Pipirig (Neamț), Bumbăcari (Bucharest), Saon (Tulcea), Slatina (Suceava), Dealu (Dâmbovița), Agapia Veche, Celic-Dere (Tulcea), Agafton (Botoșani), Ghighiu (Prahova), Dămăroaia (Bucharest), Darvari (Bucharest) etc. He taught painting at the Monastic Seminary of Neamț Monastery and at Curtea de Argeș.

- **February 25, 2021**—The Holy Synod of the Romanian Orthodox Church began the canonization process of some of the great Romanian missionary spiritual fathers who lived during the Communist period, among these Elder Sofian.

- **July 11-12, 2024**— The Holy Synod of the Romanian Orthodox Church, led by His Beatitude Patriarch Daniel, approved the canonization of 16 new Romanian Saints, among whom was Elder Sofian Boghiu. He was given the title "Venerable Confessor Sofian of Antim Monastery" with the feast day of September 16.

- **September 16, 2025**—the official proclamation of St. Sofian's canonization during the first Divine Liturgy commemorating him.

"Who Do You Say That I Am?"[6]

— Mark 8:29; Luke 9:20 —

- When some people do not find an answer to Your question: "Who do you say that I am?", then I, Lord, am glad that I can see You, God-Man and Man-God.
- In poor swaddling clothes, on the straw bed of an obscure manger in Bethlehem, I see You as a man! In the voice of angels, in the Light that envelops Your poor dwelling place, I recognize You as God!
- When You flee to Egypt out of fear of Herod, I see You as a weak human. When, in Egypt, I see the idols of the temples broken on the ground by Your arrival, I see You as God Almighty.
- When, in Nazareth, before God and men, You grow in age and understanding, I see You as a man Who has not yet reached ripe age.
- Yet, when at twelve years old You stand in the middle of the teachers in the Temple, listening to them and asking them questions, I too am amazed together with the scholars, and witness the eternal wisdom hidden in Your humanity.
- You are human when You hunger, You are human when You sleep in the boat. But when You walk on the water, when You command the storms and winds, when You feed the five thousand people with five loaves of bread, I see You as God.
- When You descend into the river and are baptized, when You complain that You do not even have a stone upon which to rest Your head, when You allow Yourself to be arrested and bound, I see You as man, befallen by human weakness.
- However, when heaven opens and from on high God the Father says: "This is My beloved Son in Whom I am well pleased" (Matt. 3:17), when You bring Your executioners to their knees, when the earth

6 Bethlehem, 1970. The text was handed to us by Elder Sofian at the end of the '90s to be published in this book.

trembles under Your feet, when the sun is darkened, not bearing to see Your Crucifixion, then I see You as God.

- When I see You dead on the Cross, I see the man of sorrows. You are human in the sealed tomb.
- When You come out of the tomb without breaking the seals, You are God.
- With these eyes, with this heart, with this faith, I too approach the poor manger in Bethlehem, which was Your crib, O Lord! I bend my knees together with the simple shepherds and the wise magi, and I bow to You my God, Who became man for me and for us all!

"Let Us Live In Light So That We Can Pass Into Light When We Leave This Life!"[7]

When we pray with repentance, we have this peace—
that God is with us • The Lord Jesus Christ never lied to us!

Dear young people full of Christian enthusiasm! Since I've been the way you now see me and know me, I've had a single comfort: God's justice. I never faltered in this illness. Sick for so long, almost eight or nine months, I nonetheless have not felt any spiritual wavering, on the contrary, I have felt a perfect peace, I could say, in God.

When we pray with repentance, we have this peace—that God is with us!

I want to encourage you to strive to acquire this peace. God has this method: when He wants, and when we are also worthy, we have His help permanently. When we begin to pray with repentance, it never seems that our suffering is more difficult than others' and we always have this peace—that God is with us and helps us in any situation, however difficult it may be for each of us. And so, I sincerely encourage you, with all my heart, to trust that God is permanently next to us, and in us, and helps us, and comforts us, and strengthens us! He is present in our life in a way we don't even suspect. God is Spirit and God lives in each Christian heart.

I thank you with all my heart for this effort of yours. It is an effort that spreads very much Christian joy. How much joy this Bethlehem, about which we sing in all our churches and homes, brings! Bethlehem, so near and so far from us, is, in the most delicate moments of people's lives, the source of joy and peace, the source of tenderness in our souls.

The Savior, the Master of the world and the entire Universe, in His humility willed to descend into our human nothingness and our human evil. Because a home in which the Mother of God could give birth would have been found if there had been love! A house could not be found,

7 A talk by Elder Sofian addressed to a group of students of ASCOR Bucharest who had come to sing Christmas Carols for the Elder and who had filled the church of Antim Monastery, at the end of the '90s. Transcription from an audio recording.

and so they chose a manger. From there, from the manger, He blesses us with His presence in the world. He blesses us each time we remember this moment of His birth and have our minds on Him and our hope in Him.

The Lord Jesus Christ never lied to us!

Truly, the Lord Jesus Christ never lied to us! He spoke the truth with divine power and certainty. God, as He promised, never abandons us, and precisely when no one helps us, precisely then is He next to us and helps us, if we pray and if we truly want to be helped by Him.

Forgive me, but I can say that I also have experienced such things in my life. When I had absolutely no human help around me, I felt fully the help of our Savior. And I wish that you have the same help!

At the same time, honor God and respect your life, because this is what God wants from us: to live in Light so that we can pass into Light after we leave this life! Live in Light in this confused world. May God help us all to be able to truly live in peace and good understanding, not only during this festive period, but also during the whole year and all our life. Amen!

THE VALUE OF THE SOUL[8]

The soul remains a great mystery • The soul "is the living imprint of the Holy Trinity in the human nature" • "We can lose everything except our soul, because if we are left with it, then we have not yet lost anything!" • Are we truly attentive to our soul's desire? • We bear within us the icon of God!

FOR WHAT WILL IT PROFIT A MAN IF HE GAINS THE WHOLE WORLD, AND LOSES HIS SOUL? OR WHAT WILL A MAN GIVE IN EXCHANGE FOR HIS SOUL? (MARK 8:36-37)

Brothers and sisters in Christ,

In these few and simple words, but full of deep meaning, the Savior reminds us of the price and incomparable value of our soul.

What is the human soul, however, and why is it so precious in the sight of God, such that nothing in this world is worthy of it?

What is this soul of ours, if Heaven itself rejoices when a lost soul returns to God (Luke 15:7)? What is the human soul, if God Himself took on flesh and sacrificed Himself for its salvation and joy?

The soul remains a great mystery

In order for us to understand what the value of the soul is and what significance it has for our earthly life, it is simplest to compare the corpse of a person who has recently died with the body of a living person. A cadaver also has bones, muscles, nerves and blood; but it doesn't move, feel, speak, or think like a living person.

What is it missing?

It is missing this hidden and unseen power breathed by God Himself into the first human being, a power which puts the body into motion and which we call the soul.

The soul is and will remain in this life a great mystery, hidden temporarily in the human body. It was compared to a heavenly diamond of great price.

8 September 21, 1969. The text was given by Elder Sofian for publication in this book at the end of the 1990s.

If we see the creatures and things of the world through it, everything shines with a beauty that surpasses all the beauties of this world. If we see tombs through the soul, they open and the dead appear as the living. If we see Heaven with the world of intelligible spirits through it, everything is illuminated, and we see the fullness of the Kingdom of life.

All people wish to discover this great mystery and to touch this heavenly diamond. But the soul cannot be seen and it cannot be touched. In vain will we search for it in muscles, in blood, in bones, in nerves, in the brain, in the heart, or in any other particle of matter.

Because, although it exists both in the body and outside the body—just as a song exists on a disc or a thought exists in the mind—the soul, being immaterial, cannot be seen nor touched.

It is a spirit placed by God in man and is the part through which our being relates to the Creator of the entire universe Himself. Because the soul is spirit, just as "God is Spirit" (John 4:24).

The soul "is the living imprint of the Holy Trinity in human nature"

When the first man was made, God said in the counsel of the Holy Trinity: "Let us make man in Our image, according to Our likeness," (Gen. 1:26) and later on we read that "God made man in His own image" (Gen. 1:27). In the beginning of Scripture we also learn that "the Lord God formed man of the dust of the ground, and breathed into his nostrils the breath of life; and man became a human being" (Gen. 2:7).

The soul is, therefore, the image of God in us according to nature, grace, and glory.

According to nature, the human soul is similar to the Father in regard to the mind [*nous*], which is the source of knowledge; it is similar to the Son in regards to the inner word, the beginning of wisdom; and it is similar to the Holy Spirit in regard to free will, which is the root of all good things.

According to grace, the soul is similar to the Son of God, because through the Sacrament of Holy Baptism the soul receives the grace of adoption, it too becoming a son of God by grace.

According to glory, the soul is similar to God Himself through the power of the heavenly light poured upon it, as the Holy Evangelist John says: "Beloved, now we are children of God; and it has not yet been revealed what we will be, but we know that when he is revealed, we shall be like Him, for we shall see Him as He is" (1 John 3:2).

Therefore, he who wants to learn what the soul is should know that it is the great masterpiece of God's counsel. It is the living imprint of the Holy Trinity in human nature.

In the Kingdom of God there is nothing more beautiful, more precious, or more pleasing than seeing the face of God, which the angels also desire to look at. They never grow tired of looking at the divine image as at an unending fountain of beauty and light. Someone said: if the image or face of God showed itself for a single moment in hell, hell would become heaven; but if for even a single moment the face of God no longer showed itself in heaven, it would become hell. We cannot forget that the human soul is created according to the image of the divine face. For this reason, the soul is the most precious treasure in the eyes of God.

In the soul lies all the power, all the worth, and all the value of the human being, precisely because it is made according to the image of God and for an unending likeness to Him.

"We can lose everything except for the soul,
because if this remains, we have not yet lost anything!"

In the soul lies all the superiority of the human being above other creatures, in it is everything that makes man the master of the universe. In the soul lie reason, understanding, and judgment, with whose help man can penetrate the secrets of nature and master it for his use. Through the gift of speech, humans can understand and draw near to one another, and through the gift of creating works of art and through all other spiritual gifts, man raises himself above all other creatures on earth.

In a word, the soul is the altar of the human being, it is the image and seal of God in man. The provenance of the soul is God, and the greatness, value, and nobility of the soul lie exactly in its divine origin.

For the salvation of this soul, God sent His own Son into the world.

For the soul, the Savior suffered on Golgotha and spilled His most precious blood on the Cross.

For the soul, the Lord established His Church on earth.

For the soul, the Kingdom of Heaven exists, with all the goodness of eternal life, which eye has not seen, nor ear has heard, "neither have entered into the heart of man" (1 Cor. 2:9).

Man's soul is, thus, the most precious thing on earth. If we were to put them on a scale, with the entire world on one side—with all its riches,

beauties, and pleasures—and on the other side a single human soul, the scale would tip towards the side of the latter. The Savior Himself says very clearly: "For what shall it profit a man, if he shall gain the whole world, and lose his own soul?" (Mark 8:36)

We can acquire all the riches on earth, we can gain all the glory and admiration of the entire world, we can obtain all the wisdom and knowledge of all the nations and all the sages, but if we have sold our soul to the devil or allowed it to be defiled by sin and to go to hell, we have lost everything. For if we do not attain salvation, everything else does not have any value in the eyes of God.

Or, said differently, we can lose everything except for the soul, because, if this remains, we have not yet lost anything! All things, in one way or another, can be remade, can be regained, other than the soul. We only have one soul, and if we lose it, we lose everything.

But how can we lose our soul? Can it be lost through death, perhaps?

No, because the soul is immortal and lives eternally even after bodily death. What kills the soul is sin, and the danger that threatens it in the next world is hell.

Are we truly attentive to the soul's longings?

If the soul is the most precious part of our being, our primary and greatest care should be for the soul and its salvation. The soul should be the center of gravity of all our preoccupations and efforts.

It is good and natural to take care of the things of the body: food, clothes, shelter, and all other things. But, Holy Scripture instructs us to concern ourselves in the first place with the soul, with its nourishment and salvation: "Is not life more than food and the body more than clothing?...Seek first the kingdom of God and His righteousness, and all these things shall be added unto you," the Savior teaches us (Matt. 6:25, 33). And when He was tempted by the devil, the Lord Christ said: "Man shall not live by bread alone, but by every word that proceedeth out of the mouth of God" (Matt. 4:4). That is, bread is indeed necessary for bodily nourishment, but it is not sufficient, it does not satisfy the entire being of a person. Because man also has a soul, and this soul also needs its own food and drink, which it longs for, and becomes weak, like the body without bread and water, if you do not give it to it.

In one of the Beatitudes, the Savior blesses those who "hunger and thirst after righteousness" (Matt. 5:6). Therefore, there is another kind of hunger than the one for bread, and another kind of thirst than the one for water. The soul hungers and thirsts like a deer for sources of water. It thirsts and longs for truth, goodness, and beauty, like a plant for the light and warmth of the sun. It cannot grow and cannot develop except under the benevolent rays of love and goodwill among people. The soul's thirst is not quenched except with the clear water of tears of repentance and prayer. The soul does not feel well except in the clean air of good deeds and the divine grace found in Church.

For its purification, the soul has the water of Baptism and repentance; for its nourishment and strengthening it has the divine supper of Holy Communion; for its sanctification and perfection in this life it has the Church and its holy servants; and as a reward for its labors on earth, God has prepared for it the joy of paradise in the other world.

But, brothers and sisters in Christ, how do we treat our soul? Have we not dethroned it from the place of great honor in which God placed it within our being? Have we not pushed it to the edge of our everyday preoccupations, cares, and anxieties? Are we truly attentive to its questions, restlessness, needs, and its desire for light, for purity, for beauty and truth?

It remains for each of us to honestly answer how he treats his own soul, for which—you should know this well—he will give an account before God, Who entrusted him with it!

We bear within ourselves the Icon of God!

Usually, we never get tired of the relentless toil and chasing after the things needed for the body's satiety. For such pursuits we find time, money, energy, and a good disposition.

When it comes to the things necessary for the soul, however, thousands of stumbling blocks appear in our path. We do not have time to go to church and not even to merely glance at a page of the Holy Bible. We do not have money to help the needy who need our support, and neither do we have the energy nor the will to fight against the temptations and passions which assault us.

We are alarmed by the smallest signs of bodily illness, and we immediately run to doctors, to medicines, but we have no care for the tremors and sufferings of the soul, wasting away from lack of food and left in disrepair. We are very saddened when we lose a sum of money, a patch of land, a coat, or a good friend, but we are not bothered in the same way when we lose our soul, staining it with the mire of lies, evil, and fornication, of drunkenness and all other soul-killing passions!

But, as much as we neglect, forget, or greatly undermine the soul's needs, that much will our life be more troubled and more unhappy.

So that we do not end up like this, we must reserve at least part of our energy and power, of our time and earnings, of our labor and worry, for our poor soul, for this secret, invisible treasure, hidden by God within our being. We should remember it as often as possible. We must free it as much as possible from the unjust and oppressive slavery to the body and passionate cares.

We should give back its right of primacy, the dignity of ruler and center of our being, our life, and our preoccupations. We should especially guard it from the mire of sins, because the soul is the image of God in us. We bear within ourselves His icon. And when we sin, it is as if we throw God's icon in the mire.

Let us clean our soul through the bath of inner tears of repentance and true confession; let us feed it with the light of beneficial knowledge, with pure feelings of mercy, righteousness, and love which ennoble the heart; let us encourage it with the determined will to do only good, a will that makes one's character strong as steel; let us strengthen it with prayer which connects us with God; let us feed it with the heavenly nourishment of Holy Communion which unites us fully with Christ, our Savior.

Therefore, let us draw near to ourselves, to our soul, as much as possible, and let us urge it to watchfulness and to doing good deeds, whispering these words of holy encouragement to it:

"My soul, my soul, arise. Why do you slumber? The end is nigh and soon you will be troubled. Be vigilant, then, that Christ your God may spare you, for He is everywhere present and fills all things."[9] Amen.

9 Kontakion of Saint Romanos the Melodist, from the Great Canon.

The Spiritual Portrait of a Vladika[10]

Recollections of 1927-1928 about His Eminence Metropolitan Visarion Puiu when he was the Bishop of Bălți-Basarabia, having three counties in his Bishopric: Hotin, Bălți, and Soroca

I met Metropolitan Visarion Puiu for the first time in the spring of 1927, when he was Bishop of Bălți-Basarabia. I was fifteen years old then.[11] Now, I am eighty-five years old. The seventy years separating me from His Eminence did not darken and did not erase anything of his vigorous and amiable portrait from that time. He was nearly fifty at the time.

Tall, spry, energetic, with a penetrating gaze, brown hair and beard, a clear and authoritative voice. He was just as friendly, good, tender, and understanding, close to the poor and lowly, while ruthless with the proud, disorganized, and irreverent, as he was severe and authoritative.

On great feasts, he would find a day in which he would eat with the humble people around him: the coachman, chauffeur, cook, housekeeper, and the two disciples in the bishop's house. When his mother was alive, she too was at these family meals. He slept little, ate little. He would not eat anything at night, but he liked to kindly entertain those invited to dinner. He almost always had guests for dinner, especially people whom he needed for different episcopal problems.

He was a sincere, open man, he did not like compromises or cunning deeds. He was an active man, endowed with an admirable managerial sense. He would travel around his eparchy, on canonical visits, exhorting priests to maintain their churches and cemeteries beautifully, to restore their old churches or to make new ones.

He built a large cathedral in the Metropolitan Center of the town of Bălți, near the town center, that was painted in the meantime. He bought some land at the edge of the town of Bălți, surrounded it with a fence,

10 Xerox copy of a manuscript written in 1997.

11 In 1927, Elder Sofian—at the time a novice at the Rughi (Soroca) skete—was sent on obedience to the city of Bălți to help Bishop Visarion Puiu.

planted a vineyard and orchard, built a palace—the Episcopal Palace; this was designed with a second floor, but only the ground floor was built, since he was sent to Cernăuţi to be the metropolitan. He built a church with the feast day of St. Parascheva in the Palace's courtyard according to the model of Meşterul Manole's church in Curtea de Argeş.

After he left the Diocese of Bălţi to be Metropolitan of Cernăuţi, I could not follow his activity there.

During the Second World War, being delegated as head of the Christian mission in Transnistria, he had a very fruitful activity there too. After returning from Transnistria, he went abroad to France, where, similarly, I do not know what he did or where he finished his tumultuous, and at the same time creative, life, at the age of eighty-five.

Lord, give rest among the righteous to Your departed servant, Visarion the Metropolitan.

Humility Means Life[12]

The most powerful weapon against the devil • What is humility? • "The closer the saints drew to God, the more sinful they saw themselves" • "Jesus Christ remains the true model of humility forever, for eternity" • False humility • Let us no longer indulge in shameful thoughts • An attentive observation of our soul is very beneficial for us • Despair not! • "We live in a very dangerous age, and, therefore, especially now we need to be strong, to be humble!" • The most humble human being

Good evening! We are happy that on this beautiful day in which we celebrate the Annunciation, we have Archimandrite Sofian Boghiu, Staretz of Antim Monastery, in our midst. The young people of ASCOR and those from the League of Students earnestly asked him to speak to us during this fasting period before the Resurrection, and we thank Father for accepting our invitation. Father chose to speak to us this evening about humility. Father Sofian, we are listening to you!

Elder Sofian: I am glad that what I will tell you this evening is under the patronage of the Savior and the Mother of God, on this day of the Annunciation of God's Incarnation in the world. Both the Savior and the Mother of God were and always are humble. The divinity of Jesus Christ descends to earth from the glory of the Holy Trinity in a human body, and the most humble nature on earth is chosen for this work: the Mother of God. Thus, the beginning of the world's reconciliation with God, through the Incarnation of the Lord Jesus Christ, takes place.

As it was announced, I'd like to speak to you, with the help of God, about the highest Christian virtue: humility. This is very good and necessary both for the society in which we live and for each person individually so that we can be received into the Kingdom of God. Without humility, the Holy Fathers tell us, one cannot reach Heaven, the Kingdom of eternal life.

For this subject, I consulted Saint John Climacus and Saint Dorotheus of Gaza from the ninth volume of the *Philokalia*.[13]

12 Conference held in the College of Law Auditorium in Bucharest on March 25, 1999.

13 ***Translator's note***: Fr. Dumitru Stăniloae's twelve volume translation of the Greek ***Philokalia*** into Romanian was a monumental effort that began in 1947 and ended in 1992 (the year of his

The most powerful weapon against the devil

Abba Anthony the Great once said: "I saw all the snares of the evil one strewn across the earth and groaning, I said: who can pass through these? And I heard a voice telling me: humble-mindedness!" Such snares sown on the earth that St. Anthony the Great saw are also spread today for people by the enemy, the devil, to confuse them on their path to God, to salvation.

In response to the question St. Anthony posed himself, why did Christ the Savior not recommend prayer, fasting, almsgiving, faith, or other good works, but rather recommended humility? Because all other good works are precious and beneficial for us Christians, but the most powerful weapon against the snares of the devil is humility. Just as pride is the most cunning weapon of the devil against us. And, O Lord, how much pride there is on earth today!

We very rarely find people who are truly humble. True humility, say the Holy Fathers, is the sole virtue that cannot be infected or darkened by the devil. Why? Because it is full of heavenly grace.

The enemy, the devil, the father of lies and pride, meddles in all good deeds and deforms them. Does someone want to fast? The enemy whispers in his ear that if he fasts, he will lose weight, will not be able to work, and will not be able to study. And he robs him of his fasting. Does someone want to pray? The devil scatters his mind, he sends impure images or sleepiness and tiredness, and in this way robs him of his prayer. Does someone want to give alms? The devil sends him fear of becoming poor, he brings stinginess and hatred of the poor and in the same way, he is tricked by the devil, by this father of lies, who robs him of all his good works.

---

death), resulting in an expanded edition of the original Greek manuscript that includes Sts. John Climacus and Dorotheus of Gaza in volume 9, St. Isaac the Syrian in volume 10, Sts. Barsanuphius and John in volume 11, and St. Isaiah the Solitary in volume 12. Not only did Fr. Stăniloae include more texts in his translation, but he also added footnote commentary that clearly reflect his personal experience of Christ as Hypostasis—Person acquired in the Communist prisons of Romania, in which he was imprisoned for his participation in the Burning Bush movement at Antim Monastery, Bucharest alongside Elder Sofian and other notable contemporary Romanian Elders such as Fr. Roman Braga and Fr. Arsenie Papacioc.

What is humility?

Humility, however, with the help of the Good God ruins all of Satan's snares. Humility and love are powerful because they originate from the very person of Christ the Savior, Who exhorts us: *Learn from Me for I am gentle and lowly of heart and you will find rest for your souls* (Matt. 11:29). God—our peace—is Himself love full of humility, Who protects His creation from the devil, the mortal enemy of man—this is how the Savior Himself calls him, the devil being the murderer of humankind from the beginning (John 8:44). Brethren, blessed is the one who has humility. Humility does not get angry, nor can it anger anyone. For what is worse than being angry and angering others? Humility does not gossip, it does not condemn anyone, it does not despise anyone. The humble person does not even despise his colleague in his mind. And if he sees him making a mistake or having one or more defects, he tells him honestly, in private, with care to not offend or embarrass him; in this way, he seeks to correct and help him truly. This is humble-mindedness. Humility is truly great and has the power to attract the grace of God to the soul.

How much turmoil there is in the world because of a lack of this humility, of this divine virtue!

Nothing, however, can defeat humility. Anything upsetting that happens to a humble person, he immediately judges and blames himself. He cannot bear someone else being blamed because of him; he cannot bear guilt being put on someone else. In such a case, he takes responsibility for it. In this way, he passes through life untroubled, without getting upset, and with complete rest.

There are two kinds of humility, as well as two kinds of pride. The first kind of pride is when someone disdains his neighbor, considers him good-for-nothing, and sees himself above him. If he does not come to his senses quickly and does not struggle to escape such a passion, the second kind of pride will slowly but surely come. In this case, he puffs himself up, resists God, and attributes his good deeds to himself, not to God, Who tells us: *Without Me, you can do nothing* (John 15:5).

Similarly, there are two kinds of humility. The first kind of humility consists in considering your neighbor wiser than yourself and putting him above yourself in everything. It means considering yourself lower than all. How difficult this is: to renounce our conceit, our pride, and to humble ourselves with all of our heart! It is very difficult, but very precious before God.

The second form of humility consists in attributing all of our success to God. This is the perfect humility of the saints. It is born in the soul naturally through the fulfillment of the divine commandments.

"The more the saints draw near to God, the more sinful they see themselves"

In the first volume of the *Philokalia* we are told that God is hidden in the fulfillment of the commandments.[14] Similarly, in the nine beatitudes, we also read this saying: *Blessed are the pure in heart for they shall see God* (Matt. 5:8).

The same thing happens to a humble person as to a tree. When trees bear much fruit, the fruits bend their branches and pull them down, but the tree that cannot bear fruit grows taller and stands upright. It is the same with the soul: when it humbles itself, it bears fruit. The more fruit it bears, the more it humbles itself.

Therefore, the more the saints draw near to God, the more sinful they see themselves. We hear this from Abraham. When he saw the Lord, he called himself *dust and ashes* (Gen 18:27). The Prophet Isaiah, when he was called to his prophetic mission, exclaimed: *Woe is me! for I am undone; because I am a man of unclean lips, and I dwell in the midst of a people of unclean lips* (Isa. 6:5). Look at the humility of the saints, at how holy their hearts were! Even when they were sent by God to help people, the truly humble ones did not obey, fleeing the opportunity to be praised. Thus did Moses ask God when he was called to lead his people out of slavery in Egypt, to send someone stronger: *O my Lord, I am not eloquent, neither heretofore, nor since thou hast spoken unto thy servant: but I am slow of speech, and of a slow tongue* (Ex. 4:10). The Prophet Jeremiah said: *Ah, Lord God! behold, I cannot speak: for I am a child* (Jer. 1:6). And, simply put, each of the saints had attained this humility as a result of fulfilling the divine commandments.

14 See Mark the Ascetic, "On the Spiritual Law: Two Hundred Texts" in ***The Philokalia: The Complete Text Vol. 1***. (London: Faber and Faber, 1979), 123: 190. The Lord is hidden in His own commandments, and He is to be found there in the measure that He is sought."

No one can put into words how this humility is born in the soul if one does not find out through experience and deeds. It must be lived. Truly humble yourself at the right moment, and in this way, you acquire this virtue. You cannot attain humility only from hearing or from the pages of religious literature. If we stop at reading spiritual books only and do not try to live what we read, we still remain empty, poor, proud, and ignorant.

When Abba Agathon in the *Sayings of the Desert Fathers* was about to die, lying on his deathbed, the brothers asked him: "Are you also afraid, Father?" And he said: "Until now I did all that I could to fulfill God's commandments, but I am a man. How can I know if my deeds were pleasing to God?...For God's judgment is one thing, and man's judgment is another."[15]

Look how St. Agathon opened our eyes to understand something about the mystery of humility.

On another occasion, Abba Sisoes told a brother: "It is no great thing to be with God in your thoughts, but it is a great thing to see yourself inferior to all creatures. It is this, coupled with hard work, that leads to humility."[16]

Whoever fulfills all these instructions experiences this great mystery, the mystery of humility, which is a divine virtue and is incomprehensible.

"Jesus Christ remains the true model of humility for all times, for eternity"

In closing, I will add this clarification: the Holy Fathers unanimously agree that our Lord Jesus Christ is the model of humility. This is shown to us by the unique act, in all the universe, of His Incarnation. Descending from divine glory to dwell among men, choosing an earthly life full of humiliation, and culminating with death on the Cross, Jesus Christ remains the true model of humility for all times, for eternity.

Now, 2000 years after His Incarnation, Christ the Savior, present in Heaven and on earth, continues to be loved but also mocked, cursed, and denied. His Mother, the Holy Virgin Mary, similarly continues to be mocked and denied. Think of the other denominations, how much they boycott, how much they humiliate the Mother of God, this saint of saints, this Holy Virgin who surpassed the angels in purity; as it is said in

15 Agathon, "Saying 29," p. 24-25.

16 Sisoes, "Saying 13," p. 214.

prayer: "more honorable than the Cherubim and more glorious beyond compare than the Seraphim"—we sing this to the Mother of God. Her enemies mock her and bring different kinds of blasphemies against her. But the Mother of God, being good and humble, forgives them and waits for them to return to the good path!

In His holy humility full of love, our Lord Jesus Christ forgives us, bears with us, and continues to love us, just as he also forgave His enemies when He was on the Cross. Let us ask Him, from the depths of our hearts, to extinguish the evil and pride in our souls and to light within us the candle of His holy humility full of divine love. That is all. As for the rest, it is left to each of us—to you, too, men and women, male and female students—to live this heavenly virtue of humility. This pleases God more than anything else. May God and His Holy Mother help us!

We thank Elder Sofian. Next, in the second part of this meeting, we invite you to ask Father questions. The first question: the fact that today, in Romania, nearly everything goes badly, is this due to our lack of humility?

I am convinced of this! If those upon whom the well-being of our country depends thought more sincerely and with more decency, many things could change in Romania. But the correction of things does not depend only on them. There must be a collaboration, a communal effort. Usually, those who lead are well off, while others suffer. When I left Antim Monastery to come here, about ten poor people stopped me, both older ones and children, asking me for money for bread. This is how we have become—with our country's plains full of wheat, and the same in Moldova, and we don't have bread!

If we do not have bread, let us have faith and humility before God, and let us ask for our daily bread—this, in the first place, is within everyone's understanding: daily bread; but above all, it is also the bread of Communion, the bread of the Holy Eucharist, that is, the Body and Blood of the Lord Jesus Christ. This is nourishment; this is the bread for our being and existence.

How many of those who are here have confessed, and how many commune? Some can only commune rarely because of certain hidden crimes, because of certain secret sins, which in the end scream—abortions! Those who murder innocent and defenseless beings cannot commune immediately because through this sin, they have defiled their body, which is the temple of the Holy Spirit.

And, therefore, the answer to the first question is that humility, love, and sincerity are very useful for correcting our lives and Romanian society in general.

False humility

Please tell us about false humility.

Here at our monastery, there is someone who does some prostrations—when he is in very good spirits—and, if you press him a bit more, he says: "Forgive me, Father, for making a gesture of byzantine humility," that is, a gesture of false humility. There are some who mimic humility: they are quiet, courteous, and respectful, but they attack you behind your back. They speak badly of you, they slander you, and the evil hidden in their heart casts out the presence of the Savior, Who says: *Learn from Me, for I am gentle and lowly in heart* (Matt. 11:29). We are talking here about inner humility, which is full of sincerity and purity. This humility, only with the lips, does not have any value—rather, it debases the virtue of humility.

In our days, does being humble not equate to letting yourself be trampled upon? What then remains of our Christian dignity? What should we do in order not to confuse these things?

I know there is a widespread belief that humility is useless humiliation. However, for the One Who humbled Himself on the Cross, with hands and feet pierced by nails and a spear plunged into his side, true, divine humility helped Him rise from the dead.

A small act of humility (just as we too are small), of decency, seriousness—is sincerity. There are also honest people around us, humble people, wise people, who do not look at the lowliness of humility, but at its truth. Truth creates. Humility is a great spiritual dignity. You all know, without me giving you details, that a proud person, full of himself, conceited, beats his chest with his fists, but others do not exist for him. He does not accept your opinion; I am stupid, but he is very smart. You do not have such people close to your heart, or so I believe. There are such kinds of people who overvalue themselves in families, universities, and all institutions. But there are also people who respond honestly and humbly in any circumstance. Whom do you choose? I think you choose a person with decency. You trust him, he is serious, and all that he produces is valuable. There are nations—for example, the German people—who make certain pleasing things that are always praised because they put honesty and diligence in them, not laziness; and we value them because they are serious people with honest souls.

Such is man: when he is humble, he is both sincere and conscientious, and whatever he does endures; while proud people's work is also superficial, done in haste, without worth or seriousness. They do not believe in anything, they do not believe in God, or, even if they do believe, they worship formally. A humble person is one who stays in touch with God through prayer. And God, because He is humble and full of love, inspires the humble person to be as fulfilled as possible in everything. It is left, however, for each person to experiment with this in his own life.

Holy Scripture and the Holy Fathers say that the Holy Spirit prays in us when we pray. How should we understand this?

We should understand it as it is written. In each one of us, from baptism, is the Kingdom of God dwelling in our spiritual heart. The Holy Apostle Paul asks us, as if it is something each one of us should know very well: *Do you not know that you are the temple of God and that the Spirit of God is within you?* (1 Cor. 3:16) That is, the Holy Spirit is within us. Not only Him, but also the entire Holy Trinity, all of the Kingdom of God is within us. There, a great inner liturgy is served. The outer liturgy is an imitation of the inner one and the divine one in the heavens. Thus, the Holy Spirit in us prays and urges us to pray.

Oh, if only we understood this cry and impulse, this urging of the Holy Spirit within us! How much He calls us, how much He urges us, how much He strengthens us! We must pray and keep our connection with the God of our fathers! Thus, the Holy Spirit prays in us and *for us with groanings that cannot be uttered*, as the Apostle of the nations says (Rom. 8:26).

Theoretically, we know that it is beneficial for us to be humble. What can we do to feel this?

This is a very difficult and necessary problem. The Desert Fathers tell us that humility is divine and can only be acquired through deeds—by living the commandments, by fulfilling them.

If we want to be humble, we should keep the Christian statutes. When you see the New Testament at home, read the Savior's Sermon on the Mount, which is found in chapters 5,6, and 7 in the Gospel of Matthew. There it talks about humility, it talks about fasting, it talks about generosity, giving, it talks about keeping the body pure, this temple of the Holy Spirit in us. Many, beginning in their youth, pervert their body—dear young people and elders—they pervert their body and have this response to their parents or friends: "Let me live my life!" What is life for them? Parties, fornication, luxury, and faithlessness. They do not need God.

I told you what conditions are required for you to be humble, but it depends on each one of us to fulfill them. The elder in the *Sayings of the Desert Fathers* says: bodily labors count very much for acquiring humility. That is, fasting, prostrations, asceticism for the soul and body, guarding the eyes so as to not see the vanities of life, guarding the mouth so as to not say bad words—*set a watch, O Lord, before my mouth, and a door of enclosure about my lips*—as we chant in the evening [vespers] service. Brothers and sisters in Christ, empty your heart of all that is evil—we realize on our own what is evil in us—and you will acquire peace of soul and rest in the Lord Jesus Christ! You will acquire humility, with the help of divine grace, with the help of spiritual and bodily asceticism!

Let us no longer indulge in shameful thoughts!

Saint Silouan the Athonite tells us that we are not humble and, therefore, we torment ourselves and those around us. Please comment on this idea.

Saint Silouan wrote a book widely circulated in the Christian world. When I read it, I felt illuminated. In this book, we find the very essence of the goal of life: to live in the Spirit of God. As he says, if we live this humility and love and goodness that the Savior calls us to, then we—each one of us—are fulfilled, full of life, full of good desires; we have the energy to work, and we have personal relationships with other people based on love.

If we do not follow the path of God, we act like enemies to one another. In our families, there are people who have not talked to one another for twenty or thirty years, even though they have the same mother and father. There are people who have not confessed or communed for many, many years. It is not possible for humility or good deeds to bear fruit in such

earthen vessels tarnished by every sin. Our body—this earthen vessel—must first be cleansed of passions.

This is how we are. We do anything in life, even sacrilege, for this clay of ours. We do everything so that this earthen vessel, which one day might fail in some way, may be well-kept. And this extraordinary, well-crafted device, created by God, this unique machinery—above any sophisticated machinery in the world—extinguishes, melts, and then rats and snakes and all the beasts of the earth assail it to feed themselves with what we, with the price of our life, gathered and put in this house of clay, in this human body.

Brothers and sisters in Christ, the human body is not for defilement, because it bears within it the grace of God, it bears the Holy Trinity. This body that we bear all of our life, on every road, will be resurrected with our soul at the Universal Judgment; they will have a life in eternity together. So, then the body must not be despised; it needs asceticism, but it also needs to be cared for, to be clean, to be healthy.

We should pass this earthly life in this way, caring for both body and soul, but the body should be secondary. When we die, the body will remain in the ground. The soul will have priority, it will be judged by God first, so that, at the end of time, at the Final Judgement, the body will also be judged together with the soul, at that time receiving the response and reward for all of our lives and for the consequences of all our actions.

Are scattered thoughts a sign of pride? Does the humble person ever have scattered thoughts?

The humble person also has scattered thoughts, according to what St. Agathon says: "I too am a man." We too are human and our thoughts wander. The devil contributes very much to this scattering. The devil has a single thought, extraordinarily important for him: not to let us pray. All of his work is to sever this connection between us and God. Then, he is satisfied, and that is why he pushes us toward scattered thoughts.

The humble person, who permanently has the Spirit of God within himself, without a doubt, when he feels estranged from God, immediately realizes it, immediately rebukes himself in his conscience, wherever he may be, and asks God and the Mother of God for help to banish this cloud of thoughts from his heart and his life. He, too, has thoughts, like any human being, but he quickly takes measures to free himself from them. While in the case of a proud person, this is his bread and butter: passionate thoughts, different kinds of images, and especially images from films on television—those films after midnight.

I do not have a TV, nor will I ever have one. I do not want such a thing, and I do not have time to watch television. But many people complain, not only the elderly but also young people revolt against these impure thoughts, against these wicked, sinful images that the television brings into their spiritual life. And they do not forget them. An impure thought sticks to their mind, and they can no longer escape it. It seems as if they have forgotten it, but when they pray, even when they are in church, in the middle of the Divine Liturgy, this dirty image comes to them, staining and defiling them within.

The humble person prays that God delivers him from this fragmentation, this estrangement from the Heavenly Father. The proud person indulges in these kinds of things. My advice is for him to stop indulging in such shameful thoughts. I tell him: "Dear young student, who have such impure thoughts and delight in these erotic films, as if you are glued to them, these images are not reality; they are a deception; they bring much harm to your soul. Think about it!" It is good for him to distance himself from such sights that defile him and to think that, after marriage, which is done with the blessing of God, a man and woman will live all of their life together.

However, if human joy consisted only in this bodily connection, there would not be so many divorces in the world, so many break-ups, and even crimes among young people who are married. Precisely because they put this physical side first, they reached the point of divorce in many cases. Where is the happiness after which you ran your whole life, up until marriage? Where is that which was told to you in films, showing you only pleasing things, beautiful on the outside? They were lies. True life is when you get married, when you have children, when you pray, when you teach your children to pray, to fast as well, to be honest, sincere, and friendly with others. This is what the world needs today, this sincere friendliness and sincere love, next to the lies and vanity that overwhelm us.

How can we be freed of bad thoughts?

With your own personal effort, that is, by banishing them. How do you banish them? You open a book or a photo album, look at an object,

begin to think about it, and cut the sinful thought. If you cannot do it so easily, then you must repent more: "Lord, I stand before You Who know all things and see me as I am. Help me, Lord, to banish this cloud of thoughts from my life!" and then something happens. But you must be full of contrition and determination to shake off and cleanse yourself of these wretched thoughts.

An attentive observation of our soul is very beneficial to us

How can humility be practiced in marriage?

Very easily. In the first place, the husband and wife should be honest with one other, not offend one another, and agree about raising children. Sometimes, it happens that in certain families, the father loves his children in a certain way, fulfilling all their desires, and they become rude. The mother tries to teach them to pray, fast, and not say shameful words. The child listens, is very intelligent and attentive, and perceives and receives his surroundings, but this discord between the mother and father is a disaster for him.

Therefore, humility in marriage in the first place means courtesy and mutual respect between husband and wife; it means a battle against pride. This must be transmitted in the family and, if possible, not only to children. Children are easily influenced—what they see at home, they do in their life.

However, other close relatives—grandchildren, great-grandchildren, brothers, and sisters-in-law—also need this heavenly virtue, this humility, which means, among other things, courtesy towards others. You should not say something that will humiliate or embarrass the other person, but you should try to help him truly. If you tell him something sincerely and with love, he feels it, hears you, and respects you. If you talk to him like a teacher, he begrudgingly accepts it but does not respect what you say. Therefore, sincerity and courtesy are the first virtues that strengthen and sustain the virtue of humility in a marriage.

Saint Silouan the Athonite urges us to reach the humility of Christ. What is this humility of Christ?

Christ the Savior tells us: *Learn from Me, for I am meek and lowly of heart: and ye shall find rest unto your souls* (Matt. 11:29). His heart, of God incarnate, is humble. He recommends this humility of heart to us, too. Because there is a humility of the mind that is mixed with pride. Humility of heart is the true one. The spiritual heart is the spiritual center of our existence. There needs to be humility in it, as there was in the Lord Jesus Christ's.

Some of the Holy Fathers say discernment is the pinnacle of virtues. This is also because humility, when understood incorrectly, can transform itself into a complete lack of a correct attitude. What can you tell us about this?

Saint Silouan the Athonite instructs us to become familiar with this idea of discernment that we find in the Holy Fathers in the *Sayings of the Desert Fathers* and the *Philokalia*. Discernment or balance in our life means going on a divine road, the middle road. We must always have this balance of life in front of us. Because there are attacks from the left or the right. Someone who is pious and desires to do the will of God and fulfill the divine commandments occupies himself with fasting, prayer, almsgiving, and a strict life, which is very good. But he must go on a balanced path! Because there are some who fast very strictly, even a total fast; and he works in a toxic environment and, for example, does not eat oil now during Great Lent. This human vehicle—this earthen vessel, as the Holy Apostle Paul calls it (2 Cor. 4:7)—also needs material for its maintenance.

If we are too harsh on our body, we get sick, we ask the doctor for help, and he puts us on a diet. Because of such an illness that someone who fasts exaggeratedly has, he is obligated to eat meat and other non-lenten foods. This is because he exaggerated instead of fasting more harshly two days a week, on Wednesday and Friday, and the rest of the week fasting normally, in moderation. And then, instead of keeping the whole fast, he eats non-lenten foods on Good Friday. This signifies a lack of discernment, a twisted understanding of the spiritual life.

Or regarding prayer, there are people who pray very much. I don't know how many akathists they say in the course of a day; however, sometimes they forget what akathists they have read. And they say "Our Father," and at some point, they say it again. They forget that they already said it. That is how scattered their mind is. This is not discernment! Discernment is this balance, this permanent observation of our soul; it means controlling ourselves, keeping a steady hand on ourselves. When we stray, we must immediately seek to return to the good path of discernment, on which the

Philokalic Fathers guide us. Having spiritual authority and experience, they said that they knew great fasters who, not having spiritual examples, fasted until they could no longer live because of illness. They saw men of prayer with very scattered minds who gained no benefit from their many prayers. They saw merciful men who gave away all their possessions to the poor, yet after that, they became proud and lost everything. And they also add that the greatest virtue is discernment, balance in life, each day of our life.

Can Christian nationalism be accused of a lack of humility?

If it is sincere, no. Because we are indebted to love our neighbor. Our neighbor, the Savior says, is anyone, even an enemy; but our neighbor is first of all my brother, my sister by blood. If I love my relatives, I also love my people, my nation. And then, if I truly love my nation, my country—without passion—I can call myself a nationalist or patriot. If this affirmation is sincere, then humility should not be lacking.

At Voronet [Monastery]—I believe all of you have been there—a wall from top to bottom depicts the Last Judgment. And there, among other things, beneath all these elements of the Judgement is also the resurrection of the nations, the nations coming to the Judgement of God. They come grouped together: Jews, Turks, and others all come to the Judgement by nation.

At that time, we will ask ourselves: if a person of my nation, being a monk, craftsman, or politician, did some good deeds, why was I not able to? The same conditions were in place for me. Therefore, this grouping of nations will also be considered at the Final Judgment, even if the Judgment will be for each person individually. Each of us will be judged throughout history in this context of the nation. The Romanian nation has very many saints; we also have very honest people of good faith. However, we also have criminals. Each will receive a response and reward based on how he lived his earthly life.

Does the Pope of Rome, believing himself to be infallible, have humility?

To say that someone never errs, humanly speaking, is a lie. I am not the one who says this, but St. John the Evangelist: *If we say that we have no sin, we deceive ourselves, and the truth is not in us* (1 John 1:8). We are sinners, we make mistakes, but we also have the possibility to correct ourselves.

If the Holy Father—as he is called—does not make mistakes, may God bless him and help him not to err, to be truly infallible, that is, without error. However, from what we know, only the Savior was without error, without sin. He was fully human, like each of us, however he did not sin. *Which of you convicts Me of sin?* (John 8:46), says Christ the Lord. The Savior had many enemies who could point their fingers at Him, but they could not find any sin in Him. He was truly infallible.

Despair not!

Father Archimandrite, please comment on the words St. Silouan heard: "Keep thy mind in hell, and despair not."

I don't quite know how to answer this. What does it mean to keep your mind in hell and not despair? I didn't find this expression in the Holy Fathers except in St. Silouan the Athonite. For me, I explained it to myself like this: in this life, hell is often in each of our hearts—when we have scandals in our family or at work, our life resembles hell. If you are in such an atmosphere, in such a situation, do not despair! God is there as well; God can raise you out of such a hell. If we do not despair, if we do not get discouraged by our human weaknesses, and if we have—through prayer—a lasting and permanent connection with God, we can be saved.

But you can also be saved without analyzing this problem, this question. You can be saved. Be truly humble, and you will acquire love; have humble love, and I assure you that you will be saved. I also believe this for myself.

How did you practice humility in the hell of the Communist prisons?

In the Communist prisons, where I spent a number of years, all who were in the cell with me prayed, repented, made up for their sins, and regretted them; they were on this road of repentance. They were humble, honest, and led a Christian life. I tell you honestly that many times, I felt better in prison than outside.

I have been in a monastery from a young age and here I had all that I needed for physical and spiritual life. It was somewhat the same situation in prison—we had what was strictly necessary in order to pass from one day to another. Life there was preoccupied with spiritual things. One would learn texts from Holy Scripture by heart, at a time when you were not allowed to enter prison with a scrap of paper or the tip of a pencil. On

the sole of a boot, greased with soap suds, one would write with a tool that was stolen from outside, once when we were taken out to clean air. And in this way, one would write a passage from the Gospel of St. Matthew, a passage from the Gospel of St. John, from the Epistles of St. James. And how were these passages learned? Knock, knock, knock with Morse code through the walls. Some older prisoners began their time in prison when Bibles were allowed in, and they learned these passages from them. They learned these holy things and transmitted them through sound, through Morse code through walls—people were able to learn them in this way. They would write a short text learned by heart after each of them had inscribed it on the tablet of his heart and memory. And so, they learned these holy texts with such meager means!

There was a Christian atmosphere in prison. All of the insults from the guards were blows aimed at purifying us of pride. You were humble by necessity, but we are called to be humble by our free will. If we do not humble ourselves by our free will, others humble us from outside, they insult us and say all kinds of harsh words to us. And so, there was a humble atmosphere in prison. Humble by necessity, but also by choice, because in the difficulties there, nearly everyone felt the peace of Christ alive in his heart.

Referring not only to the situation in prison, what is the difference between being humble and being humiliated?

One helps the other. If, because of pride, we don't like to be humiliated, we suffer, because we don't accept the humiliation. For someone to call me stupid and many other things, and for me to not react or defend myself! However, only when we accept this humiliation from the outside do we attain humility. If you do not accept it, you suffer.

There is a connection between humiliation and humility, because through humiliation comes humility, if the humiliation is accepted from within. The Savior was humiliated—He was humiliated by people. But He was also humble in His divinity, the source of His humility and love. If humiliation is not accepted, a revolt appears within ourselves. If humiliation is accepted, it becomes humility, and then it is united with prayer, and you pray for your enemy who humiliated you. If you reach this state, you have humility, and you bear it before God.

Father, how can we renounce intellectual pride?

Intellectual pride is a kind of madness! Because it seems that everyone revolves around you, that you are the pillar of light for all of humanity, both past and future. This is pride of the highest level. It is very foolish because there have always been people more learned than me, more skilled than me, more beautiful than me, wiser than me—many in the past, but also in the present and they will appear in the future as well. Such that to make myself the center of intelligence, the center of centers, is a lack of decency in the first place. And it is good for such a person to come to his senses. Maybe he doesn't need a doctor, but it's good for him to fast, to pray to God, to read some spiritual things, to realize what planet he is on. And, if he is sincere at the same time, he will heal; if not, he dies a madman.

Maybe I am wrong, but it seems to me that some people have a greater predisposition to humility. What is your opinion?

I agree with this idea and congratulate such people, but they should be truly humble. This virtue approaches perfect holiness. The saints were truly great ascetics, they did not attribute anything good to themselves, but only to God.

I am afraid of people who consider humility to be cowardice. Humility is a great dignity, a dignity to which the Savior also urges us. The Mother of God, this earthly being who is higher than all women and all girls in the world, is the most humble creation of God. The Mother of God! And through her, God blessed us with the birth of Christ the Savior for Him to bring us true teachings, the true Bread of life, by which we exist. Thus, humility—as much as it may be, only let it be correct—is very welcomed; it draws us close to the holiness and humility of the saints.

To teach their spiritual children humility, some elders use harshness. Is this method correct?

There are some exceptions. There are, for example, sinners in the *Sayings of the Desert Fathers* and in everyday life who want to repent, but something within them does not let them. And then they slap themselves a bit. When you are home alone, by yourself, you remember your sins, and so that God will not punish you, you punish yourself.

In the *Sayings* there are such cases: they punish themselves by hitting themselves. For example, a young man wanted to be able to pray with tears. And he asked for them, and they didn't come—he was hardened at heart. And then he took off his shirt, and with a wet towel made into a rope, he hit himself on the back: "You don't want to weep? I'll give you tears so that you cry," he said to himself. So, there are similar cases of the harshness of humility.

If God gives you tears, if He gives you such repentance for your sins, then you have acquired humility. However, it must be preserved afterward. Humility is also difficult to preserve. If you do not cultivate it, it becomes extinguished. Who knows what temptations come upon you, and you remain as you were before! Just like with the Jesus Prayer. If you say it continually, with humility and asceticism, with self-control, it binds to our heart, to our life, but if we no longer practice it, it extinguishes, it stops.

"We live in a very dangerous age, and therefore, especially now, we must be strong, we must be humble!"

Can you give a definition of humility for a young person...And what are the methods for arriving at humility?

The definition of humility is the same for a young person and for other Christians. You can extract the definition of humility from all that I have said until now. A young person, in order to humble himself, should examine his conscience more often, as the Christians of old did. Each night the Christian would think, beginning with the morning and up until that moment, what he did right and what he did wrong; and he would discover that he did more wrong than good. He does this today, he does it tomorrow, and so he begins to know himself, to know that within him reigns more sin and evil than good and virtue. And then, if this young man is serious, he starts on a sincere path of goodness.

Because goodness, dear listeners, goodness is necessary both in this life and of benefit to society, but it is also beneficial in the life to come. Saint Paul says that nothing impure enters the Kingdom of God (Eph. 5:5). We must purify ourselves, to throw off all the dirt from ourselves, all the dead weight of sins, and we must cleanse ourselves day after day so that we can become human, in the first place. Written with a capital "H": Human!

This is what Scripture wants to make us, this is what God wants: for us to be true humans, to have human goodness in us. Humility can be likened to human goodness.

Sadly, in the world today there is very little human goodness. Everyone is greedy and wants to acquire millions of dollars, while others don't even have bread.

Therefore, this young person should think over everything I have said. To live a futile life, to live in sin, in fornication, in drunkenness, in useless parties, is a waste of time and a loss of eternity, the eternal joy for which we are created. The Lord did not make us for hell, He made us for Heaven, but for the Heaven in which nothing impure enters. It follows that in this life, we must live in such a way that we prepare ourselves daily for the dawn of eternal life, which is full of light, joy, holiness, and the peace of God.

Father, do you think the claims that the signs of the last times are rather evident today are exaggerated?

Maybe they are exaggerated in a way. They talk about the Antichrist, his number, and certain things that will come. First, the year 2000. A millennium has passed, and now another comes, the second, and the world expects a cataclysm or something similar. Such a cataclysm began last night in Serbia with this war.[17]

We don't know what thoughts God has about the end of the world. Even the Apostles asked the Lord Jesus Christ: *Tell us, when shall these things be? and what shall be the sign of thy coming, and of the end of the world?* (Matt. 24:3) The Savior responded to them: *of that day and hour knoweth no man, no, not the angels of heaven, but my Father only* (Matt. 24:36). He, as man, Jesus Christ as man, didn't know when the end of the world would be. In his second epistle, the Holy Apostle Paul writes that if the time of the end of the world is postponed, it is because God patiently endures, wanting to gain as many believers as possible for His Kingdom (2 Pet. 3:9). From those who are born and are not killed through abortion or by other means, who knows what saints God will appoint. Thus, if the Savior does not allow Himself to give an answer to the Apostles, how can I allow myself? This is a mystery of God.

17 He is referring to the NATO bombing of Yugoslavia that began on March 24, 1999. *Translator's note.*

However, the end of the world for me and each one of you is when I die and you die. Then everything is finished! We can't do any good deeds after death. We die forever. I think this is the answer. The end of the world, in fact, is our end. Until the last moment, we need to prepare ourselves in order to make ourselves worthy as much as possible for eternal life. The Savior tells us that at the Last Judgment, each person will give an account for every idle word spoken in life (Matt. 12:36). This is extraordinary! We are full of these idle words. We don't get rid of them, they gather within us, and at the Last Judgment we will be confronted by them if we don't repent, if we don't confess sincerely.

In relation to the previous question, from your experience as a spiritual father, what do you think about the spiritual state of Romanians in the present moment, or in general of humanity, compared to other periods? Some claims that refer to the end times are in fact based on how the spiritual atmosphere of our days is perceived.

Saint Paul and St. John the Evangelist speak about the Antichrist, for example. However, throughout history, without a doubt there were more pious periods with more faith. I am thinking of the Middle Ages; many saints appeared amid the people living then, but there were also many evil people. However, the proportion of good people seemed to be greater than those who were bad. The devil hunted Christians then as well, leading them towards perdition. But now, in our times, it is as if the devil has gained very much power over the consciences of people who lack piety and the grace of God.

I learned not long ago that in America, for example, there is a temple of the devil with six floors in a city. A temple of the devil! There are satanists—you know them—in our society today, satanists who have certain vows, teachings, and a creed of their own totally against Christianity.

In the past, there were pagans, and they had temples—as there are today, for example, Masonic temples. Whoever has been to America has seen that in each town, there is a church of the Annunciation, then a Masonic temple, a church of the Ascension, and then a Masonic temple. There are many Masonic temples on the streets or the large boulevards of America. Masons are not friends of Christians; they are their enemies. Hundreds and hundreds of years ago, there were pagan temples, but

Christianity overcame these temples. Either it toppled them, or they were deserted by their believers who converted to Christianity. Now there are institutions that desire total destruction of Christianity; and, in the first place, there is the devil with his temples.

Thus, we live in a very dangerous time, and for this reason, especially now, we must be strong, we must be humble! The devil is proud, while God is humble. And in the name of pride, the devil conquers because man likes to be proud, not humble. And then very many pass over—in record numbers—to the devil's side, and he strengthens his kingdom. Therefore, we must protect ourselves, but you must also protect those around you, and help them to walk in the way of God, which is the way of life. The other road is the way of death, of darkness, of lies. This is all that I can tell you.

In Romanian mass media, we are told that Masonry is a philanthropic organization that desires the good of humanity. Whom should we believe?

Freemasons also do good, but we don't know what evil hides within this good. For example, I am thinking of poor America again. I went there for my eyes—I have eye problems—and, even though my eyesight was poor, I saw very wealthy stores, one hundred meters long or longer, with everything: from needles to helicopters. You find sweets, baked goods, fruit, and every material good in an American store such as this. In America there is also a temple of the devil, there are possessed people or satanists, there are these Masonic temples. Thus, things are mixed together. A poor fish, in the water, in the ocean, clings to a bit of bread (or whatever is on the end of a hook) and eats it greedily, because it is hungry; and the hook remains in his throat and the fisherman pulls it out and puts it on the grill.

These earthly goods that attract us are similar. He who offers them to us wants to close our minds and keep our eyes only on them. And the soul, which is of extraordinary value—*what shall a man give in exchange for his soul?* (Mark 8:37), asks the Savior—waits like a beggar, no one takes care of him, and he stays in our body as if in a prison. What we do is not good. We should not limit ourselves only to material goods, because they only feed the body which afterwards becomes food for worms. But the soul—which will remain for eternity and will be united with the

resurrected body—is empty of good deeds, empty of virtues, empty of God. Therefore, we should not delude ourselves like the fish that loses its life for a morsel of food.

The most humble human being

Since today is the Feast of the Annunciation, please tell us about the humility shown by the Mother of God when she replied to the Archangel Gabriel: be it unto me according to Thy word (Luke 1:38).

I will answer, but I see that questions keep coming from the auditorium, and there is a stack of other questions next to me. I wonder if you have other plans as well.

There is a priest here from Basarabia who wants to leave for Iași and the train is at 9:00PM. But, because we are talking about God, about the Holy Virgin and our salvation, about humility—this great virtue—I will try to answer.

The Mother of God, as I have said, is a human being with the highest degree of holiness and humility. The Mother of God learned humility in the Temple. Until the age of about fourteen years, the Mother of God stayed in the Temple in Jerusalem under the guidance of the elderly priests and elderly women there. She acquired humility in this way, theoretically first of all, but then she conformed to all that was ordained and acquired humility of heart, true humility.

When the Archangel Gabriel told the Mother of God that she will bear a Son, she asked with humility: *How shall this be, seeing I know not a man?* (Luke 1:34). And the Archangel answered her: *The Holy Ghost shall come upon thee, and the power of the Highest shall overshadow thee* (Luke 1:35). And then, in her humility, even though she had this impediment in her holy and pure heart, says this 'yes' with acceptance: *be it unto me according to thy word!* (Luke 1:38). She accepted what was impossible according to all of human logic: for a woman to give birth without knowing a man. This is her humility.

Later on, the Mother of God realizes that she is serving God and the salvation of humankind, and she utters these words of thanksgiving: *My soul doth magnify the Lord* (Luke 1:46) and all the other stichera that are chanted in Church. She knew what fruit her humility, her acceptance, would bring. She knew how much joy there would be for the world and how much humility there would be for her. She, too, was mocked and grieved by others her whole life, but she modestly receives the Good News and brings Jesus Christ, the Son of the Heavenly Father, into the world as the fruit of her humility. This is the great humility of the Mother of God!

If we ever think that we are humble, aren't we proud?

He who is truly humble does not think: "Oh, how humble I am!" because he is a laughingstock. If you are genuinely humble, you do not have these thoughts—you simply do not have them.

The saints always see their smallest sins. An elderly woman from the countryside told me in confession: "Father, I sinned. A chick came by the hen next to me, and I went like this with my hand and hit its wing, and it weighs on my conscience." Because she pushed away a chick from the hen, she thought that she had committed a great sin. This woman was a being with a pure soul, truly humble. The saints are like this. The smallest stains on their consciences are great sins for them. So that when the thought that "I am humble" comes, you are far from being humble. Or "I am beautiful," or "I am smart," or "What nice clothes I have," and she looks in the mirror the whole day. These are the signs of foolish pride.

Father, please tell me how I should act around a person who rejects spiritual advice with much verbal aggression? Is it good to insist or to be quiet and to pray?

You should pray for him.

What will happen to those who say: "I know that God loves me and helps me, because every time I needed help He helped me" but they do not do anything to become closer to God? How can they be helped to understand that the road to God passes through humility?

If they live correctly according to their conscience, they will meet with humility.

Some centuries ago, in difficult times similar to those of today, people were asked to increase their repentance, which led to humility. Why is something like this not done today as well?

Because of the lack of humility. In 1947, our country was beset by famine, famine from top to bottom. At the time, there was a poor worker

here at our monastery (some towers were built for the large church), the old man Jacob, they called him. He carried construction material with a wheelbarrow. And I asked him: "Old man Jacob, how are you doing?" And he answered, crying: "Look, I can't take this hunger anymore. I receive a salary of 400,000 lei—in '47—and it is enough for only a kilogram of flour. But I don't have anything to eat it with. And I can't do my work." Such poverty exists today as it did then, but in humility. That is why what the person who asked the question wants to happen cannot happen.

Father, what do inner humility and external humility mean?

Yes, it is a great difference, as between the soul and the body. Inner humility is the Savior's humility, humility of the heart. External humility is false reverences and words of false greeting—he greets you to your face, but behind your back, he curses you: "How stupid he is!" And when he speaks like this, he shows that he does not have humility of heart, which is steadfast. Humility of heart is humility for all times. The other, the external one, is false and deceitful.

Father, please tell us whether the difficulty in admitting one's sins in confession is due to pride or other causes, and how can one struggle against this difficulty?

How can one struggle? For example, if a sick person goes to the doctor and, even though his liver hurts, he only says: "Doctor, I get dizzy sometimes", then the doctor gives him aspirin. But if he says: "Doctor, I feel terrible—for example, he is epileptic—I fall without realizing it, writhe on the ground, hit myself, and then I am in pain; what should I do?" Then, the doctor applies the treatment for epilepsy and helps him. But, if he is insincere with the doctor, he is insincere with his own conscience, and he cannot be helped.

The same thing also happens to the person who goes insincerely to the doctor of spiritual illnesses, that is, the father confessor. The fact that he confesses is a waste of time. You must come to confession with tears, listening to your conscience that is filled with different kinds of things, not befitting man: evil deeds, dangerous to my neighbor, my family, myself, and my soul; I go to confession filled with contrition, and I present myself before God Who is present next to the priest at that time. Then God inspires the priest with what to tell the one confessing, and in this way, he helps the believer to heal, giving him an answer fitting to his state of death.

If we do not succeed in acquiring the Prayer of the Heart, is it good to say it mechanically?

It is not good to say it mechanically because that means we are not sincere with ourselves. Jesus Christ is engaged with us in the Prayer of the Heart. So, it is very beneficial for us to pray with attention to each word we say before God. And even if we do not receive an answer immediately, we must be patient and know that the answer to the Prayer of the Heart is the classic one of the descent of the mind into the heart. That is, what you think, you should also feel.

If you say the prayer with attention, the fact that you call on the Name of Jesus Christ in your life will help you very much; it gives you an increase of faith, increase in piety, increase in goodness, increase in self-knowledge. Because we are speaking about the Name of Jesus, which is a powerful name. Called upon within us, it works. It is a long road until the mind descends into the heart, but calling on Him with attention, with vigilance and humility, this name works within us and helps us grow spiritually.

Thank you!

On the Unexpected Hour of Death[18]

An unexpected death can even take young people by surprise • Death often takes people unprepared • Why does God not allow us to know the hour of our death? • "Let us sanctify our life through the Holy Mysteries!"

Brothers and sisters in Christ,

At the gates of the City of Nain—as we find in the seventh chapter of the Holy Gospel according to Luke—two convoys of people met: a sad funeral procession was leaving the town, in which a widowed mother, heartbroken by pain, was taking her only son to the cemetery, and from outside the town the Lord Jesus Christ was coming, followed by a group of His disciples and a great multitude of people. The Lord Jesus, touched by the poor widow's great pain, approaches her and tells her: "Do not cry!" Then, drawing near to the coffin of the young man, her only son, He utters His heavenly words: *Young man, I say unto thee, arise!* (Luke 7:14). And the one who had been dead until that moment sat up and began to talk. In the midst of the great silence that fell upon the two convoys, the Savior presented the young man alive to his mother. The poor mother may have cried more afterwards, but her tears were tears of joy, because her pain had ceased. The multitude was stricken by fear, and all praised God for this resurrection from the dead accomplished before everyone's eyes.

An unexpected death can even take young people by surprise

The young man from Nain who unexpectedly died shows each of us that an unexpected death can take not only the elderly by surprise, but also even young people.

Usually a young person—and not only young—thinks about everything except death; he does not even want to think about such a thing. If someone reminds him about this, he laughs with contempt or at least indifference, as if he will never die, and, thus, it is not fitting to cloud his life with such

18 20th Sunday after Pentecost, 1986. The sermon was preserved in a manuscript and edited by Elder Sofian at the end of the 1990s.

thoughts; as if death only happens to other people, but not for him as well. Still, death comes unexpectedly for the child in the crib, for the indifferent teenager, and for the elderly person whitened by age.

Holy Scripture tells us that the time of death, just as *the day of the Lord, cometh as a thief in the night* (1 Thess. 5:2). You know that the thief never announces when he is coming to steal. He appears when you do not expect, when all are sleeping without a care. Death often does the same thing! When a person thinks his life is not threatened by any danger, when he buries himself in daily cares as if in a deep sleep, exactly then does death come to cut short the wanderings of his life.

Death often takes people unprepared

In the book of the Prophet Daniel in the Bible, we are told about the dream of King Nebuchadnezzar of Babylon. One night, this powerful king of Babylon dreamt of a giant tree with its top reaching to the sky and branches stretching to the ends of the earth. The tree's leaves were beautiful, and the fruit was large and delicious, and humans and all living things fed from their seeds. But, when the tree grew to be even higher, a voice from heaven was heard saying: *Hew down the tree, and cut off his branches, shake off his leaves, and scatter his fruit* (Dan. 4:14). King Nebuchadnezzar was horrified. At his request, the Prophet Daniel interpreted his dream which signified the violent end of Nebuchadnezzar's life, as a punishment for his iniquities.

But the dream, with the command to *cut down the tree*, also signifies each person's pitiful end. Because what else is man than a blade of grass cut or plucked from the root, which, at God's command, falls as if hit by lightning?

Sometimes it happens that we know someone in our neighborhood who has everything and is highly regarded by those around him who see and praise him like a beautiful tree full of fruit. The branches of his family stretch far and wide with many relatives. He is young and healthy, and everyone around him wishes him "many years." But, exactly at the moment when his happiness seems to not be overshadowed by a single cloud, suddenly, the terrible voice resounds for him too: *Cut down the tree!* And the command is immediately fulfilled, and death strikes him unexpectedly—choked by cancer or heart disease, crushed by an accident that no one wishes for, or hit by sudden death in another form. Those

around him are surprised to learn that he who was full of life a few hours ago has been extinguished from the present world forever.

How many occurrences like this have you not seen around yourselves, in your families, or among those you know? What is most painful, however, is not only the fact that death comes unexpectedly, but especially that it surprises people when they are unprepared to leave this life.

We cannot know how prepared or unprepared for death was the young man from Nain. However, being the only son of a widow, lacking the guidance and authority of his father, maybe he too had accumulated enough sins common to young people before the unexpected moment of death. On the way to the cemetery, however, this young man had the unique chance of meeting the Master of life and death Himself, the Lord Jesus Christ, Who, touched by the mother's tears, called the young man back to this earthly life. Without a doubt, the young man saw an unforgettable scene there, such that he lived the rest of his life with more vigilance than other young people his age. But how many people can have the astounding experience of the son of the widow of Nain? Almost none!

Still, how many young people—and not only young people—in our times, unprepared for the moment of death, continue their lives in disarray, with indifference, as if they will never die? If you could have a conversation with such a young person after he crossed the threshold into the other world, you could ask him: "What did you do, young man? You ruined yourself forever! Because your soul was full of sins: you did not listen to your parents, you did not fear God, and you often cursed and denied Him, you did not care for prayer, you did not avoid carnal sins, you did not think of the consequences of your misdeeds, you did not ponder about your soul and the Judgement of God. You ruined yourself for eternity, because the tree of your life was not only cut down without warning, but it will also be thrown into the fire." In response, the young person, after tasting death and seeing what is beyond, will not laugh mockingly, but will fully repent for his lack of sobriety and wisdom, but then it will be too late.

Similar dreadful surprises can happen to anyone, anywhere, and at any age.

Why does God not allow us to know the time of our death?

Maybe at some point this question has come to mind for each of you: why did God not leave a definite sign by which we can know that death is approaching and be able to prepare ourselves in this way ahead of time? Some of the Holy Fathers answer that God did not want for us to know the final moment of our life so that we consider each moment of our life as the final one, and thus be prepared to depart this world at any moment! The Savior Himself teaches us this in the Parable of the Ten Virgins when He says: *Watch therefore, for ye know neither the day nor the hour wherein the Son of Man cometh* (Matt. 25:13).

Nonetheless, let us imagine that we knew beforehand the day and time when we would die. Would this knowledge be beneficial for our soul? Not at all. Such a discovery would not be useful for us, and I believe that a terrible terror would overtake people's souls. Out of fear, some would lose their minds. Others, from a feeling of despair, knowing that they only have a little bit left to live, would spend their life in the most ugly pleasures. We cannot know how many out of a hundred would think of their soul and the Final Judgment.

Thus, it is better that God ordained for us not to know the time of our end, but rather to be ready anytime to give an account for our deeds without being ashamed of the way in which we lived our life.

"Let us sanctify our lives through the Holy Mysteries!"

No one can escape death. We are all indebted to pay this common tribute when God will arrange it for each of us.

If the hour of our death is unknown to us and we are instructed to watch and prepare ourselves as for the greatest final exam of our life on earth, then our waiting for the last moment should not be a passive state, without effort, and full of fear, but rather, it must be a serene waiting accompanied by steadfast work, full of zeal and joy. However, at the same time we must have unceasing care to keep—as much as possible—our soul honest, our heart pure, and our body clean of sins, knowing that our body is the temple of the Holy Spirit in us (1 Cor. 6:19). We must care for the body by giving it all that it needs to a degree that we do not awaken or spark its bad desires.

Let us meditate on the fact that all things pass, all things flow, and we walk the paths of life together with them. Just as Fall strips trees of their leaves and their sap begins to dry out, so too our life diminishes each year, each month, and each hour.

The flower of youth wilts, the light of earthly joys extinguishes, difficult old age approaches, friends die, those near to us distance themselves and abandon us. The graves of loved ones languish without a sound, only the souls of some of our dead are now in God's hands. Thus, our life passes, thus each of us passes, like a shadow on the face of the earth, until no one sees us, until almost everyone forgets us, until we are dead and there is no recollection of us in anyone's heart.

Therefore, let us sanctify our lives through the Holy Mysteries given to people by God! Let us live in good understanding with one another! Let us not gossip about each other, let us not deceive one another, let us not envy or hate one another, but, on the contrary, let us endeavor to live as brothers, knowing that we are all sons of the same Heavenly Father Whom we call "our Father!" Let us strive to live our transitory life as the Holy Apostle Paul instructs us: *Forbearing one another, and forgiving one another, if any man have a quarrel against any: even as Christ forgave you, so also do ye. And above all these things put on charity, which is the bond of perfectness. And let the peace of God rule in your hearts, to the which also ye are called in one body; and be ye thankful* (Col. 3:13-15). Amen.

Words at the Beginning of Lent[19]

The effort of fasting "is proof that we truly love God" • "Is not this the fast that I have chosen?"

Fasting, in general, is restraint and temperance. Temperance in food, drink, and idle and superfluous talk; self control and restraint from every harmful thing.

The effort of fasting "is proof that we truly love God"

Both in the Old and in the New Testament, the Prophets, Apostles, and all the Holy Fathers throughout the Church's history put a very great price on the practice of fasting for body and soul, by this seeking to overcome the evil within us. Practically speaking, it is not at all easy to always watch yourself, to resist the temptations from within and without, to cut your will, to humble your body and soul with a true desire of defeating the evil within you and conforming yourself to the will of God. Therefore, the effort of fasting is considered a sacrifice of soul and body offered to God, and, at the same time, it is proof that we truly love God, fulfilling His ancient command given to our ancestors from the beginning of the world.

A complete fast—a Christian fast well-pleasing to God—is always accompanied by prayer and almsgiving, these being considered the two wings of prayer by the Holy Fathers.

The emphasis must fall especially on fasting for the soul. If we leave ourselves enslaved by ugly desires, by passions, then despite all the bodily fasting we do, we drive God's grace away from us and lose the reward of fasting.

Because look: one fasts but argues with and sues his brother in order to wrongfully steal his goods. Another fasts with the body, but becomes angry, speaks poorly, reproaches, and defames his fellow human being.

19 Article published in the newspaper titled ***Schimbarea la Faţă*** [***Transfiguration***], edited by ASCOR Bucharest [Association of Romanian Orthodox Christian Students], no. 2, 1997.

Another has a stomach empty of food, but his heart is full of evil, egotism, envy, and impure thoughts. He eats neither meat nor dairy, but he kills the honor and good name of his fellow man through slander, lies, and condemnation.

"Is not this the fast that I have chosen?"

Is this not the fast that I have chosen? asks the Lord through the Prophet Isaiah. *To loose the bands of wickedness, to undo the heavy burdens, and to let the oppressed go free, and that ye break every yoke? Is it not to deal thy bread to the hungry, and that thou bring the poor that are cast out to thy house? When thou seest the naked, that thou cover him; and that thou hide not thyself from thine own flesh? Then shall thy light break forth as the morning, and thine health shall spring forth speedily: and thy righteousness shall go before thee; the glory of the Lord shall be thy reward. Then shalt thou call, and the Lord shall answer; thou shalt cry, and he shall say, Here I am* (Isa. 58: 6-9).

Therefore, if you truly fast, open your egotistical heart to the needy, and just as you restrain your mouth from food, so too restrain it from lying, from cursing, from condemnation, from gossiping, and from all other sins that act through words.

The Holy Fathers, great teachers and ascetics of the world, highly praise fasting and recommend it persistently. Here are some of their words: "Fasting is health and peace of soul and body"; "Fasting is the quenching of bodily lusts, freedom from evil dreams, purity of prayer, guarding of the mind, the door to compunction, humble sighs for one's sins, the beginning and foundation of every spiritual work that is well-pleasing to God." And St. Basil the Great adds: "If people used fasting to guide all their deeds, there would no longer be any obstacle for deep peace to reign in all the world; nations would no longer rise up against one another, armies would no longer fight. If fasting reigned, weapons would no longer be made, tribunals would no longer convene, there would be no one left in prisons; forests and deserts would no longer have brigands, towns denouncers, and seas pirates. If people were disciples of fasting, then as Job says, the voice of the one asking for tribute would not be heard. If fasting governed our life, then life would not be as full of tears and sorrow. Fasting would have taught everyone to restrain themselves not only from food, but also to banish love of money, greed, as well as any other passion. If these sins were driven away, nothing would stop us from living a life of full peace and spiritual equanimity."[20]

These are only a fraction of the blessings and fruits of fasting, which we too can acquire with the help of divine grace and our steadfast effort.

Blessed are those Christians who diligently follow the rule of the four fasts throughout the year, together with Wednesdays and Fridays, as our fathers and grandfathers did, in order to renew the body, illuminate the soul, and change our entire life for the better. May God help us!

20 Translation of a text quoted by Saint Sofian from: Sfântul Vasile cel Mare, ***Omilii*** și ***cuvântări***, ediția a III-a, în col. ***Părinți*** și ***Scriitori Bisericești***, vol. 1, traducere de Pr. Prof. Dumitru Fecioru, Editura Basilica, București, 2009, p. 65 [Saint Basil the Great, ***Homilies and Teachings***, 3rd edition, in ***Church Fathers and Writers***, vol. 1, trans. Rev. Dr. Dumitru Fecioru, Basilica Publishing House, Bucharest, 2009, p. 65].

ENCOUNTERING FOR PRAYER[21]

"It is not good to pray only with our lips!" • He who does not pray is like a bird without wings • The Jesus Prayer "burns all our inner impurity like a heavenly fire" • Feeling God's presence in our life • "The prayers of those in prison were like those of the Holy Fathers" • The Prayer of the Heart is very possible in modern life • The Kingdom of God is within us • Christian life is mystical, hidden • "The Mother of God responds right away to a prayer done with all one's desire, with all one's being" • "This is what I advise young people: to have balance, wisdom, prayer"

We celebrate this day in a special way. Our spiritual shepherd, His Beatitude the Patriarch, celebrates ten years as Patriarch. This morning, after the Divine Liturgy was served at the Patriarchal Cathedral, numerous important speeches were given that showed all the toil, all the difficulties, and all the beautiful fruits that appeared during these ten years through the care, stability, and wisdom of Patriarch Teoctist. This evening, please send him a thought and prayer for the coming years. May God protect and keep him in the front of the Church because he is a good and true spiritual father. With all our hearts, let us truly wish him to live many blessed, fruitful years.

Apart from the festivities surrounding the Patriarch, November 14th gives us another reason to rejoice: the feast of St. Gregory Palamas, the theologian of prayer. During a very difficult time for the practice of the Jesus Prayer—when there were many disputes and unjust criticisms regarding such an activity, this great, God-inspired theologian appeared who, through his understanding and especially through the grace of the Holy Spirit, very clearly explained what this prayer that unites man with God consists of.

Why is the commemoration of St. Gregory Palamas at the beginning of the Advent Fast? As you know, we begin the fast before the Feast of the Savior's Nativity tomorrow morning. And we need a lot of prayer during Lent, just as prayer needs fasting. Without a communion between these two practices, our spiritual life limps along.

21 Conference held with the Association of Romanian Orthodox Christian Students (ASCOR) in the College of Law Auditorium in Bucharest on November 14, 1996.

Thus, today, at the invitation of the students of ASCOR (Association of Romanian Orthodox Christian Students)—my spiritual brothers and sisters—I'm here, before you all, trying to say a few words about prayer.

Honored audience, the Holy Apostle Paul, speaking about the importance of good deeds in the Christian life, also gives us this instruction: *Pray without ceasing* (1 Thess. 5:17). As you know, God is spirit and presence. *I am that I am* (Ex. 3:14), God Himself says to the Prophet Moses in front of the Burning Bush on Sinai. And there is no greater joy than our communion with the Living God through prayer.

"It is not good to pray only with our lips!"

What is prayer? We all know it. Before this talk started, we were already in prayer—the Paraklesis to the Mother of God from Putna Monastery was being chanted. In the *Philokalia,* we learn that prayer means our mind speaking with God.

When we pray, when we tell God about all of our sorrows and ask Him to help us in our troubles, it is fitting to let go of all worldly cares from our mind—as is chanted during the Liturgy in the Cherubic hymn—and to think of only Him. We are speaking with God Himself! It is not good to pray only with our lips, while our mind is far from the words of the prayer! This is disrespect and sin. *How can you expect God to pay attention to your prayers*—a Holy Father asks us—*if you do not pay attention to your own prayers? You do not know what you are saying!*

Prayer done with devotion, with a pure heart, requires a certain preparation, dear students; it requires guarding our senses. The Prophet Moses was not able to approach the Burning Bush on Sinai until he took off his sandals because God warned him that in front of him was holy ground (Ex. 3:5). Nearly every place in which we pray is holy because God is present there in a hidden way. Therefore, we, too, are ready so that this inner spotlight of our life is open to the conversation of our mind with God. Before beginning to pray, let's strive to banish every passionate thought from our hearts.

It is beneficial to give our prayer and heart their due respect and thereby to listen to the Savior Who exhorts us: *But you, when you pray, go into your room, and when you have shut your door, pray to your Father who is in the secret place; and your Father who sees in secret will reward you openly* (Matt. 6:6).

The inner closet is the heart, and the senses are the door. Therefore, they must be tightly shut because attacks come through them during prayer.

Prayer must be done with perseverance, according to the many examples we have in the Holy Gospel. Let's recall the pagan woman, the Canaanite woman who shouted desperately after the Savior to heal her demonized daughter. Although the Savior does not seem to hear, in the end, He heals her daughter, even from a distance (Matt. 15:22-28). Let's recall Bartimaeus, the blind man from Jericho. People asked him to be quiet, but on the contrary, he shouted even louder. And hearing him, Jesus healed his blindness (Mark 10:46-52).

We may ask ourselves: when does God answer our prayers more quickly? The answer can be given in multiple ways. A sure path is when our prayer is accompanied by fasting, almsgiving, and a blameless life. Almsgiving and fasting are the two wings of prayer. These three good deeds—prayer, fasting, and almsgiving—interweave and work together for our benefit.

Similarly, our prayers are heard very quickly when we ask the Mother of God and the saints (friends) of God for help, and when these prayers are done by many believers gathered together. The Holy Apostle Peter was imprisoned by Herod, with his feet in stocks, but the unceasing prayers that many believers said for him before God were so powerful that the heavenly Father sent an angel from Heaven and, wondrously, freed Peter from prison (Acts 12:3-11). So, it often happens that God responds to our prayers done with devotion.

He who does not pray is like a bird without wings

However, there are also quite a few cases when God does not fulfill our prayers. For what reason? Because many people, as I said, pray only with their lips, and their mind wanders everywhere. Our attention flies away from the words of the prayers. Our Savior rebukes those who pray in this way, saying: *These people honor Me with their lips; but their heart is far from Me* (Matt. 15:8).

Likewise, God does not listen to our prayers when—without us being aware—we ask for something harmful for our lives. A person I know, when he was in prison, continually asked to be taken outside to work—still in prison but to work outside in the fresh air. Because life inside the cell had become very difficult and unsupportable for him. God continually postponed responding to his request. Later, however, he realized why his prayer was not answered: many who left to work in the fields—under pressure from the guards, in forced labor—died there, in the fields, or the Delta. And many—almost all—who did not die returned to their prison cells sick. Thus, God did not fulfill his request when he was praying for it because he could have died there.

This also happens in certain cases when we ask God for something and do not receive it. God, Who knows precisely the entire course of our life from when we are born until we die, knows what we need and do not need, what is beneficial and what is detrimental for us. Therefore, in His omniscience and wisdom, He does what is best for our life. Even though we are sinners, God still loves us and desires the best for us. And, in certain situations, God wants to help us without listening to our prayers that are harmful to our soul.

What should we ask God in our prayers? Because many people ask for worthless things. Let us ask Him for health of body and soul; let us ask Him for clarity of mind and wisdom so that we do not stray from His path; let us ask Him for goodness of soul and humility of heart. Let us ask Him for discernment in all that we do and the conviction that when we die, we will give an account before the Judgment seat of God for how we lived our life on earth. Let us ask Him for zeal to read Holy Scripture, to understand it, and to fulfill God's commandments. Let us ask Him for what is worthy of Him and what He alone can give us: the grace of the Holy Spirit and the salvation of our souls. Let us ask Him for the great gift of seeing our sins. Let us ask Him to help us seek the Kingdom of God and His righteousness first in all our lives. Let us ask God for all of these things in our prayers.

What happens to the one who does not pray? Sadly, many people do not pray and consider this practice of the Christian life to be worthless. He who does not pray stumbles very easily and falls into sin. He who does not pray has no strength in his battle with the storms of life. He is like a soldier without a weapon, like a bird without wings or a reed shaken in whatever direction the wind blows, and only before God does he not bow to ask and serve Him. He is like a fish on dry land, as St. John Chrysostom tells us.[22]

22 Saint John Chrysostom, ***Homily on the Poor Man Lazarus.***

If Christ the Savior spent entire nights in prayer, what must we do to be saved? They who do not pray languish in the kingdom of material things, are not written in the Book of Life in Heaven, and do not have a place in the Kingdom of God. At God's Judgment, that no one escapes, they will be told: *I know you not!* (Matt. 25:12).

What are the benefits of prayer? Through prayer, we can acquire whatever we ask from God. Our prayers must only be worthy of God. They must be done with a pure heart, perseverance, and humility. Christ the Savior Himself promises us this when He says: *And whatever things you ask in prayer, believing, you will receive* (Matt. 21:22). And again: *Ask and it shall be given you* (Luke 11:9).

He who prays with all of his heart, immersing himself in the words of the prayer, together with the fulfillment of his requests, also receives the inner peace that the world cannot give—the peace promised by the Savior, Who says: *Peace I leave with you, my peace I give to you: not as the world gives do I give it to you* (John 14:27). And, in this way, we have a sense of certainty, we feel that we are not alone in the world with other people only, but that the God of our fathers, Who watches over and protects us in this earthly life, is with us.

Sometimes, God does not immediately fulfill our prayers, as I said. Saint Monika—the mother of Blessed Augustine—prayed to God for eighteen years to bring her son to the faith. Her persistence in prayer pleased God. And He truly listened to her, bringing her son onto the path of salvation, and not just in any way, but endowed with all the beauty of Christian experience given by divine grace. Since we do not know if all our prayers are for our benefit, it is always good to end our prayers with these words: *Lord, You Who know all things, help me so that my prayer to You may be fulfilled according to Your holy will! Lord, may Your will be done in my life!*

The Jesus Prayer "burns all our inner impurity like a heavenly fire"

Honored audience, alongside all of the problems that I talked about up to now, there is another kind of prayer: calling on the Name of the Lord, called the Jesus Prayer, mental prayer, or the Prayer of the Heart.

It is a powerful prayer comprised of these words: "Lord Jesus Christ, Son of God, have mercy on me, a sinner!" This prayer is short, you can say it anywhere and anytime, standing or walking.

In modern life—in life's rush, when we do not have time for long prayers in our room, in front of icons and lit candles—we can say this prayer anywhere and at any time. Both at school and at the store, at the factory and studio, we can say the prayer in the secret of our heart. And Jesus Christ, Who is always present in our life, listens to our prayer that is dedicated to His powerful Name. I heard many of you say that you know about the Jesus Prayer. I know many young and old people who say this prayer and are even advanced in this prayer. I was very glad each time I learned that such Christians exist.

We find the following words of the Savior in Holy Scripture: *Whatever you ask the Father in My name, He will give you* (John 16:23), so that the Father may be glorified in the Son. And again: *If you ask anything in My name, I will do it* (John 14:14). In the name of our Lord Jesus Christ, the Holy Apostles and Holy Fathers worked miracles, healing the sick and casting out demons from people.

This prayer is called the Jesus Prayer because, at its core, it contains the name of our Lord Jesus Christ, a powerful name, as I said. It is also called *mental prayer* because, in its first phase, it is said with the mind. And it is called the *Prayer of the Heart* because, after much time spent saying it attentively, it descends from the mind into the spiritual heart.

The Jesus Prayer is within everyone's grasp, and it can be said in three ways: the way we talk (as I am talking now), in our mind, or in a whisper. It can also be said in the rhythm of our breath—when we sit on a stool, keeping our head lowered slightly to the left and two fingers of our right hand pressing lightly on our clothing, above the place of the heart.

This prayer of calling on the Lord's name must be said unceasingly, day and night, in any place we may be and any work we may be doing. However, practically speaking, especially for beginners, it is difficult to say it unceasingly, and therefore it can be said alternatively with the seven daily services of the Church, morning and evening prayers, the Paraklesis and Akathist to the Mother of God, and similarly the Akathist to our Lord Jesus Christ which is tied to the Lord's name, with all the attributes of the Savior Christ in the context of communal prayer.

Especially for monastics, it is good for mental prayer to be done four or five times a day, at least fifteen minutes each time. But, without a doubt, this prayer can also be said by lay people, by any of you, according to each person's zeal, at least three times in twenty-four hours, for fifteen minutes

at a time. This prayer must be said often so that it can penetrate our heart, the center of our being.

And we must keep one more thing in mind: when we say the prayer, we must be attentive so that each word of the prayer falls on the place of the spiritual heart, which is two fingers above the place of the carnal heart, the physiological heart. This place, discovered by the Holy Fathers who were great men of prayer, is the spiritual center of our being.

This holy prayer must be done with the blessing and guidance of a spiritual father who usually also practices it. It is meant to help us purify our mind and heart of impure thoughts and desires. Repeatedly calling on the Lord's name burns up our inner impurities like a heavenly fire.

Feeling God's presence in our life

The ultimate aim of this prayer is for the mind to descend into the heart, unifying these two centers of human nature (the mind and heart) and achieving a perfect harmony between them. Usually, a person thinks one thing but feels something else. He speaks well of the person in front of him, but in his mind and heart, in his depths, he curses him. When we unite these two centers, a person becomes a spiritual unity, and then he is whole, as God made him in the beginning: a whole human being. We achieve this holy ideal of our life on earth through the Prayer of the Heart.

However, until we attain this ultimate aim of our inner ennoblement and sanctification, of the uplifting of our human nature rent by passions, we need a severe effort of dispassion, of battling with ourselves (which is not at all easy), of banishing the evil from our mind and heart, and of concentrating our mind, which is constantly distracted during prayer, as I said before. If we were not helped from above in this effort, our battle with ourselves would almost be hopeless. For our comfort and strengthening, we have the experiences and teachings of the Holy Fathers, that we find in the *Lives of the Saints* and all patristic literature, to help us.

Even if the great joy of the mind descending into the heart is delayed, because this happens only with the help of God and when God wants, our sincere and steadfast effort to frequently call on the Lord's name is very beneficial. Through this prayer (simple as it is), we acquire the sense of God's presence in our life. We feel that we are not alone with other people only but that He is present. We feel His real help in our life through the strength of patiently bearing temptations and difficulties. We feel how this prayer strengthens us in our faith, increases our love for God and others, and illuminates our mind to understand the Holy Scripture more deeply. It helps us feel that heavenly joys are infinitely greater and more beautiful than earthly joys.

All of these heavenly blessings are like a down payment for entering into communion with Christ and with the grace of God, tasting bit by bit, while still in this life, the joys and the happy state of the next life, as much as it is possible for us humans.

May the Good God help us attain this holy ideal of the union of mind and heart—in fact, our union with God. Then, our battle with ourselves eases, the holy prayer repeats itself unceasingly in our heart day and night, as Scripture says: *I sleep, but my heart is awake* (Song 5:2). In this prayer, spiritual joy surpasses all earthly joy. With humility, perseverance, and love, with time and without time, with hope in God and desire, let us say this holy prayer: "Lord Jesus Christ, Son of God, have mercy on me, a sinner!" Amen.

"The prayers of the prisoners were like those of the Holy Fathers!"

Father Archimandrite, what should be the daily prayer rule of a student?

There once was a pair of students in Athens—Gregory and Basil—who greatly impressed their contemporaries. Today we call one of them Basil the Great and the other Gregory the Theologian. They were a blessed pair of students who, alongside their studies, also studied the Gospels. These young people only knew two paths: one led to school and the other to church. Students nowadays should similarly weave prayer and study into their lives. I do not know how they should make their schedule, however, alongside bodily nourishment that, whether we want to or not, we seek and partake of, we also need spiritual nourishment, without which we die; we die even though we live. We die spiritually and become barren, hardened, dry, unfeeling, evil, jealous, proud, and so on. Therefore, it is good to feed ourselves with both one and the other. As the Savior Christ says: *But seek first the kingdom of God and His righteousness, and all these things shall be added to you* (Matt. 6:33).

Prayer—this connection to holiness, to the source of life and wisdom—helps us to learn what is good and to rid our mind of darkness so that it becomes luminous. It helps us remove the hardened layers covering our heart—hardened layers that make us insensitive to the word of God.

Thus, we should emphasize growing closer to God and everything else will come almost automatically. That is, we should not have holes in our life, saying prayers for only one day or one moment, while the rest of our life is spent in other preoccupations. Each day should be marked by prayer and other human, student responsibilities. Without this alternation, our life limps along; it is an ill, insufficient, empty life.

For young people, I especially recommend the Jesus Prayer, which is a short prayer that can be said everywhere in every condition. It is difficult to recommend a longer prayer rule. This prayer, said with all one's heart and especially with humility, helps. Before one begins saying psalms, paraklesis, and akathists, this prayer can help very much.

In the *Journal of Joy*, Fr. Nicolae Steinhardt quotes Kierkegaard, who says many people believe that when they pray, they pray so that God can listen to them, but in reality, it is exactly the opposite: when a person prays, he begins to listen to God. What can you tell us about these statements?

It is true that when people pray, they expect something from God—help that only He can give. Often, our prayers, our requests to other people are in vain. However, if we begin to pray, we begin to understand God's guidance for our life, which is a great benefit and true profit for us. Because God never teaches us with malintent, but always for our benefit.

What can you tell us about the power of prayer that some people had in prison?

We were so well-guarded, so constrained in prison that we could only think upwards, vertically, to God. Usually, a person prays fervently when he is in trouble. And the prisons were truly great trials. The prayers of those in the Communist prisons were received by God. With all the misery and evil commanded against the poor prisoners, they all had a serenity and joy that could only come from above, from God.

The prayers of those in prison were like those of the Holy Fathers in the desert or like the martyrs burnt at the stake, who, with a fire burning beneath them, were joyful and thanked God for the sacrifice they were bringing before His holiness. The prayers of those in prison, of the political prisoners, were similar. For us today, their prayers and way of life suggest the thought that it is good to humble ourselves, to struggle, to lead an ascetic life—as much as possible—through fasting, prayer, prostrations, forgiving the insults we receive in life, patiently enduring without complaining, and then our prayers will be received by God, just as the ones of those in the Communist prisons.

Please share a few words with us on the biblical theme of the "Burning Bush."

"The Burning Bush," as we know very well, is a biblical fact: a blessed event in which the Prophet Moses, having fled from Pharaoh's house in Egypt and reached the area of Mount Sinai, was tending his father in law's sheep. Stopping in front of a bush (a tree that burned in flames and was not consumed), Moses wanted to draw near to this fire. And then he was told from above: "And he said, draw not nigh hither: put off thy shoes from off thy feet, for the place whereon thou standest is holy ground" (Cf. Ex. 3:5). Someone was speaking to him from within the bush—God was speaking to him. This bush, in our Orthodox Church's theology, is a symbol for the Mother of God, who was the mother of God incarnate. She had the holy, heavenly fire—Jesus Christ—within her being, but she remained unburnt, unharmed, yet deified. The "Burning Bush" is also a symbol of unceasing prayer. He who prays unceasingly is like the bush that burned but was not consumed. We are always in the fire of God—this blaze of light and power. The more we burn, the more luminous and closer to God we become. This is the meaning of the "Burning Bush."

Please also tell us something about the "Burning Bush" spiritual movement at Antim Monastery.

The "Burning Bush" spiritual movement was born at the beginning of the Communist rule. On the road and in everyday life there was turmoil and an effort on the side of enemy powers to change all that was ancient, rooted, beautiful, and stable into a new way that we know and have lived.

Within all this turmoil, at Antim Monastery, in the library, we talked about the Jesus Prayer, the issue of confession, and this inner work of dispassion, all based on Holy Tradition, the practice of the Holy Fathers, and the ascetic experience of the Church over the course of two millennia. Beginning in 1945, we organized conferences for about six years, especially on Sundays.

This communal work was very pleasant. Unfortunately, it took place in a closed circle because it could not be extended very much due to the tumult outside of our monastery life.

There were big personalities who protected us, such as Fr. Stăniloae, Fr. Benedict Ghiuş, Professor Alexandru Mironescu, Dr. Vasile Voiculescu, author Ion Marin Sadoveanu, and others. Many young people participated, many students who, afterwards—poor people—suffered in prison. They came there, thirsting to learn something about inner life. And they would leave very well-fed spiritually. Once the speaker finished his talk, there were public questions, different kinds of questions, like I am asked now. And those who wanted to and were able to would answer them. There was a dialogue, a tapestry of spiritual ideas, thoughts, and desires that nourished the listeners very much.

Is it true that all who participated in the "Burning Bush" were imprisoned? What was the reason for their imprisonment?

There is a saying: "Whoever is not with us is against us." Those who governed us required everyone to be like them. However, without contradicting them, we did not agree with the Marxists. They were intelligent—because the devil is very intelligent—and they were led by this spirit of evil. They realized that we were not with them, that we were against them, and then they rounded us up where they found us and closely watched us for many years, just in case we were against them. These were the consequences of our meetings.

The Prayer of the Heart has great importance in modern life

In the current conditions of life, how can we receive the gift of the Prayer of the Heart, knowing that Christians' minds today are much more scattered than those of Christians in the past?

What you are saying is true, this is how it is. Life today is tumultuous, without pause, full of movement. However, this prayer is very short. The prayers of the hermits lasted all day and night. A saint in the *Philokalia* says that he prayed from morning until night, and when he grew tired praying, he would read Holy Scripture. His life was permanently engaged with God. His prayer was static—a kind of prayer that forced him to stay in place.

For modern life, it is as if God especially appointed this short prayer: "Lord Jesus Christ, Son of God, have mercy on me, the sinner," as I said it or as you know it; or at least the summation of these words: "Jesus, have mercy!" However rushed we may be in everyday life—maybe you are in a class, listening to a lecture at the university, or at the studio, factory, on the road, or talking with someone—we can say, "Jesus, have mercy!" quite frequently. On the one hand, we say "Jesus"—God, with all His Kingdom, Who illuminates the plane of our Christian life, and on the other hand, "have mercy on me"—which reflects our fallen state of lowliness, misery, and tribulations we often encounter. Let us at least say these words throughout our life. This short prayer can be said as frequently as possible, as busy as we may be. I knew someone with the Prayer of the Heart, whom I know precisely that he prayed unceasingly. When he would speak, for example, about certain very important things from his life experienced during the Russian Bolshevik Revolution, his heart would be praying; the prayer had descended into his heart. And when this prayer descends into the heart, then just as we breathe, so too do we pray.

In conclusion, we can say that in modern life, with all its rush and our unrest, we can nourish ourselves in a truly pleasing way with this prayer.

How can we discover what path we should take: marriage or monasticism?

Marriage is the usual path of life. At the beginning of the world, there was a pair of humans: our ancestors, Adam and Eve. God gave them the commandment to be fruitful and multiply. Thus, the family is, first of all, the foundation of human society. Through marriage, man and woman become creators, multiplying the human race. This way of life is a general calling.

Monasticism is a biblical exhortation, and only he who has a calling, who is urged from the depths of his being, comes to the monastic life. Therefore, there is a great distinction between one way of life and the other. The monastic has one mission and the family another.

Family life, with its cares and everyday problems, often looks only downwards or horizontally—it does not have time to look upwards as well. He who comes to the monastery, especially for this particular aim—communion with God—can intervene to draw the attention and enlighten the minds and habits of people, telling them that there is also another, unending life beyond this earthly life; thus, to think beyond the grave, which we often forget to do. We agonize and work from dawn to dusk for our everyday bread, for shelter and parties, but forget that we

will die one day and have to give an account for every idle word spoken in our life, as the Savior Himself tells us (Matt. 12:36). The monastic and the priest who shepherds us have a duty to keep the banner raised and enlighten the darkness of our everyday life. I believe this is the mission of the monastic in comparison to that of the family.

In the present moment, there is a strong increase in the influence of images, especially through television. Do you think this affects the power of people's prayer?

Television, this modern tool of communication, is both good and bad. It is good when you know how to choose what is beneficial from it, and it is bad when it transmits, through images, things that trouble us, that especially trouble young people. I am referring to images of inappropriate or even pornographic films. I met many young people, not only parents of young people, who are against these sinful images that trouble the minds and senses of those who watch the television screen.

During St. Basil the Great's time, young people would come to him and ask him what attitude they should have towards pagan books. It was a critical period between paganism and Christianity. Pagan learning, especially Greek, was enjoyable, but you could also find inappropriate things in it. St. Basil gave them very practical advice:

"Thus, precisely following the example of bees, we too must partake of the writings of profane authors; for bees neither go haphazardly to any single flower nor do they try to gather all that they find in the flowers upon which they land, but they take whatever they need for their work, and the rest they happily leave. If we are wise, let us take what benefits us and what is true from books."[23]

Therefore, St. Basil the Great's advice is good for television as well. Television can be beneficial, because we discover certain things that we do not find in ordinary news, which we do not even have time to browse. We find certain scientific or even spiritual communications. However, we also find flowers that neither have nectar nor pollen, and it is good not to look at them—at those shows that are poisonous to the mind,

23 Sfântul Vasile cel Mare, ***Omilii*** și ***cuvântări***, ediția a III-a, în col. ***Părinți*** și ***Scriitori Bisericești***, vol. 1, traducere de Pr. Prof. Dumitru Fecioru, Editura Basilica, București, 2009, p. 325 [Saint Basil the Great, ***Homilies and Teachings***, 3rd edition, in ***Church Fathers and Writers***, vol. 1, trans. Rev. Dr. Dumitru Fecioru, Basilica Publishing House, Bucharest, 2009, p. 325].

imagination, and heart of the viewer.

Father, what do you think about those who practice the Prayer of the Heart, but adopt teachings that are foreign to Orthodoxy—for example, yoga or parapsychology?

I believe that God does not listen to their prayers. These practices are foreign to our people, our mentality, and are not born through Christ or for Christ. It is a kind of hypocrisy in prayer, a delusion; things are mixed up. However, the Jesus Prayer and yoga practices are as far apart as the earth is from the sky.

Similarly, there are witches who tell the future using certain icons. We are led astray if we ask for a consultation from these witches. The Spirit of God cannot be reconciled with lies, with this hypocrisy. You will know these people who mix the Jesus Prayer with yoga from their deeds. If we look carefully and attentively at their lives, we usually see that they have gone astray; their life is not that of a Christian. Even in yoga, there are certain questionable things that usually happen, many inappropriate things. Those who practice yoga know what I am referring to.

Why is a spiritual father needed for the practice of the Prayer of the Heart?

A spiritual father is needed because this prayer said unceasingly—said very often for many years—brings certain special states to the one practicing it. For example, a warmth appears here, in the right part of the heart, above the physical heart. A sign appears, and the one who prays and does not know what purpose this prayer has can become proud—who knows what he can think about himself. And the spiritual father can tell him that this state of warmth is natural: "Be calm, keep going." That is, on this path of the Prayer of the Heart, certain new problems can appear for the one who prays. He does not understand them, does not know how to resolve them, and the spiritual father who practices this prayer can respond precisely to his confusion.

The Kingdom of God is within us

Tell us about tears during prayer. Can tears during prayer also be from the devil?

Very much so! From the devil, but also from our nature. The great pain we experience in our everyday life is eased by crying, by tears. However,

there are also tears of hysteria or tears of joy for earthly success. There are also spiritual tears that come with more difficulty—tears of repentance! They are very well received by God and come when we regret certain ugly deeds committed in our life, when we repent with all of our heart. There are also tears of our prayer of faith. These tears are pleasing to God. All other bodily ones relieve us somewhat of this psychological pressure but are only of immediate benefit; they do not help with prayer.

What is wordless prayer, and "prayer like fire" which St. John Cassian's Spiritual Discourses[24] speak about?

Prayer like fire or prayer without words is the Prayer of the Heart, which I mentioned. It appears when our heart prays without words, day and night; when the grace of God works within us to such a degree that everything within us burns like a fire similar to the Holy Light in Jerusalem. You know that the Holy Light has appeared for hundreds of years in Jerusalem on Holy Saturday. At the beginning, this Light does not burn you; you can put your hand in it, you can put it on your face and it does not burn you. However, it is a light, a flame, just like the flame of the Burning Bush on Sinai that did not consume the bush, the tree there. The flame in the praying heart discussed in St. John Cassian's writings is similar: a fire that does not consume, but burns and gives light, just as God enlightens our mind and heart when we desire something divine.

Can prayer replace Communion, as we read in the life of certain hermits?

Prayer cannot replace Holy Communion. The Divine Eucharist has its role, and prayer has a preparatory role in receiving the Holy Body and Blood of the Lord Jesus Christ.

Saint Mary of Egypt only through prayer, without communion, after forty-seven years as a hermit in the Jordan desert, had reached the point of being lifted off the ground in prayer, without being communed. However, we all need Holy Communion. Saint Zosimas—who came to her in the desert and communed her—put the seal and confirmation on this honor St. Mary had of being lifted off the ground in prayer; her body had become

24 *Sfântul Ioan Casian, Scrieri alese,* în *col. Părinți* și *Scriitori Bisericești, vol. 57, traducere de Prof. Vasile Cojocaru* și *Prof. David Popescu, Editura Institutului Biblic* și *de Misiune al Bisericii Ortodoxe Române, București, 1990, p. 468.*

so light that she would be lifted off the ground in prayer. However, she absolutely needed the Holy Eucharist. After she communed, the saint passed away. The second time St. Zosimas came with the Holy Gifts, he did not find her alive. She had received her allotment of holiness through her first and final communion, after forty-seven years of eremitic life. Thus, prayer has its purpose, and Holy Communion is the fulfillment of this purpose.

What purpose does prayer said with the lips serve for learning the Prayer of the Heart?

A person adorned with the recitation of psalms, akathists, and canons can say this short prayer I mentioned orally. However, when you say it with the mouth, the mind often wanders far and wide, as I said. Therefore, it is good for us to make an effort to concentrate more. If we do not succeed all at once, we can repeat the prayer. We should repeat it, repent for our wandering mind, and ask the Good God to help us collect our mind within ourselves. This goes for any prayer we say: reading psalms (which are very beautiful, very powerful), the Paraklesis to the Mother of God, the Canon to our Guardian Angel, the Canon of Repentance, the Canons to the Mother of God, very beautiful things. If our minds were concentrated on every word of the prayer, the benefit would be great for us.

But, because our mind wanders, after we pray, we are the same people that we were before praying; nothing happens within us! I look at what happens in our church: prayers are said, and the Divine Liturgy is celebrated (the Divine Liturgy is the most powerful prayer of all Church services). Then, a homily is given. After the service and homily have finished, a great commotion takes place. Each person speaks about totally different matters than what was heard in church up until then. Proof that almost nothing remained in the minds and hearts of those who listened because they were continuously distracted and scattered.

Therefore, we must concentrate on every word of the prayers we say—whether out loud, quietly, or internally. If we are not able to pay attention, we repeat the prayer once, twice, three times, four times, because the prayer we say without attention has no value; it does not receive a response from God because it is done only with the lips, while the heart is "far from Me," as the Savior says (Matt. 15:8). Concentration on the words of the prayer must be in such a way that it leads us towards ourselves, to the center in which God is hidden within us.

The Savior tells us that the Kingdom of God is within us (Luke 17:21), and St. Paul tells us that the body is "the temple of the Holy Spirit" (1 Cor. 6:19). The Holy Spirit dwells within us! The Kingdom of God is within us! Here, within ourselves, we must say our prayers and all our invocations when we utter them to God, the Mother of God, and all the saints. And if the mind is in another place, these lessons, exhortations, and prayers do not return to us, but remain floating in the ether; we do not benefit from them. It is as if we looked into a shop window filled with all kinds of goods, but a glass is between us and them—we cannot put our hand on them. And so it happens with our inattention that interposes between us and our prayer. May this obstacle not exist!

The Christian life is mystical, it is secret

What should I do if my spiritual father, who does not practice mental prayer, considers that it is not necessary for young people to practice it, urging them towards a social Christianity, rather than a mystical Christianity?

For me, a Christian life that is not mystical at the same time, that is, secret, connected to God, does not exist. I do not know of a true Christian who is not a mystic at the same time. I am referring to a Christian who communes with the Holy Mysteries, who confesses, who sanctifies his inner life. This is a mystical, secret, hidden state: "But you, when you pray, go into your room, and when you have shut your door, pray to your Father who is in the secret place" (Matt. 6:6). How can you pray without thinking that this Heavenly Father is hidden somewhere and sees the state of your soul? How can you be worldly, only earthly, lacking this spirit, this energy of the soul, which, if it is not in us, then this well-oiled machine—our body—is nothing, disintegrates, and wild beasts eat it?

Within each one of us is a secret, mystical center. All our good relationships with those around us stem from this center: our love, goodness, mercy, humility, meekness, courtesy. All are connected to this mystical center within us, where God and His Kingdom reside.

Thus, I don't know how a Christian life without prayer, without this mystical center, without this place of God in us, would look. Social life? Even the pagans had a social life, but they were concerned only with the horizontal plane of existence. The Lord Jesus Christ, however, tells us in the Sermon on the Mount: "Seek first the Kingdom of God and His righteousness, and all these things shall be added to you" (Matt. 6:33). Thus, I do not believe that engaging in social life is an impediment if at the same time you have an undying spring within you coming from God's presence within you.

Are the prayers of those who have not confessed in many years, or those who live in sin, heard by God?

If the prayers are said like those of the Publican in the Gospel (Luke 18:13)—with humility, pain of heart, without judging others, asking for forgiveness for the misdeeds committed, then God listens to anyone. God became incarnate for sinners. The thief on the cross only said a few words, and he was forgiven (Luke 23:40-43). We find this idea that some of you may know in the Church Fathers: *Blessed is the thief! All of his life he stole, and in the end he stole Paradise.*

Thus, God listens to anyone's prayer that is said with humility, repentance, and regret for all that was evil in his life until then, until the moment in which he thought that God exists and then realized that he too must give an answer before the heavenly Father for all he did on earth.

Are there temptations from the left and the right? What does this mean?

Yes, there are temptations from the left and temptations from the right. Those from the left are very well known: drunkenness, laziness, fornication, theft, vengeance, anger, etc. Those from the right are unhealthy exaggerations of good deeds, such as exaggerated fasting. Fasting is appointed by the Church to help us cleanse ourselves spiritually and physically. Fasting should not only be bodily, but also spiritual. Today, I actually heard something very interesting: someone said that he met a group of people who did not eat cheese because it was made with rennet, thus, a little bit of blood was mixed into the cheese. This is an exaggeration. Nowhere in the lives of the Holy Fathers do we find such a scrupulous and, at the same time, false analysis. If fasting is not done with discernment, if it is not united with the goodness of heart, guarding the mouth, and abstaining from condemning others, then it is not beneficial but actually poisonous. You can waste away and die of hunger, but if you have something against your neighbor and you speak badly of him

behind his back, your fasting is in vain. So the same deeds, done with the good intention of sanctifying our life, when they are exaggerated, become a cause of falling to the right. You go on the wrong path through good deeds.

Therefore, it is good to ask God for wisdom to illuminate the path of our life, so that we may go on this royal road (*via aurea*, the golden way, as the Holy Fathers call it), so that we do not err. Fasting should be done with wisdom, abstinence should be true abstinence, guarding the senses should be sincere guarding, repentance should be sincere repentance, prayers should be as many as possible, but they should be done with attention, contrition, and humility, and then everything goes well.

However long prayers may be, if they are said only with the lips, they are not received by God. Some poor Christians read akathists and psalms—many psalms and akathists—but they only realize after much time has passed that they said them only with their mouths. Their heart and mind were absent from what they were saying. Such prayers help very little.

Sometimes, during evening and morning prayers, we don't always have the same spiritual state or disposition. Sometimes we are very tired. Is it good then to shorten our prayer, or to continue it?

If we can make the effort of being attentive when we are tired, we should continue the prayer. If we cannot, God knows the real and sincere state of our life. When we are truly tired and our mind is scattered, we should at least say one or two prayers, a few prostrations, and then we can rest. If we manage to wake up during the night, we can continue this prayer. The rule for prayer is that it should be done consciously, being attentive to what you say to God, because He is a permanent presence, He knows us, sees us, and hears us in every moment. We should be the same way—just as present and attentive when we speak with Him.

Why is prayer said to be a dialogue with God when, in reality, only we speak?

It is still a dialogue because God is the One Who listens to our prayers. When we speak with someone, there are two of us—there is the other who listens, sympathizes, and agrees with what we say. It is the same with prayer. It can also be a response from the heavenly Father when God listens to our prayer, and then it is still a dialogue, communication, and communion with Him.

"The Mother of God immediately responds to prayer done with complete longing, with all one's being"

Is it good for a group of faithful friends to do evening, morning, or other prayers together?

Elder Sofian: Prayer done in a group is very well received by God. I was telling you that while St. Peter was imprisoned, many Christians gathered together, praying for him somewhere else, in a house. All had their minds and souls directed to God. They all asked for the same help; they all prayed for the same goal: that St. Peter be delivered from death because the next day, he was supposed to be taken out of prison and executed in the sight of the people of Jerusalem. They all prayed with the same longing and the same intention, and God listened to their prayer (Acts 12:13-17). When many people pray together, it is a beautiful thing, but under one condition: all must be attentive to the words of the prayer.

Private prayer is better, it seems to me, because when my mind wanders, I come back, repeat the prayer, am attentive, repent, and linger on a page or paragraph of the prayer. If there are many people, I cannot make all of them stop and start the prayer again from where my thoughts wandered. That is why I say: prayer as a group is very good when all have the same thought of prayer and are attentive to what they are saying; but if cases of inattention happen (as I said about myself), private prayer is better—each person prays individually in the secret of their life.

I am confused about some of the prayers to the Mother of God, for example, when we call her "the only quick helper." How should I understand this?

The Mother of God is the Mother of our Savior Christ. A mother is always very sensitive to her son, to her child. If anything happens to her child, a mother is very easily moved. If her son is in a difficult situation, even if he treated her badly until then, she gets worried very quickly and does not know how to help him escape from that impasse more quickly. The earthly mother! I have met many cases like this in my life as a priest.

The Birthgiver of God is a great exception: she is the mother of God incarnate! Being on the Cross, Jesus Christ put His Mother in the care of His beloved disciple, the Holy Apostle John, telling him: "Behold,

your mother!" (John 19:27) Through this entrustment during the most difficult moment in the earthly life of the Lord Jesus Christ, the Mother of God becomes our mother, of us on earth. She truly prays for us and is our great intercessor before God.

The Mother of God and St. John the Baptist, these two great witnesses of the Savior Jesus Christ, have much influence before the Just Judge. When we address the Mother of God, she intercedes for us before the Savior: "Lord, You Whom I carried in my arms, Whom I raised during Your earthly life, help me in my prayer and help these people who pray to me!" In the akathist for the Dormition of the Mother of God, the Holy Virgin says: "O Heavenly King, receive all who pray to You and call on my name for help, so that none leave without being aided and listened to" (Ikos 10). Truly, the Mother's prayer is received by her Son, because He is God full of love.

I will tell you a story from prison that someone who had been a political prisoner and had been in prison for twenty years recounted to me. A young man who had grown old in prison. During an extraordinarily difficult interrogation, his patience ended, and he set his mind on finding a way to end his life. And he remembered, however, that when he was free, his grandmother would tell him: "When you have a great trial, pray to the Mother of God!" And, he said: "I didn't have the courage to pray to the Savior because of my mistakes, but I prayed to the Mother of God, who lived on earth like us." A short prayer said in desperation: "O Mother of God, I can't bear the pain and pressure inflicted on me here any longer. Help me!" He was praying in his cell. And, a few moments later, he saw a woman in white with a baby in her arms entering through the tall door of the room: "You called me. I will help you. Be at peace!" And she left. Afterward, he was no longer called in for interrogations. He was moved to a different location, to the North Pole, somewhere in Vorkuta. Then, all his life—he lived in prison for many more years—he had very much peace in his soul, even though the external suffering was quite difficult from time to time. The Mother of God helped him the moment after he prayed fervently. I know of this event from the one who experienced it; he told it to me. And in prison, one does not lie. In prison, each person says what is on his heart. The poor person told me what happened to him and how the problem was resolved.

This is what the Mother of God does, she is a quick helper. But the prayer must be said from all of one's being, with all of one's longing, strength, and trust, said in desperation—and the prayer will be fulfilled the following moment. You do not need much time or lengthy prayers. Sometimes, we need long prayers to calm down, collect ourselves, and be able to concentrate. Other times, in such difficult moments, you receive a response right then and there; the Mother of God answers you.

Father Archimandrite, do you think that in the Romanian Orthodox Church's calendar, there should be a day to commemorate those who died in the Communist prisons?

It is good for us to pray for those who died in prison, this is a very good Christian deed. Among those who died in prison, there are many who need our prayers. Only saints do not need our prayers. We pray to them so that they may intercede for us before God. But for others who passed from this life and are now beyond, possibly weighed down by some heavy, unforgiven sins, the Church's prayers and our personal prayers are very beneficial for them.

How can we get all earthly cares out of our minds during prayer? What should I do if I have a hardened heart and don't feel anything when I say the prayer?

We should repent for our dryness while we pray. We must repent before God and say: "Lord, I am like the barren, dry, untilled earth"—-as the psalmist says (Ps. 62:3); "Help me! Send down Your grace upon my heart which thirsts for You!" A private, personal prayer can be said there and then, in the secret of your heart. An examination of your conscience is also necessary; there are certain difficulties, we have certain reasons for being hard-hearted.

Usually, our sins harden us. We did certain evil things, there are some people we cannot forgive, and so our heart is covered by a thick layer of stone, because of this hatred toward our neighbor. Let us pray for God to tear this veil, to open our hearts to what is beneficial again, and to make it impermeable to all earthly cares. This contrition for our sin and hidden prayer of repentance to God will tear down the veil of hard-heartedness and unfeeling that grips us.

At a certain moment, I say the prayer mechanically, without it reaching my

soul. It's as if the prayer has become dull. Can prayer become routine?

It is good to repeat it then; to repeat the prayer, and to make an effort to think about what we are saying. We should ask God for a quick renewal of prayer—there and then. And something will happen to us.

"This is what I advise young people: to have balance, wisdom, prayer"

Father, for now, I don't believe in God with all of my heart. Is it a sin for me to only pray to Him because I am afraid of Him?

It is good to pray like that. There is an event in the Gospel: when the Savior is descending from Mount Tabor after the miracle of the Transfiguration, he meets the other apostles (without the three who were with Christ) and a man with a demon-possessed son. They were all in turmoil. The man had asked the apostles to heal the possessed child; however, they could not free him, and there was a kind of contempt toward them. The father approached Jesus, saying: "Teacher, I brought You my son, who has a mute spirit. And wherever it seizes him, it throws him down; he foams at the mouth, gnashes his teeth, and becomes rigid. So, I spoke to Your disciples, that they should cast it out, but they could not....But if You can do anything, have compassion on us and help us" (Mark 9:17-18, 22). The Lord Jesus said to him: "If you can believe, all things are possible to him that believes" (Mark 9:23). The father immediately responded with tears in his eyes: "Lord, I believe; help my unbelief" (Mark 9:24). He believed, but not fully; he was on the road of faith. And the Savior healed both him and his son. The Savior increases this little faith—that some of the apostles also had at a certain time—if we persevere in drawing near to Him and continue to pray to Him to help us, to give us full faith. And He gives it to us!

If we don't have a spiritual father, does that mean we are not good Christians?

When we are sick, we need a doctor. But despite being sick, we may be stubborn and not go to the doctor. The doctor waits for you or doesn't even know that you are sick, and you wallow in your sins and pain. This is how such a state is.

That is, we need confession to unburden the weight of our sins and mistakes. Sometimes, we feel this need, so we tell someone. We tell a friend what is weighing on us. That person listens to us, maybe comforts us or encourages us with a word, yet we remain the same, with this burden that clings to our being. If, however, you tell a spiritual father your sorrows, alongside the fact that he listens to you and gives you some guidance, he unbinds you; that is, he lifts your sins and annihilates the burden. And he is not the one who does it, because we don't have this power, but Christ Who is present, near at hand in every confession, next to every person who confesses. He forgives and blesses and eases us of this burden.

Therefore, if someone does not confess, it is his loss. He remains weighed down, and this burden hardens his heart during prayer. He is very much at risk of falling into different kinds of troubles and temptations in his life, and he can no longer think of God's gifts; he does not recognize them, and they do not have room within him. That is why a spiritual father is needed to help us and guide us to this small gate through which we can connect with the heavenly Father. Through the grace of priesthood, the spiritual father forgives our sins, and we can thus approach the essence of life, which is God.

Can marriage in any way be an impediment on the path of the Prayer of the Heart?

It can be an impediment, but I know married people who also pray very fruitfully with this prayer. It is difficult, but still possible for a person to pray even if he is married and has a family. If he succeeds in convincing the rest of his family to follow this path, then their life will be much easier and more beautiful.

Please comment on the biblical verse: "For where your treasure is, there will your heart be also" (Luke 12:34).

I believe that there is no need to make a complicated commentary on this matter if we think that, truly, what makes us most passionate also attracts our attention.

Treasure presupposes, first of all, money, dollars. There are people who have no other care than to become rich. Nowadays, there are three categories of people: poor, middle class, and very wealthy. I believe that those who are very rich often have their heart where their money is. They think about how to stack one on top of the other so that their treasure grows more and more. If they also have spiritual preoccupations, when they pray, when they read the Holy Scripture, the Philokalia, or other

blessed texts, their attention is divided between the place of their treasure, the means of increasing it, and what is said in the holy writings; yet often their mind wanders more to where the material treasure is than to where the spiritual treasure is. Thus, it is said: "Where your treasure is, there will your heart be also." I believe everyone can recognize this in his own life.

The saints, however, had a completely different way of thinking. St. Anthony, for example, renounced and rid himself of all his earthly belongings after the death of his parents. Although he had inherited great wealth, his heart did not get attached to it; rather, he divided it among the poor. And then he could not think about this treasure; he had another one in the Kingdom of God. And alone, with only a shoulder bag, he left for the desert. Therefore, where his true treasure was (in God, for Whom he had sold everything), his heart was also.

Thus did all those who left their belongings, these men of God, who lived permanently in prayer and meditation, with their minds bound to this reality beyond life on earth, in eternity. Their heart was where their treasure was, where God was, where grace was, where the Sacraments were, where joy for eternal life after death was.

Father Archimandrite, at the end of this conference, maybe you would like to give one more word for the benefit of young people.

I have a very good opinion about young people, because they, through a kind of inner impetus, spurred on by the grace of God, orient themselves with hope towards the heavenly Father. They draw near to Him through prayer. Children, young people, many of them (God knows how many there are) have this faith, not learned in school, because only recently was religious education introduced in schools. They have a faith learned by ear, as some who are musically talented learn by ear. These young people learn the faith in this way—from the Church, from a book that fell into their hands, from the Bible, the New Testament, the Philokalia. And faith takes root in them. They pray and feel that this prayer makes them well, helps them, illuminates their mind, and gives balance to their life. Then, they keep on this road of faith. Sometimes, it happens that their mother or father is actually against them on this path of the Church.

What do I recommend to young people? To walk on the path of salvation, to be realistic in life, balanced, to neither slip to the left in these common passions of life, nor to the right, exaggerating certain things.

They should not join dangerous circles that draw them into all sorts of evil deeds. Young people who do not have complete wisdom should gather it from the Holy Books and ask God for it in prayer. They should strive not to fall into drunkenness. They should preserve their bodies pure because our bodies will resurrect in the General Judgment. Therefore, it is good to take care that our body is pure and holy and can continue on this road of Light into the Kingdom of God, together with our soul.

This is what I advise young people: to have balance, wisdom, prayer, watchfulness of the heart, guarding their minds, mouths, and hearts. If they have all this spiritual protection, their lives will be stable and honest, both here on earth and beyond.

We are all very thankful to you!

Humility: Gateway to the Kingdom

Recollections from the Communist Prisons[25]

I saw suffering as a penance for my sins • God is truly good! • The Holy Spirit can bring something extraordinary to our hearts

To the degree that you have a broken and humble heart, you become more free within, and then God descends into you. Our purpose on earth is to fill ourselves with God. And we can only fill ourselves with God through humility. This path of acquiring humility must be the foundation of our life.

Humility means that God is beside you in everything. We do not become someone through cheap pride, but only through humility. Without humility, we cannot feel God's greatness, Who is humble. The devil has been very proud from the beginning. The proud person follows an incorrect path. He judges according to human logic and says that humility is a lack of dignity. In this way, he loses, slowly but surely, the very essence of life. And, finally, he remains empty-handed for the eternity that we enter.

To live in humility means to live a genuine life, while to live in pride is an artificial life. Therefore, each time you are humbled, bear it and pray: "Lord, receive this humiliation in place of the humility I lack. May this humiliation make up for the pride from which I cannot free myself by my own will."

I saw suffering as a penance for my sins

I was imprisoned in the Communist prisons and only God knows how unjust it was there, how much hate, how much evil; it is as though you cannot even describe it in words. Wherever you looked, there was only

25 A number of recollections from Communist prisons were gathered in this chapter—handwritten notes or audio/video recordings—that Elder Sofian imparted to certain close disciples from 1994-2001.

hatred. But, by God's mercy, I could pray and was so peaceful! I would pray and it was as if all their hatred was directed at someone else.

When I was greatly tormented, I tried not to revolt, not to protest. I would think: "Let me recall how I've sinned before God, for which I am now suffering this injustice." And I would think about different sins of mine, which only God and I knew, and I saw the suffering as a penance for my sins and did not revolt. A penance that I accepted with full, inner freedom. I would think that I too am evil, sinful, and have sinned before God; I would think that maybe I am worse than all the guards combined. I would think that maybe if I were better, they would not be as bad; thus, I, too, was guilty of their evil. When I would think in this way, I no longer felt any bit of revolt in my heart, I would forgive everyone, and I could pray for them. I almost no longer felt the suffering they inflicted on me. I tell you honestly that when I could do all this and could think of my sins, I felt such great joy, peace, and richness of love in my heart that it was as if I were flying, even though I was in prison.

We were not unjustly sentenced, even if the accusations against us were false. In prison, I became more aware of the multitude of my "subtle" sins—sins from the right. Maybe those of us who initiated the Burning Bush Movement became proud thinking that, through our prayers, we had the high calling of delivering the country from its impasse. Maybe, within our hearts, we judged others who committed all kinds of blasphemies. Maybe we participated in pompous, large celebrations with much self-aggrandizement. And God rightfully cleansed us like gold in the fire.

I endured very great humiliation in prison, with my mind on God, my sins, and people's suffering. I had never heard such dirty words until I ended up in prison. The guards spoke very vulgarly, especially to the priests. They would hit us with whatever they could find, with their hands and feet. I would not say anything to them. I would think that I deserved it for my sins, and prayer would grow within me like a fire. One of the political prisoners would tell me indignantly: "Why don't you say anything to these terrible people, father?" I remained silent and felt that if I responded to the guards, the prayer would have stopped.

We were shut in a tiny cell, tightly packed, with an open bucket for necessities, infected air, permanent toilet smell, with the lights on day and night. We were spied on through a peephole at all times. The food

was very scarce and miserable. We were physically emaciated; we did not have air and had become blue.

God is truly good!

We could be killed dozens of times a day in prison. Then I promised the Good God that if He let me hear confessions again in freedom, no one would leave from me without some good advice, without help, or without being listened to, despite all his sins. We suffered so that you who now run to Church can be at peace with everyone.

I tell you in all sincerity: I believe, with all of my being, that God is good! I always felt this. In prison, I found all of my guilt before God, even in the most subtle aspects, and God was very present in my life; He was always very alive and very good; truly very good! Maybe I was not so guilty. Maybe others were guilty too, since we were all there, behind bars. I was not interested, however, at all in their sins; I was not interested if others were or were not to blame, and neither am I interested in this now.

I was so preoccupied with seeing my sins, that even at night I talked in my sleep and asked for forgiveness from God. And the same guards who watched the doors listened by the bars to what I was saying. And the following day they would call me in for an interrogation and tell me what I had said in my sleep, because of my spiritual turmoil. At night I would say: "Lord, forgive me a sinner!" And during the day they would shout at me: "Sinner! Sinful priest!" And they would repeat all that I had said at night in my dreams, God knows how.

The Holy Spirit can bring something extraordinary to our hearts

I never felt abandoned in prison. I felt a presence that kept me alive and in a state of inner peace. Prayer was much more personal in prison than outside.

I wanted to say this: it is very important for us to be aware of how unworthy we are before God. We must not blame anyone except ourselves. We must always repent, with all of our heart. I am not angry at those who did evil to me in life. I remember them, yet I do not have anything against them, I do not bring to mind any painful memories. If I do not find myself guilty in a real way, and I do not repent from the depths of my soul, I cannot pray more deeply, and I cannot have the full joy of prayer. If you have these two—humility and forgiveness of others—you will begin to feel how you acquire within yourself something from God, something extraordinary! Only the Holy Spirit can bring this "something" in our heart.

I did not hate any of the enemies who oppressed us; God helped me not to regret the fact that I was imprisoned. They needed me there as well so that, with our Romanian brothers, we could all suffer the wrath that came upon the country. In prison, I came to better know the suffering of the Romanian people. People of all social strata were imprisoned there. I learned some things from them that I had not been attentive to during the period of freedom. I learned what the purpose of suffering was for me, and in this way, I better understood certain problems that I was confronting in my life. Life in prison was quite hard. However, the whole country was suffering, not only in the Communist prisons but outside, too. I can also say that I had more happy days in prison than after I gained my freedom, happiness comes from within, not from the outside.

Seek to do as much good as possible around you, love your neighbors, pray as much as possible with the Jesus Prayer, do not speak badly of anyone, and in this way, you will have peace of heart. May the Good God and the Mother of God help you unceasingly in any place you may be!

Love For Enemies[26]

Let us confront evil with good! • Am I not at all to blame? •
It is very important to pray for those who hate us

Man is born to live in union with his fellow human beings. He feels lonely and unhappy as long as he is alone and isolated. Therefore, man seeks society, friendship, and family. But, curiously, although people feel each other's absence, although they long for and seek one another, nonetheless, after they meet, after not much time, many of them argue, do not get along, separate, and hate one another.

An old Latin proverb says that man is a wolf to other men: *Homo homini lupus est*. Sadly, this proverb is always true and current because, ever since the human race has existed, from Cain and Abel, the sons of Adam, until our days, although there are intelligent beings who bear within themselves the image of God, the majority of people cannot bear one another, and they often hate and tear each other apart and bite one another, worse than beasts. They are upset and troubled by a single insult. They explode in anger at a petty injustice. After anger comes arguing, and from arguing comes enmity, then revenge. Calumnies, feuds, fights, trials, underhanded blows, and wars all come from here.

Thus, instead of looking as a family of siblings, as God wanted us to be from the beginning, human society has the appearance of a fierce battlefield. Culture and civilization did not bring much change from this point of view. Only the weapons of war have changed. From the perspective of evil and revenge, there is not a single difference between our wild ancestors in caves and their descendants in the twentieth century.

We may ask ourselves: who can heal this continually open, bleeding wound, this shortcoming of human life? Who can reconcile our [human] nature's desire to live in society with our evil and hostile impulses? What can each of us do to live in peace and on good terms with our neighbor?

The Savior responds to all of these questions in chapter six of the Holy Gospel according to Luke: "Love your enemies, do good to those who hate you [...] And just as you want men to do to you, you also do to them

26 Undated manuscript.

likewise" (Luke 6:27-31). How good it would be if each one of us lived according to this rule!

Let us confront evil with good!

Therefore, let us do good and treat others as we would like them to treat us. This is the natural measure of humanity. Then, let us do good not only to those who love us, but also to those who hate us—that is, we must love our enemies. This is the supreme measure of Christian love.

Brothers and sisters in Christ, the first of the two Gospel commandments we mentioned is easier to fulfill, although good deeds are often repaid with evil, disdain, and insults.

But none of the commandments in Holy Scripture receive such opposition from our human nature as the commandment to love our enemies.

I often had the opportunity to meet people who hated each other. Men or women who have terrible enemies. Some of them come here to the Holy Altar and ask us to pray for God to punish their enemies for all the evil they did to them. We respond that we will not pray for God to punish them, but to pacify and calm their hatred, which is oftentimes unjust.

Yet, when I occasionally dared to advise them to reconcile, to do all that lies within their power to end this enmity between them, which torments them in the depth of their being, they answered me: "How can I reconcile and how can I forgive, Father, the one who mocks me, who slanders me in front of everyone, turns his face away in disdain each time he sees me? He hurts me, curses me, or threatens me with death!" I take their word for it and realize that they suffer greatly.

We know that, unfortunately, there are such people who offend and trouble their fellow human beings without a reason, only with the desire and pleasure of doing evil to others. But still, how must we treat such people? Should we respond to them with the same measure of evil? "An eye for an eye, and a tooth for a tooth?" (Deut. 19:21). Should we repay them according to their deeds? Should we hate them, curse them, and condemn them as they do us?

If we treat them according to the measure of their evil, our enemies will become even worse, and our life around them will become more difficult and bitter day by day: a life of hell! If you respond to evil with

evil, it only seems like you cure and escape the evil. In fact, you make the wound deeper! If, however, you confront evil with good, the power of evil weakens because the enemy no longer has anyone to fight with. Left alone, he burns with anger a bit longer, and then he calms down.

We know, however, that in the eyes of the world, if you receive insults and physical blows with meekness and self-control, if you ask for forgiveness—even though he is more guilty than you—you are considered by many to be cowardly or faint-hearted, or someone who lacks personality. Conversely, if you hit back and seek to take revenge, you are considered a man of action, a dignified, honorable man.

But God, the Father of all, does not like such an honor. He wants us to reconcile and live together as brothers. He wants good to triumph through gentleness, not through violence. "Learn from Me"—the Savior tells us—"for I am gentle and lowly in heart: and ye shall find rest for your souls" (Matt. 11:29). He asks us to be good and gentle not only with those who are good, who treat us well, but to treat especially those who are evil with unfeigned goodness and patient endurance, in order to pacify them, as God does with us, for He is merciful and kind to the ungrateful and evil (Luke 6:35).

Better to let yourself be humiliated by people and honored by God, remaining in the service of the good, enduring, forgiving, and praying, rather than taking revenge on your fellow man who is your enemy, and therefore lose the goodness of God.

Am I not at all to blame?"

Brothers and sisters, when we speak about forgiveness and reconciliation, we often only think of our enemies, who in different ways wrong and hate us. This is natural. But, at the same time, we must think about ourselves: are we not also others' enemies? Do we not also do evil to others and wrong them? Maybe others are better and more blameless than we are, and we wrongfully hate them. Maybe not they, but we are actually the cause of our turmoil and enmities!

Therefore, finding ourselves in enmity with someone, it is good to examine our thoughts and ask ourselves honestly: "Am I not at all to blame? Is only he to blame? If my conscience does not prick me for certain evil and hidden deeds that I cannot see or do not want to recognize, then is my conscience not darkened by sin? Is he, whom I consider my enemy, in any way better than myself, and I, in my darkness, wrongfully hate him?"

If, searching within ourselves in this manner, we discover a certain guilt and realize that he too is right, we go to the other person, ask for forgiveness with humility, and the wound heals.

It is very important to pray for those who hate us

We know from experience that poisons are harmful to our body. Nonetheless, some of them, used in certain doses by doctors, heal certain illnesses. So too—for ourselves—are our enemies. Used by God in certain measures known only to Him, they heal us of spiritual defects and, especially, heal us of pride, abuses, certain passions, and overconfidence in ourselves. For such reasons, too, we are commanded to love and to pray for our enemies.

And there is another very important reason why we need to pray for our enemies. For example, in our life, we meet an evil person who stays the same, without changing, someone who unjustly wrongs us out of the abundance of his evil. Such a person is often under the control of an evil spirit. It urges him to act in this way, and without realizing it, he becomes a tool of the devil, who, in fact, is the real and great enemy of the human race and, thus, the enemy of each of us individually.

Such a wicked person, through his own evil deeds, breaks his connection with God, Who is the source of good, and from a son of God by grace, as he became through the sacrament of Holy Baptism, now, driven by passions and evil, becomes a son of the devil. He is like one dead before his natural death. He should not be cursed because he is already under a curse. Without him realizing it, he greatly needs God's help, to Whom he can no longer pray. Evil has captured and hardened his heart. He needs others' prayers and especially the prayers of those whom he hated and oppressed. This enemy becomes like those who crucified the Savior, and the one who was wrongfully persecuted becomes, in a sense, like the One Crucified on the Cross, Who prayed for His murderers, saying: "Father, forgive them, for they know no what they do" (Luke 23:34). Although they thought they knew what they were doing!

Practically, it is difficult to bear unjust humiliations, to respond with good instead of evil, to forgive from the heart, and to pray for the good of your enemy. It is difficult to sincerely rejoice in his joys, to empathize with him, and to truly feel sorry when you hear that your enemy is suffering greatly. Only with God's help can you acquire such feelings full of kindness and goodness for the one who is hostile to you! Therefore, we need to pray very much in these situations so that God can inspire us with such feelings.

When God sees your patience, your good thoughts, and the gentleness of your heart, He will pacify and humble your enemy as well, and He will comfort you with an inexpressible peace and joy poured into your soul, and He will prepare a large reward for you in the Heavenly Kingdom.

May the Good God help us resolve our conflicts with our enemies, praying for them and pacifying them. And when we pray with the "Our Father" and say the words, "and forgive us our trespasses, as we forgive those who trespass against us," may we not prove to be liars because we did not forgive, and thus fall into condemnation; but, because we truly forgave those who did evil to us, let us ask the Most Good and Heavenly Father to also forgive us all of our trespasses. Amen.

Thoughts on the Sunday of Orthodoxy[27]

1. He who observes and experiences how the life of the Church unfolds during this period realizes that we have entered a special order; we breathe a different spiritual air. Great Lent is like a time from another world, richer in meaning and spiritual fruit. It is like the secret heart of the liturgical year and a spring of holiness for all the days of the year.

2. Today, with God's help, we finish the first week of the Resurrection Fast. The sanctity of this Lenten period is great and undeniable. Whether we realize it or not, it penetrates us, with or without our will. Until the great day of the Lord's Resurrection, we move through a special spiritual atmosphere, in which each Sunday of Lent shines like a bright star. We ascend these Sundays like steps leading to the great height of meeting the Resurrected Jesus Christ. These Sundays of Great Lent speak to our mind and heart with the power of a divine discovery, reminding us that our life here in the world is founded on a secret [heavenly] order, and that our life here on earth is imbued with heavenly tidings.

3. Today, the first Sunday of Lent, called the Sunday of Orthodoxy, is especially one such day that is full of spiritual meaning. It is the doorway to the other feasts of Lent until the great feast of Holy Pascha. And the ordering of these days of Lent, between the first and last Sunday, that is, between the Sunday of Orthodoxy and that of the Lord's Resurrection, is not accidental. The whole path of our salvation is contained within these two Sundays, and we cannot see the light of the Resurrection in the age to come if we do not orient ourselves to it by going through the door of Orthodoxy.

4. But what does the Sunday of Orthodoxy mean for us, Orthodox Christians, and what spiritual memories do we celebrate today?

5. Beloved, we can say it concisely, from the start: today, our Church celebrates the fullness of its faith.

27 Extracts from missing pages of a manuscript of incomplete homilies on the Sunday of Orthodoxy.

6. Eight-and-a-half centuries after the Incarnation of Christ the Savior, after it had won all its dogmas and right worship of God by blood and grace, on a Sunday like today, the Holy Church permanently established its treasure of spiritual teaching, fully established and clearly articulated, such that through it the world could be made worthy of union with God and eternal life with Him.

7. By an ordinance from above, the reason that led to the celebration of the Sunday of Orthodoxy was the triumph of the Church over its adversaries: those who fought against icons.

8. For, in the eighth century, a heresy was born in the Christian world, spread by certain emperors, seeking the complete destruction of holy icons. Yet, the word Orthodoxy means, as we know, "right worship."

9. The right worship of God could not be complete so long as the images of God and His saints, present in icons, were not glorified. Therefore, the day in which the Church reacquired its icons—and, together with them, its right worship—was called the Sunday of Orthodoxy.

10. The Sunday of Orthodoxy is not only a simple recollection of a past historical event, but it is the day on which Orthodoxy, with holy power, affirms its faith for all ages. Year after year, the Sunday of Orthodoxy also has something to tell us, in our day and age, addressing a calling to us. Year after year, we, too, must ask ourselves what Orthodoxy means for each Christian soul and what our duty is to our holy faith.

11. Orthodoxy means correct and unshakeable faith in the true God. The essence of Orthodoxy is Christ the Savior Himself, alive and present in our midst. In the heart of Orthodoxy, just as on her holy altars, the Savior is forever present, alive, and continually acting upon us. Although He is invisible, He is present in our life, as He Himself said: "Lo, I am with you always, even unto the end of the world!" (Matt. 28:20).

12. But who can speak of the power that God gives us during prayer, which is the soul of Orthodoxy? Who can ever speak of the consolation that Orthodoxy gives us in the services for our dearly departed? Who can ever speak of God's parental care for us in our illnesses, trials, and all kinds of needs? Who can ever speak of the fullness and nimbleness

that God gives us in the sacrament of Holy Communion? Who can ever speak of the special joy that we feel on the great feast days of Christianity? Someone once said: if you want to know what is in the center of the earth, look down from the top of a volcano! If you want to know what is in the center of Orthodoxy, go to an Orthodox church for the Paschal vigil—the empress of our Christian feasts. Only then will you understand the immense force of resurrection that the Savior brings into the world through the holy establishment of Orthodoxy. Truly, no one word in the human language can encompass all that Orthodoxy is.

13. Above all, the Sunday of Orthodoxy is a celebration of the triumph of right Christian worship. A holy remembrance dominates this day; for the history of the Church, it signified the end of many centuries of turmoil and struggle for the right faith, the victorious end that crowned the asceticism and self-sacrifice of the confessors of the Living God.

14. Just like its divine Founder, that is, like the Savior of the world, Who reached the

15. Resurrection only after passing through torture, the Cross, and suffering, so too did His Church, from the beginning, not gain any of Its holy and salvific truths without first passing through trials, battles, and difficulties, out of which, however, it always emerged brighter and stronger. The battle against holy icons was a great trial through which the right-worshiping faith passed. It was a period of nearly a century and a half in which one of the Church's most precious truths, namely the veneration of the image of God, was attacked. A persecution similar to that unleashed by the Roman pagan emperors at the beginning of Christianity was commanded in the eighth-ninth centuries by the self-proclaimed Christian emperors, who were wicked and pagan at heart. The Church bled, suffered, and endured hardships from these blows, but it also fought and, in the end, completely triumphed.

16. The devotion of those of you who choose this Holy Sunday of Orthodoxy to draw near and unite yourselves with our Savior through the Holy Sacraments is living proof of living out the right worship of God. This is the cornerstone of Orthodoxy: the God-Man Jesus Christ Himself given to the world, even in this age, as a guarantee for eternal life with Him in the age to come, in heavenly right worship, where may God

make us worthy to see Him face to face and to partake of Him more fully to the endless ages. Amen!

17. Today, brothers and sisters in Christ, is the name day of our holy faith; it is the name day of Holy Orthodoxy's divine glory.

18. The word orthodox is of Greek origin and means right glory or right faith. Orthodoxy is the Church of God as it was established by our Lord Jesus Christ, as it was understood and experienced by the Holy Apostles, Holy Martyrs, Holy Fathers, and our fathers and forefathers who neither strayed to the right nor the left, but kept the right path, the right and steadfast faith, as Holy Scripture exhorts us: "be thou faithful unto death, and I will give thee a crown of life" (Rev. 2:10), as well as, "to him that overcometh will I give to eat of the tree of life, which is in the midst of the paradise of God" (Rev. 2:7).

Icons: Living Signs of Divine Blessings[28]

1. Icons are spiritual dams that block all the evil one's assaults upon a person's life. At the same time, they are a secret ladder on which God descends to meet the believer.

2. If the very existence of icons is based on the Incarnation of the Son of God, this Incarnation, in turn, is strengthened and attested by the image of the One incarnate.

3. The icon is a guarantee of the reality of the divine Incarnation. Therefore, in the eyes of the Church, denying the Savior's icon is the same as denying the Lord's Incarnation, denying the entire economy of our salvation.

4. That is why we defend holy icons not only for their didactic role or aesthetic aspects but also because icons constitute the very basis of the Christian faith and of our salvation. This is how we can explain the unwavering decision of those who honor holy icons to defend them even at the price of their lives.

5. The icon of a saint is the image of a spiritual human being who dwelt among us at one point, sanctified his life in this world, and passed beyond to the Kingdom of God. From there, with the help of divine grace, the saints help us form a connection with them through prayer. Standing next to an icon, it is as if we are standing next to a window, a channel through which one can communicate with a person who was once in history, in this earthly reality. All of the spiritual world is living and present, and if you address it, you receive a response. This is the relationship between us and an icon; this is the relationship between us and the saints.

6. In religious mural paintings in which the human figure appears so frequently, beginning with God incarnate, Jesus Christ, and the Mother of God, down to the least known person in the world of the saints, there are so many presences that add a special value to the place of worship. The

28 Notes on pages of a manuscript.

wall itself is ennobled by participating in the spiritual life. Similar to the human being, the wall becomes the body, and the mural painting, with the world of saints, becomes the soul. Thus, the mural decor gives life to the wall. And if the grace of consecration is added to such a place through the service of the consecration of the church, then the church becomes a Holy Place, a true House of God, a place of worship.

7. In the nineteenth century, a completely undesirable phenomenon took place for our church painting. Thus, concomitantly with our orientation to the West on a political and cultural level, especially in the second half of the nineteenth century, a short-lived change in the good taste of our people occurred, in that it preferred realistic, Renaissance-style painting in place of our venerable eastern art, reaching the point of destroying admirable fresco paintings and covering them with realistic oil paintings, as it happened with the paintings in the Tismana Monastery church and the mural paintings of the "Doamnei" Church in Bucharest. Sadly, this wind of "modern fashion" in relation to traditional painting infiltrated the neighboring countries as well: Bulgaria, Serbia, Russia, and even Greece. However, thankfully, this temptation did not last long. During the first few decades of the twentieth century, a movement to return "home" to the original, to our traditional painting, began.

8. Just as on the Mount of Transfiguration [Tabor], the Savior's human body became like a luminous vestment of His divinity but did not cease being a human body, so too, after His Resurrection and Ascension to the right hand of the Father, this Holy Body, clothed in His divine glory, preserves its human nature for eternity.

9. In the icon of the Savior, we depict His holy body with His face, as the iconographic tradition has preserved it. But, in the same icon, we contemplate His Divine nature, eternally united to His human nature depicted in the icon.

10. In his letter to Leo the Isaurian, St. Gregory II, Pope of Rome, says that we cannot depict God the Father in icons because we do not know how He looks. If we had seen and known God the Father as we saw and knew His Son, we would have tried to describe and depict Him in art. In icons, we only depict what is revealed: the incarnate person of the Son of God—Jesus Christ—and the Holy Spirit in the form of a dove

and tongues of fire. We depict the Father symbolically through a blessing hand—coming out of the sky—which generally indicates the presence of the divine.

11. We do not say that icons are God. For us Christians, an icon is an image of a heavenly being. It represents heavenly nature, just as photographs represent the images of our parents, siblings, and friends.

12. In Holy Scripture, we have very harsh, condemning words about idols, but not a single word against honoring icons. We find the biblical foundation for the veneration of icons in the following verses:

— "And the Word was made flesh" (John 1:14);

— Jesus Christ incarnate is "the image of the invisible God" (Col. 1:15);

— Jesus Christ is the "express image of his person" (Heb. 1:3);

— "He who sees me, sees him who sent me" (John 12:45);

— The Holy Spirit was seen descending like a dove (Matt. 3:16), and in the form of tongues "of fire" upon the heads of the Holy Apostles (Acts 2:3).

12. Icons are not idols but living signs of divine blessings in our life and Christian homes.

13. The most precious purpose of an icon is for us to actually move beyond it, not stop at merely viewing it. In the spirit of Holy Orthodoxy, we believe and confess that: the reverence shown to an icon ascends to its original image. Therefore, when we are in front of an icon, we do not say: "Icon, help me!" but, looking with faith at the image depicted on it, we pray: Lord, have mercy on me! Most Holy Theotokos save us! Holy Guardian Angel, protect me! Saint Nicholas, Saint Paraskevi, pray to God for us!

14. He who does not honor icons does not honor the saints whose prototypes are imprinted on icons. Icons show us the inheritors of incorruption and the Kingdom of God who began their holy lives here on earth. The Holy Spirit dwelt in them in a real way, even in this life.

15. Therefore, a natural and organic relationship exists between honoring the saints and venerating icons.

16. The spiritual experience of holiness is communicated to us through icons. They also teach us the truths of the faith, being rightly named scripture in images. Icons also have a significant educational role in our formation as citizens of this world and the Kingdom of God.

17. Therefore, praying before an icon, or only attentively looking at one, it reminds us of the life portrayed on the icon and urges us to watch over our life and live correctly, as if before God, Who sees all: our eyes should see with purity, our ears should hear what is beneficial, our hearts should not be harboring evil thoughts, and the body that will rise on the Day of Judgment should be kept without stain, clean of any filth or vice. That is, we must strive to live our life as the saint in the icon lived, before whom we pray.

18. The icon urges us, therefore, to pray and model our own lives on the model of the one depicted on it. Its quiet presence, humble and full of grace, always reminds us of the existence beyond us towards which we are going.

19. Icons are visible signs of the invisible God. They are the invisible presence of God in a visible space. All Christian life seeks nothing other than to experience the invisible life of Heaven now, on earth. Icons exist precisely to give us a real sense of God's presence in our midst.

20. God is, without a doubt, everywhere present in the same form. But He is present in a more special and powerful way in everything that is directly connected to His manifestations.

21. But what were and are God's greatest manifestations if not, first of all, His Incarnation, with all the events connected to it, followed by His manifestations through the lives of His Saints, with our Most Holy Mother of God in the forefront?

22. That is why icons truly bring heaven itself down to earth. All of heaven depicted upon an icon bows down over us and secretly looks at us: the Holy Trinity, holy angels, and all the saints descend from an icon and fill our life from childhood to death.

23. A blessed icon transmits, thus, something of the beauty of divine glory through material means, visible to the bodily eyes. For this reason, the Holy Fathers say that an icon is venerable and holy, because it transmits the divine state of its prototype and because the grace that dwelled in the prototype can now be found present in its icon. Through it, as through a window open to eternity, we address the holy persons depicted in the icon who are in the Kingdom of God, asking them for the help we need. With this awareness, the Orthodox Christian kneels before an icon and prays with tears, convinced that his prayer is heard, and he truly feels a great spiritual relief and receives a comforting response to his prayers.

TRANSFORMATION[29]

Can society still be changed? • The emphasis must be put on prayer • Zeal for God • The steps of the Prayer of the Heart • The fruits of the Jesus Prayer • Living prayer

Father, can you give us a word of advice?

Elder Sofian: You are thirsty to gather something very valuable from me, but—as I am now sick—I am less generous with such advice. I can say some words, I can give you some advice that is not so valuable, but at least do it, brothers.

Pray! Do not live without prayer! God is present in each moment, within our reach, He is present everywhere. Anytime, any day, at least a little, pray with much attention, not with superficiality. Pray with all your heart. Pray, for example, with an "Our Father," said slowly, concentrated, at least once or twice a day. And advise other people to pray and give alms or help others.

Even if you are a student and have to study, it is still good to be active and to do something for others. We can be saved, and we can be worthy through what we do for those near us. Remember this: each day, it is good to do at least a good deed, an act of charity, as small as it may be. A good deed is the most valuable of all the things we do in our relationship with God.

Look at St. Antim Ivireanul who highly praises good deeds. Although he was a stranger to us Romanians, he did many good works in the more than twenty-five years he lived in Romania.

Alongside other obligations which you fulfill, do not forget to visit the sick; help them in whatever way and however much you can. A sick person always needs money or medicine.

In conclusion, let us try each day to do a good deed, as small as it may be. The Savior tells us that for a cup of water that we give to a thirsty person, we will not lose our reward.

29 Elder Sofian responded to these questions over the course of 2000-2001. The chapter was revisited and completed by Elder Sofian at the end of 2001. The interviews in the present volume were done by the editor.

Can society still be changed?

How do you think the relationship between material and spiritual conditions in Romania has evolved since 1990?

A person progresses from the point of view of faith when he is limited materially. After the Revolution, many hoped it would be much better, at least from a material perspective. However, in general, those who had the opportunity continued to become wealthy, while those who were less cunning and maybe more honest remained in their state from before and continued to be poor. Some poor people have become closer to God, others swear and curse the rich.

We all notice that there is more external freedom than in Communism, but sadly, there is also the appeal of other denominations that come from rich countries and ruin our Orthodox faithful; they destroy their understanding of our faith.

After 1990, we were expecting a return to faith, to a good, harmonious life, but, on the contrary, we see that it is a bitter life. Some live very comfortably and don't know what to do with their money, while others, poor people, nearly die of hunger. They come to the monastery's gates and ask for a loaf of bread. This begging is not normal because the country is rich, the soil produces as it has until now, but the wealthy people are not honest. Those with more possessions are not more open, more generous, or with more faith.

In this regard, the Savior, Who is the Master of the universe and is present in each of our lives, humbles Himself to the point that He appears in the person of a beggar and asks you to help Him. But if you see him in the form of someone who is still young, you shout: "Go to work!" You don't realize that in fact you are not helping Christ. Some people exhaust their possessions and don't have anything left to eat. It is very difficult to endure such conditions, especially when you have to take care of children. Then, if we help these people, they will be grateful, and maybe they will help us when they become better off. This way, life goes on normally.

It is good for the poor person to confess with maximum sincerity and to forgive from his heart all whom he is angry at, often because of mere trifles (or at least to pray daily for them); but if he does not complain and does not revolt against those who have and do not want to give, at the critical moment, when he truly can no longer go on, God helps him.

If instead of praying to God, he curses and swears those who have, then alongside his material poverty, he also has a spiritual one and is lost to God. Not all poor people are saved, but only those who have goodness, who have a spiritual life.

Similarly, there are also millionaires and billionaires. They usually want to have even more. They must be conscious of the fact that if they are not merciful in this life, they will go there where they will not have anything. And those who do not have anything here but respect the Christian way of life will have everything in the next life. If I amass money and don't give it to anyone, I live in a continuous lie. I keep my money, and then death comes. However, when I help my neighbor live a decent life, all of us can be more easily saved. This is how I understand this life.

Father, some say that since we are a student association, we should fight to change society. How should we respond to them?

I advise you never to take such exhortations seriously—that you, young people of ASCOR, are called to change society. You will be totally destroyed if you follow this advice. We must only become good Christians and sociable people. Other denominations are agitators and organizers of parades. It is very difficult to change society now. It continues along the path on which it started. What we can do today is to change ourselves and become a light for those around us, whether at home or at work.

Then, think of the fact that even during the Savior's time, there was a secret police like there is today. And then—as now—there were people who noted every word spoken by the Lord Jesus Christ in order to catch Him with something. And the poor believers—as in all the ages that followed since—were running after the Word of God, after Truth. Thus, ASCOR should seek to be at peace with God, and every one of its members should be a son of God according to grace. These are the things that are truly pleasing to God. For this reason, the Eternal Son became incarnate; He died on the cross to reconcile us with God.

It is very important for you all not to become proud. If you are proud, you will not advance spiritually. Be decent, be modest. Don't become proud because all that we have is given to us either by God, our teachers, or other people who are older than us. Everything is given to us.

I wish that God helps you to grow in all that is good and worthy and to finish your exams and university studies with which you are engaged. When you finish them, tell yourselves the words that a father said to his son who had completed his BA degree: "My dear, only now are you beginning your studies." I also completed two degrees: Arts and Theology. But after I finished them, I continued to learn. So, I wish for you to study well, because the world puts a high price on someone with a degree, on a scholar.

You know that the Holy Apostle Paul says that nothing impure will enter the Kingdom of God (Eph. 5:5). That is why it is good for you to strive toward a life that is holy. Tell the truth! God is Truth!

Therefore, seek to be close to God and yourselves by being honest in your souls! Keep this sincerity in your hearts, this purity, this honesty toward others, because we have enough liars. Be pure! May God give you health!

The emphasis must be put on prayer

The specific work of ASCOR is spreading the faith to college students. What advice can you give us so that we can best fulfill this mission?

The emphasis must be put on prayer, being aware of the fact that it is not we who are doing something positive, but God Himself.

What can we do so we can genuinely be the followers of the Association of Romanian Christian Students (ASCR) that was active between the two world wars—this spiritual milieu that included Mircea Vulcanescu, Sandu Tudor, and other future members of the "Burning Bush" movement?

You should deepen your spiritual life and your cultural formation. Proud culture is one thing, and spiritual culture is another. During those times, Romanians were free. Now, after the Communists intruded into our society (and they were the enemies of the faith), things have greatly changed. In the period between the two world wars, many young people had a spiritual zeal that was almost natural, as the zeal of small children; it was as if God had raised them this way, as if He was directly taking care of them, even more than their parents did. It was as if God was preparing them, giving them wisdom, as He is giving to some young people in our days. The young people of those times were prepared for this severe trial—Communism; and it might be the case that things could repeat

themselves in some way in our days. The most important thing we should learn from these more than forty years of Communist occupation is that we should always try to be good Christians; we should try to have more love.

A young person who worked for many years in mass media said that day by day, television and the internet are more harmful than helpful to us for our spiritual life. What do you think of this statement?

Very true! From what I hear as well, especially from young people, I believe that this statement is very true. These people tell me of the disgust and emptiness that television often leaves in their souls. And it is not only about this emptiness but also some abominations that penetrate their minds. There are especially certain programs after midnight that pervert young people, stain them, defile them.

I don't have a TV, and I am at peace, but I hear how people complain about it. For this reason, I didn't want to buy one. Once, someone gave me a TV, but I refused; I told him, "I am sorry, but I have no time for this." Of course, there are also some good things on television or the internet. However, at the same time, television captures your eyes; it is a way to make you blind, and then it communicates certain things that defile you; it doesn't communicate to you something that would truly benefit you. People of today watch television, go on the internet, watch the news. They are also confronted with anti-Christian propaganda. Especially some young people who are not prepared, who don't know anything about Jesus Christ, hear all kinds of malevolent ideas. Then, TV takes away from you the time in which you could read a book, pray, meditate, rest, or talk to someone. But, if you focus on a TV show so that you do not miss anything, then in the end, TV influences you in such a way that you become robbed spiritually.

Father Staretz, we have two questions from theology students. They teach us many things in the School of Theology, but it is difficult to cover everything. What should we give the most importance to?

Concentrate in the first place on the Holy Scripture and on the writings of the Holy Fathers who explain the Scripture. They are the primary sources for the teaching of the Church.

What advice would you like to give to professors at the School of Theology?

I cannot advise these professors since they are more prepared than me. How can I instruct people with PhDs in Theology? I do not have a PhD. They already know the advice that I could give them. So then they should do that which they know the Lord Jesus Christ asks of them.

I will only remind you of this virtue of love. The Savior taught us to love one another, to love the truth and God. Then, the emphasis must always be put on deeds. The Lord Jesus Christ says: "Whoever practices and teaches these commandments will be called great in the Kingdom of Heaven" (Matt. 5:19). Professors teach young people who enter theological schools to lead a Christian life. And the Christian life is a divine life. Christianity established itself through a practical life, through holiness, and not through haughty science. This life in God was missing in the pagan world. Christianity brought this holiness according to the model of God. Absolute holiness is in God.

All of these professors know better than I do what holiness means, what a life lived in holiness means.

Zeal for God

How can a believer know that within him is the grace of God and that it is not a delusion?

He realizes this from the inner peace that the one in whom the grace of God dwells has. The person who does not have grace is, first of all, troubled; he does not have peace. Whatever he says, he does not have peace. The world today is at war; it is troubled because of passions, and therefore, we all need this peace—inner peace. It can be obtained when we ask God for help and when we make efforts to overcome the urge to sin.

Even the neo-protestants say they have peace in their faith...

What kind of peace can they have without the Holy Cross, without the Mother of God, without the Holy Mysteries? They talk about Jesus Christ. But our Lord Jesus Christ is very humble. These sectants are anything but humble. I also ask myself: what kind of peace can the neo-protestants have? We should not confuse spiritual peace with the apparent peace of sectants.

What does the Savior refer to when He says: "I came to send fire on the earth, and how I wish it were already kindled!" (Luke 12:49).

This fire is the zeal for God. The Savior desires us all to have a strong zeal for divine things, as the Christians of the first centuries had. This divine fire that the Savior brought into the world was lit by the love for God that zealous Christians have always had.

The martyrs' hearts were burning with a yearning for God. This internal fire helped them defy all torments. Today, we are cold like ice, we are people who are almost dead. We don't have this internal fire anymore, and neither do we have this elementary zeal. We are experiencing a hardening of our hearts today—we can't focus, we can't pray attentively before God.

The zeal for God was stronger in the first centuries. It functions like an internal fire that determines you to perform any action, however difficult, as if you do it for God and for your salvation—both for your own good and for helping your neighbor. This is how I understand this verse.

The steps of the Prayer of the Heart

What are the steps of the Prayer of the Heart?

The first step is prayer done with the lips. We say it (when we are alone), the same way we speak, simply or in the rhythm of prolonged breathing.

The second step is mental prayer. That is, we say it not only with the lips, but also with the mind. With much attention, first of all! Here, our battle with the mind intervenes. When you see that your mind has slipped to another place, you don't give in. You humble yourself and you struggle to pray with much attention. We reproach ourselves because, even when we stand before God, our thoughts are defiled, or our minds are far from Him. And we force ourselves until the mind humbles itself and directs itself, pure, toward God.

We should especially ask the Savior to deliver us Himself from the attacks of the enemy, the devil, which overtake us during prayer. If the mind wanders to the office when you are praying or you quarrel with enemies, you exert yourself in vain; in that case, the mind cannot nourish itself with the Holy Spirit. And the enemy works in this way: precisely during the time you pray, he attacks you with unclean thoughts and images that defile your heart and mind and thus spoil your prayer. Or he sends you other kinds of thoughts: "You have some shirts to wash," "You forgot to water the flowers," and so on. But if you try hard and cry with much longing to God, then these powers of darkness weaken or even disappear; and then we can pray with a clean mind, that is to say, all of our attention focuses on God.

The third step is the Prayer of the Heart. The mind and heart unite, and our attention is concentrated within the heart. That is where the prayer is accomplished. The mind descends to the heart, and there, in the depth of the heart, it begins to pray. It is what the Psalmist says: "Out of the depths I have cried to You: O Lord, Lord, hear my voice" (Ps. 129:1). On this step, our prayer gushes from the depth of the heart. I am not speaking about the physical heart, but the spiritual heart, the center of the human being, which is detected by the Holy Fathers a bit higher--with two fingers—than the left breast.

When the mind unites with the spiritual heart, only then do we become whole, pure beings. Because we usually think one thing and say something else. How many times have we surprised our own selves with this profoundly false state of being. You say to someone, "I forgive you," but you have not healed the wound within yourself, you have not erased his fault from your heart, you always bring it to mind. We cannot be in agreement with ourselves. The Jesus Prayer is the only prayer which has this gift, this power to unite the two centers of our being into one, making us honest, spiritual people.

The fruits of the Jesus Prayer

It often happens to those who practice the Prayer of the Heart that, when they wake up from sleep, they feel how the prayer utters itself within themselves, similar to how we hear our heartbeats without our control or command. And a great joy is produced there, a rush of spiritual light. Christians find themselves singing "Holy God" or "O Champion General" and good thoughts begin to be born in them, truly spiritual thoughts, and they fully feel the grace that overflows into them. And on the final stage of prayer, this step is accompanied by seeing the uncreated light.

What are the fruits of the Jesus Prayer?

The fruits of this prayer are hard to fathom. But these truly spiritual things remain as an ideal, like a very distant horizon. To begin with, we should call simply on the name of Jesus, uttering this prayer many times, with much attention on each word. It is very helpful to be aware that we are invoking Someone, that we are addressing Someone. It is good to realize that we are weak and helpless, and this "have mercy on me" comprises all of the Church's prayers and our cries to God in one phrase. We should begin simply, uttering these words everywhere, wherever we find ourselves, but with much attention. And, at the same time, with care to renounce all passions and impure thoughts.

And little by little, to the measure of our humility, we are illuminated from within and feel that we are not alone, we feel that there is Someone with us in each moment and cares for us. At the same time, our zeal for all that is holy increases—compared to our normal state in which we are very stubborn and careless. Maybe you have noticed that in the evening, when you want to pray, you fall asleep with your head on the prayer book--from exhaustion or boredom; whereas if you have to do something which you like (other than prayer), you can easily spend the whole night awake doing it.

The Church Fathers tell us that when prayer attaches itself to us (with the help of God and by calling on the name of Jesus), we leave everything aside, and the mere thought about prayer is a true joy. It is as if the desire for prayer consumes us. We feel it as a voice, as a reproach within us; it is something that always urges us: You are not praying? Pray!" Prayer itself teaches us how to pray, and later on, it utters itself on its own in our hearts, even at night. But, for us to arrive at these fruits, much struggle is needed, much perseverance, much patience and especially much humility. And little by little, with God's mercy, prayer begins to pour into us.

In the beginning, it is difficult, the mind runs everywhere, but the grace of God helps us. The Holy Fathers say: "Give 'Lord, Jesus Christ' to this fickle mind!" The Prayer of the Heart is true spiritual nourishment. Sometimes, it is shortened to a few words: "Jesus, have mercy on me!" From the Jesus Prayer sprang this "Lord have mercy!" with which we usually pray during services; from this call on the name of the Lord, this powerful name.

Mental prayer helps us very much to clean ourselves from within and to sow within ourselves love for what is truly beautiful and uplifting in life, not for petty things in which we get caught up with such foolishness.

Living prayer

Thus, in the morning, if you can't take the time to pray before your icons, then at least while you are on the street, on the road you are taking, say "Lord Jesus" in the secret of your heart. Because our mind does not stay quiet. It quarrels, it threatens... And so, it is better to call on the name of the Lord, which can truly protect and sanctify us. The Savior says: "Ask, and it will be given to you" (Luke 11:9). Through all of our good deeds, we can win love for God, but most of all through prayer. Therefore, we should say the prayer as frequently and with as much attention as possible.

What else can you tell us about the lack of attention during prayer?

This lack of attention when we stand before God in prayer is a great offense, a true blasphemy toward Him. God is very good and very attentive to each of our lives. If not even a strand of hair or even the most insignificant insect is overlooked by Him, all the more is God's attention directed to the human being. We are the ones absent from this meeting with Him. God does not expect a formal prayer from us, but a conscious, living prayer. You should have this awareness that you are calling on God in your life and that He will respond and can help you. Prayer attracts this protection from God over you, and this occurs all the more when we say the Prayer of the Heart.

There is also the prayer which is called spiritual vision or contemplative prayer. When the Christian arrives at this step, he is filled by the Holy Spirit, and he sees and understands certain things which fill him with the awe that St. Paul speaks of: "And I know a man—whether in the body or out of the body, I do not know, God knows—who was taken up to Heaven and heard ineffable words, which man cannot utter" (2 Cor. 12:3-4).

We have not arrived there yet. Let us start from the lower steps. Let us begin by battling the thoughts that come to us during prayer. Let us set aside the cares of life which occupy our minds night and day! Let us steal as many moments of our time as possible and dedicate them to God by praying! Let us hold ourselves firmly, with all of our energy, against the enemy who wants to steal this little drop of time devoted to God. And little by little, with the help of the Good God, we also will ascend towards pure prayer.

Thank you, Father Staretz!

Spiritual Blindness[30]

Spiritual blindness is more dangerous than the physical one • Where does spiritual blindness come from? • Biblical examples of spiritual blindness • Let us not forget about our spiritual eyes! • Let us admit we are suffering from spiritual blindness! • The spiritual "ointment" of grace

Christian brothers and sisters,

Many diseases and sufferings torment peoples' lives. But the greatest suffering seems to be blindness. Unable to work in order to make a living, the blind usually beg. From all the categories of beggars in this world, blind people impress in a distinct way those who walk by them. However much someone may be stingy with beggars, or however much he may be against them, it is impossible for him not to be touched even a little by a hand extended by a blind man.

Something similar happened to the blind man of Jericho—whose name was Bartimaeus, as we find out in the gospel written by St. Mark. He was sitting on the edge of the road, begging for alms. He was by the side of the road that came from Jericho and went to Jerusalem. Many people passed by on this road, and I believe many helped him. And still, he continued to remain miserable, however many alms he may have gathered.

Spiritual blindness is more dangerous than the physical one!

His misery consisted of the fact that he could not see the person who gave him alms, nor could he see what he was receiving, he could not see his own hand into which alms were placed, and he could not see himself. For these reasons at least, we can say that physical blindness is one of the most miserable states in a person's life.

A person does not have only physical eyes, but also spiritual eyes. The physical ones are similar to the eyes of other creatures on earth: horses, wolves, and many others. Spiritual eyes however are like the eyes of angels and the eyes of God.

30 The 31st Sunday after Pentecost, January 22, 1984. Typewritten homily, revised by Fr. Sofian in 2000.

Thus, because man has two kinds of eyes, physical and spiritual, a person's blindness can also be physical and spiritual. Physical blindness can result from birth, an accident, or an illness. Due to physical blindness, we cannot see this material world, and neither can we see ourselves. We cannot go without a guide, and we cannot rejoice over light, colors, and all the beautiful things in the visible world.

Spiritual blindness is, however, much more dangerous than the physical one, and such a blind man is more miserable than the blind Bartimaeus from today's Holy Gospel (Luke 18:35-43). If the physically blind man does not see the physical sun and its light, the spiritually blind man does not see the Sun of righteousness and the Father of lights, with the radiance of His grace. He does not recognize the One Who gives him incorruptible goods—life, soul, immortality—nor does he see himself as he truly is.

Where does spiritual blindness come from?

We can ask ourselves: where does this spiritual blindness come from?

The answer may seem unpleasant to us, but this is the truth: spiritual blindness often comes through the eyes of the body. The eyes are the two lights of the face, but they are also like two bodiless hands stretched forth, like two bridges upon which sin can be brought from the outside to the inside of our soul.

Looking passionately at worldly delights, the image of those delights descends from the mind into the heart, and there, in the inner chamber of the spiritual heart, where God and His Kingdom should dwell unceasingly, therein darkness descends and sin is committed. On this matter, the Savior teaches us: "The lamp of the body is the eye; if therefore your eye is good, your whole body will be full of light. But if your eye is bad, your whole body will be full of darkness" (Matt. 6:22-23). And in another place, He says this: "whoever looks at a woman to lust for her he has already committed adultery with her in his heart" (Matt. 5:28). Or vice-versa, the woman who looks at a man with lust has also committed a sin in her heart. And sin darkens the inner eyes, and a person becomes darkened and blind.

Biblical examples of spiritual blindness

The Bible, this magnum opus of humankind, offers us many examples of spiritual blindness from the beginning of the world. I will mention a few examples. Thus, in the book of Genesis, we learn that the woman—the first woman in the world—saw that the fruit of the tree of knowledge of good and evil was pleasing to look at and good to eat. And she took it, ate it, and gave it to her husband too (Gen. 3:6). And their eyes were truly opened, however not like the angels' or God's, as the serpent promised them, but their eyes were opened like those of sinners, and they saw that they were naked (Gen. 3:5). Their eyes were opened, but Heaven was closed to them (Gen. 5:7).

Later, still in the book of Genesis, we read that "the sons of God, seeing that the daughters of men were beautiful, and they took wives for themselves of all whom they chose... Then the Lord saw that the wickedness of man was great in the earth and that every intent of the thoughts of his heart was only evil continually. And the Lord was sorry that he had made man on the earth" (Gen. 6:2, 5-6).

For their spiritual blindness and their terrible sins, the cities of Sodom and Gomorrah were destroyed by fire and covered by the waters of the Dead Sea (Gen. 19:16-26).

Because of his physical eyes, Samson was blinded; Samson, who saw Delilah, desired her, and thus, blinded in his soul, was defeated by a woman—he who thousands of people could not defeat (Jdg. 16).

Holofernes was blinded by Judith, who, with her trappings, stole his eyes; with her beauty, she stole his heart, and with a sword, she cut off his head (Jdt. 13).

King David was blinded by the desire of his eyes when he saw Bathsheba, the wife of Uriah (2 Kgs. 11), as were the two elders of Babylon seeing Susanna when she bathed. Herod was blinded seeing Salome, the daughter of Herodias, dancing (Mark 6:21-26); and even the wise Solomon was spiritually blinded by the foreign women and sinned before God (1 Kgs. 11:3-4).

There are many similar examples in Holy Scripture and, without a doubt, many more in peoples' lives throughout history.

Through these open windows of our eyes, together with the temptations quoted from the Bible, entire waves of other fantasies and desires enter into us, such as pride, greed for possessions and wealth, envy, anger, drunkenness, sights that trouble our imagination. Successively or all at once, they darken the light within the soul and shake the entire life of man.

Let us not forget about our spiritual eyes!

Man is not made by God only for this earthly world, but this world is for us only a battlefield, a stadium for testing the spiritual and physical powers, with which the Christian—doing good deeds and spreading light around him—tries to emerge victorious and be worthy of the prize, that is, the joy of the next, unending life.

We are given these physical eyes precisely to navigate this world, to see where we are going, to inform ourselves and understand the realities here, and to rejoice in a blameless way over all the good and beautiful things that surround us.

But this is not all. These physical eyes are also given to us to keep them continuously in connection with the luminous eyes of our soul, through which we can understand the true meaning of existence and, in this way, know the Master of life Himself, Who said: "I am the Way, the Truth, and the Life" (John 14:6).

Therefore, alongside the many cares of our earthly lives, we should never forget about the vision within, about our spiritual eyes, so that they may in no way be overshadowed or darkened by passions, but that they may be clean and luminous like the eyes of babies or even the eyes of angels. And if it is said about certain things or beings that are dear to us like the light of our eyes, then all the more should the light of our souls be dear to us, this part within us which is the essence of the human being and gives it meaning.

Let us admit we are suffering from spiritual blindness!

It is a great danger for each one of us when our soul is sick, when we are blinded by passions and we do not realize that we are sick.

"If you were blind, you would have no sin, but now you say: We see. Therefore, your sin remains with you," the Savior tells the Pharisees (John 9:41). In other words, the Savior tells them: "If you recognized your blindness, you would be without sin, because you would pray to Me to heal you. But you pretend to see the truth, when in fact you are blind and do not want to be healed by Me."

When a person realizes that he is sick and asks for guidance from someone, runs to the doctor, and prays to God—he does something to escape from the illness that threatens his health. But if he remains indifferent, the illness spreads, and one day, he becomes bedridden or dies. The same thing also happens with the illness within, with the blindness or even the death of the soul.

For many of us, the words of Revelation are fulfilled, in which God tells us: "I know your works, that you have a name, that you are alive, but you are dead. Be watchful and strengthen the things which remain, that are ready to die" (Rev. 3:1-2). What are these deadly works that we have and carry with us, which darken our souls so that we die, yet we are still alive? Here are some of them: pride, envy, anger, drunkenness, fornication, greed, sloth, superficiality, disbelief, lack of love, unjust judgment of our neighbors, etc.

How many families fall apart because of the passions and the non-permissible relationships one or the other spouse has? How many wives mourn the bitterness of their marriage when the husband comes home late drunk, makes a scandal, scares and beats her and the children, and later on, he abandons his family and gets mixed up with another woman? How many Christians pray to God only when they face some trouble, but when everything goes well, they forget about God and the soul and lead an ugly life, lacking anything good?

The spiritual "ointment" of grace

Such deeds, Christian brothers, are like dark shadows, heavy shadows, which envelop our soul and our conscience, making us sick unto death.

In conclusion, I will quote—still from the book of Revelation—he words of God which are fitting, to different degrees, for each of us:

"I know your works, that you are neither cold nor hot. Oh, if you were cold or hot! So then, because you are lukewarm, and neither hot nor cold, I will spit you out of My mouth. Because you say, 'I am rich, have become wealthy, and need nothing'—and you do not know that you are wretched, miserable, and poor, blind, and naked.

I counsel you to buy from Me gold tried in the furnace, that you may be rich; and white garments, that you may be clothed, that the shame of your nakedness may not be revealed; and anoint your eyes with eyesalve, that you may see.

As many as I love, I rebuke and chasten. Therefore, be zealous and repent. Behold, I stand at the door and knock. If anyone hears My voice and opens the door, I will come in to him and dine with him, and he with Me" (Rev. 3:15-20).

May the Good God help us to see our own sins, to free ourselves and escape from them. Let us pray to our heavenly Father to grant us tears of repentance and the spiritual "ointment" of His grace so that He may fully heal the illness of our spiritual eyes and, with His light, illuminate our inner world, darkened by passions. May our Savior, He Who is greatly desired, grant us the white garments of purity of body and soul, so that we can know God in truth and receive the Great Doctor, the Mystical and Heavenly guest—Jesus Christ. He waits at the door of the heart of each of us, and He is ready to help us and heal us of all our weaknesses.

Let us ask Him to come to us, into our life, into our heart, into our family and society!

Let us ask Him with humility and love, saying: "Come, Jesus Christ, come to us too! Amen!

Discernment[31]

The experience of the Prayer of the Heart • Father Ioan Kulighin in Romania. The "Burning Bush" meetings • Spiritual personalities from the interwar period in Romania • The pitfalls of false faith • Discernment. How will it be under the Antichrist's dominion? • Humility and love, attributes of Orthodox life • Faith of young people • The importance of a spiritual father • Sin is a great obstacle to true freedom • Why can we not say the Prayer of the Heart?

Please tell us about one or two important spiritual people whom you met.

Elder Sofian: I would briefly refer to the Russian priest Ioan Kulighin, about whom I spoke on another occasion. I met him at the time when he left Russia immediately after the war,[32] when the Russians forced the German army to turn back. Father Ioan, roughly sixty years old, was the spiritual father of Metropolitan Nicholas of Rostov at that time.

Father Ioan entered the famous Optina Monastery at a young age. As a novice—according to what he said—he lived for a long time at Optina Skete, which was near the monastery, attached to it.

Father Ioan Kulighin

After the Revolution, in 1991, I had the desire to see where Fr. Ioan Kulighin grew up, and I went to Optina Monastery. It is at the edge of a forest. The large church is today restored after the Communists stored tractors in it. I told the monks there about Fr. Ioan. They didn't know anything about him, because Father was taken from there by the Communists when he was still a novice at the monastery. I recounted his life to them, and they added him to their diptychs, and now Father is again there, in his place.

31 The interview was taken in 2000 and revisited and completed by Elder Sofian in 2001 and 2002.

32 Saint Sofian is referring to World War II.

The experience of the Prayer of the Heart

At Optina Skete there were twelve younger novices and four spiritual fathers. Each day, these novices would confess, and the confessor would help them feel very light. After daily confession, they felt light like birds. There they practiced the Jesus Prayer; after a time they were no longer beginners, but experienced practitioners!

Concerning unceasing prayer, a very important problem is the descent of the mind into the heart. These young men, among whom was also Fr. Ioan Kulighin, to begin with, adopted the first part of the prayer. They prayed daily. Persevering, in the end, Fr. Ioan acquired this prayer with all that is most precious: the union of the mind with the heart.

Because, until the mind descends to the heart, a person is double: he thinks one thing and feels another. He can never acquire true unity within his soul. When the mind reaches the heart, then what a person thinks, that he feels, that he speaks, and that he does. Only then can he be called a sincere person. Until he reaches this high spiritual state, he can praise you with very beautiful words that you hear, but at the same time, behind your back, he can curse you or speak badly of you. When the mind enters the heart, a person becomes truly united and sincere. Then, the heart becomes pure. Those with pure hearts, says the sixth Beatitude, will see God (Matt. 5:8).

God has His dwelling in the hidden heart of a person. There, in this spiritual heart, is the temple of the Holy Spirit in us. There resides the Savior after our baptism. The mind of the one who prays, which until then usually wanders about and is restless, descends into this place as well.

Father Ioan had this experience which is difficult to acquire; he had attained it already when the Russian Revolution started. Then the Communists shot or killed with the sword many of the old monks in Optina, while the young men were arrested and sent to forced labor.

Father Ioan was taken from the daily peace and joy in which he lived at Optina and was taken to a Bolshevik revolutionary construction site—by a river—where they were forced to work on all kinds of projects, as also happened here [in Romania]. There were many young people there, regular people, who mocked and cursed the whole revolutionary movement in Russia. Father Ioan worked so calmly, that he attracted others' attention: "Why are you so happy, what happened to you? You have a very difficult life here." But he responded simply: "I have Christ, I have everything. I don't have any kind of trouble." Because he was praying ceaselessly, he was joyful, he was content, and he felt Christ present in his heart, even though he labored greatly in that hell. Of course, many didn't understand, poor people, because they were young at the time, with preoccupations similar to those of young people today.

We read in the lives of the martyrs that they were singing psalms while a fire was burning underneath them. Similarly, Fr. Ioan worked not in a fire, but in water that went up to his knees during the winter—those terrible Russian winters. This is how Fr. Ioan endured that very grim, very difficult life until he was put in prison.

The Communists had the opportunity to learn a great deal from the prisoners because when a person is constrained in prison he is forced to say everything he knows; even what he doesn't want to say, he is forced to say it there. Optina had been a very powerful spiritual center; many Russian writers went there, and without a doubt, over time they became enemies of the revolutionaries. Thus, the Communists wanted to learn as much as possible from the young men who had lived in Optina. So, Fr. Ioan was drained of all he knew, at that age, about other people who were of interest to the Russian Secret Police. Afterward, he was taken out of prison for hard labor, and then again put in prison, such that he knew very well the Communist prisons of that period.

When this Bolshevik persecution eased a bit and they used other methods of surveillance, they allowed more freedom to the Church, and so the Metropolitan of Rostov (with whom Fr. Ioan's destiny would be tied) began to lead a more active life. In the meantime, there were no priests anymore, because the majority had been executed; there remained only those who were freed from prison. Fr. Ioan had retained his integrity because, with the help of the Jesus Prayer, his being had not been exhausted, even with all the persecutions and sufferings that he endured while imprisoned.

Father Kulighin was a man of great integrity and he had a very good memory. Because it was very difficult for someone to write and read even a few pages of Christian writing, Father was forced to store some of the writings of the Holy Fathers in his mind. As he had a very clear mind, he managed to learn many things by heart. He would quote with great precision from the writings of the Philokalic Holy Fathers. And at the same time, do you know why his words were powerful? Because he lived

what the Holy Fathers wrote. And his words were words that impressed and attracted, and this convinced Metropolitan Nicholas to take him as his protopresbyter. Father Ioan was thus both the confessor and the protopresbyter of the Metropolitan.

Father Ioan Kulighin in Romania. The "Burning Bush" meetings

After some time, the balance of the war seemed to shift to the side of the Germans who were advancing rapidly on the territories of the Soviet Union. However, in the end, the Germans were forced to retreat, and Metropolitan Nicholas fled Russia when he learned that the Bolsheviks were again near Rostov. With him were Fr. Ioan, a deacon, the Metropolitan's sister—who was a nun—and a friend of hers. After they arrived in Bucharest, the Metropolitan went to the Patriarchate, as was the norm. At the time, the Patriarch of Romania was His All Holiness Nicodim Munteanul, who in his youth had studied in Kiev, and thus he knew Russian very well; he agreed with the Metropolitan of Rostov that his entourage be housed at the Nifon House in Cernica Monastery.

In the meantime, Fr. Ioan—who was an authentic spiritual man—looked for a place to renew his spiritual life. Someone directed him to Antim Monastery (at the time the Burning Bush had already begun).

One day he left by himself from Cernica to Bucharest. On the tram, he asked where Antim Monastery was, and a young man responded in Russian: "I know where, I will take you there if you need it. My name is Leontie, I am from Basarabia, I know Russian as well as Romanian, and so I can help you." This young man had been a soldier in the Soviet army (he was dressed as a civilian then, the army being in decay). In this way, Fr. Ioan appeared at Antim Monastery in 1945 while I was also there.

He came to Antim on a Sunday evening before Vespers; after the Vespers service, the Paraklesis to the Mother of God was chanted, like today. I invited him first to the service in the church, and after that, we began to get to know each other. Father Benedict Ghius was present, and brother Andrei Scrima, the disciple of Anton Dumitru—professor of logic and philosophy at the University; Sandu Tudor was also present, who later would become Fr. Daniel Teodorescu (he initiated the Burning Bush). Thus, Fr. Ioan met these people on a Sunday evening in October. He stayed with us for the night, and afterward, for two years, he came every Saturday evening to be at the vigil. He served with us, and after the Divine Liturgy on the following day, stayed there, and in the evening participated in the meetings of the Burning Bush.

At these meetings, there was usually first a conference about the Burning Bush—which is a symbol of the Mother of God and unceasing prayer—and afterward, in the form of a seminar, there were questions and, of course, answers. Father Ioan was also present.

The conferences were held in the Monastery library (in the area to the right); the room and stairs were always filled with people in the audience.

Once, when the second part with questions began, Fr. Ioan added some instructions on the Jesus Prayer to one of the answers. Afterward, he became a very important person at each meeting, and at almost all the Sunday evening meetings that followed, people especially asked him questions. He knew many things, he spoke beautifully, in Russian, of course, and brother Leontie translated. Today some people write about the Burning Bush, imagining what we discussed, and what problems were addressed at these conferences. The essence of the Burning Bush meetings was the deepening of the knowledge of the Divine Liturgy and the tradition of the Prayer of the Heart.

Toward the end of 1946, Fr. Ioan and Br. Leontie were arrested by the Soviet army and taken to the tribunal in Bucharest, prosecuted, and imprisoned. Some Romanians were imprisoned with him as well. Father kept in touch with us through them. Some were freed and would come to us and bring news or certain things from Fr. Kulighin. At the time the prisons were less severe than in the period that followed; later on, when we were also arrested and imprisoned, life in prison and at the secret police [jails] became very harsh.

Father Ioan was forced to choose between life in prison and capital punishment. Father chose life in prison. He said that life in prison was not foreign to him, and that in the Communist prisons, many discouraged people thought that everything ended there, in prison, and he could help lift their spirits. He preferred a life sentence. However, he was transferred from Bucharest to Odessa, and there, at a certain moment, for his meekness, old age, and past, he was taken out of his cell into the prison courtyard, to the open air (the open air meant very much for those of us who were imprisoned). There was a kind of garden in that courtyard and he occupied himself with taking care of the flowers. Father Ioan eventually died in the prison in Odessa. God knows where he is buried, if

something remains of his body. This is, in short, the life of a great spiritual father whom I knew, Fr. Ioan Kulighin.

Father Sofian, you were born and lived for many years in Basarabia, and because of this, maybe you can clarify a problem for us: from within the Russian people there emerged great spiritual personalities, like Fr. Ioan Kulighin whom you knew. We can also mention well-known saints, like St. Seraphim of Sarov, the saints of the Pecerska Lavra, or St. Silouan the Athonite. At the same time, however, the Russians stole Basarabia from us, the northern part of Bucovina, our treasure (and now they don't want to give it back); the Russians also deported or killed thousands of Romanians. How do you explain the fact that amid this nation, there existed simultaneously these two extremes of radically different people?

The Russian people are a large nation, a giant nation, so it has room for saints and soulless people to live together.

Spiritual personalities from the interwar period in Romania

Can you tell us more about other great spiritual fathers that you have known?

I would say a few more words about Fr. Georghe Rosca, to whom I confessed for approximately ten years. Professor Virgil Candea also confessed to His Reverence. Father Rosca was a very cultured priest. He had a deep knowledge of Scripture. He knew Russian very well and translated many useful writings into Romanian, among which I would rank the *Sbornicul* [a collection of writings on the Jesus Prayer, similar to *The Art of Prayer* by Igumen Chariton] first. He was also from Basarabia. He knew very many practical and spiritual things. And he was especially a very skilled spiritual father, a good guide of the Prayer of the Heart.

I remember Fr. Ghelasie (who was a kind of hermit) and Fr. Teodosie; I confessed to them during my time at the seminary of Cernica Monastery (between 1932 and 1940). I felt the presence of divine grace and the fragrance of sainthood around Hieromonk Ghelasie. Before 1945, at Cernica Monastery, there was a high spiritual life, due especially to the old monks, among whom were these two very good instructors. For us students at the time, these Fathers were special people.

Another great spiritual father and a man with a very good soul was Fr. Benedict Ghius. Father Benedict received a special blessing from Fr. Ioan Kulighin, equal to an initiation into the Jesus Prayer.

Among the people arrested in the evening of June 13-14, 1958, and condemned to hard years in prison (for "subversive activity" within the Burning Bush organization) were, first of all, Fr. Daniil Teodorescu and Fr. Benedict Ghius—the initiators of this Christian movement, who maintained the flame of the Burning Bush, which burned but was not consumed.

Those of us who participated in the conferences at Antim saw each other again for the first time since our arrest during the trial, in the Court of the Military Tribunal of Bucharest, and then at Jilava. At Aiud we only saw each other partially. We also met briefly after four years in the forced labor colony at Salcia, close to Braila.

While we were at Jilava (squeezed into a large cell, with walls blackened by oil), Fr. Benedict, with a luminous face, imposed himself from the beginning, with his gentle, convincing, and wise words, as a great comfort for all of us present—officers, priests, doctors, monks, young and old. The presence of Fr. Benedict made us completely forget the misery in which we found ourselves.

In the forced labor colony at Salcia we met again with Fr. Benedict and other colleagues from the Burning Bush and were with them for more than two years. Especially on Sundays, groups formed in the courtyard of the prison, and there was at least one priest in each group. The largest group was the one surrounding Fr. Benedict.

He would pray for everyone, and then he would talk to us from Holy Scripture and the Holy Fathers, from history and his own life. He spoke to us from his inexhaustible wealth of knowledge and the fullness of his heart ruled by grace. Father's words, full of light and encouragement, went straight to our hearts, like true spiritual nourishment, gladdening us and strengthening us, so that we endured the sufferings of prison much more easily, and at the same time our faith in the God of our fathers increased.

What can you tell us about Sandu Tudor, who was the principal initiator of the spiritual movement the Burning Bush?

In his civilian life, Fr. Daniil was a journalist. He had his own car and plane (he was also a pilot). But, at the same time, he also had a great zeal for truth. He went to Mt. Athos for a while and met a very spiritual Elder who greatly impressed him. When he returned from the Garden

of the Mother of God [as Mt. Athos is known], he felt a calling toward a different life, a spiritual life.

At that time, I was a student at the Cernica Monastery Seminary. Those in charge of the Seminary would sometimes ask Sandu Tudor to give talks to the students. Even though his daily life involved worldly preoccupations, he would talk to us about the Holy Fathers, and especially about the Jesus Prayer. He had already begun to practice at that time. He was not a banal person, but very original and fully alive. When he felt a certain lassitude in those around him, he would say something that invigorated you, even though he sometimes chastised you. He was a man with a beautiful and very dynamic soul; he was always thinking of new things. He was curious, in the good sense of the word, that is, he was an eternal seeker. Sandu Tudor had a direct style and you couldn't really compromise with him. He would say things directly to your face, without hiding. After he was tonsured a monk, he became even more direct.

One could write a voluminous book about Fr. Daniil. At some time, when he was still in the world, he sympathized with the left-wing movement. He was a correct and sincere man, and he really believed that the Marxists wanted to help people in need. When he realized the actual situation, he stopped supporting the Communists, and in the end, they killed him in prison.

I visited him at his house before he became a monk. He had an impressive library (that the Communists destroyed) and was very cultured. He and Nae Ionescu were very cultured people, true intellectuals who valued the Church very much. Nae Ionescu had read all the Patristic volumes from the *Migne* collection. When we were at Antim, we bought this collection from him. Sandu Tudor was on the same level.

Many intellectuals preoccupied with problems related to Christian life would come to him with questions. If you had any confusion, it would be made clear after talking with him. He read the latest books, especially literary ones, even after coming to Antim Monastery. Alexandru Mironescu told him once: "Sandu—they were old friends—you are an insufferable man, but you are extraordinary!" So he was. You had to endure many ways in which he would say you are a fool and other such things, but, at the same time, he had a loving way of being in which he made you overlook all that he had said and you ended up liking him. Father Daniil was also a very good poet. "The Akathist Hymn of the

Burning Bush" that he composed is one of the most profound poems ever written to honor the Mother of God.

After being tonsured as a monk, he became very simple, in food and all things. In addition to the depth of culture he possessed, one could also see in him a sincere spiritual life. We met only once in prison at Aiud; we smiled at each other, but we could not say anything. Soon after, Fr. Daniil—the name he took when he received the Great Schema—became a martyr and went to the Kingdom of God with the Prayer of the Heart. He was helped and instructed very much in this work of unceasing prayer by Fr. Ioan Kulighin. Sandu Tudor, just like Vasile Voiclescu, authentically acquired the Jesus Prayer because they sought it with all of their heart.

What impressed you most about Fr. Dumitru Staniloae?

The calm with which he would talk about divine things—his calm and certainty. He would speak, for example, about the Holy Spirit, about the works of the Holy Spirit. He talked as if he was referring to normal, natural things. In fact, they were normal, but they presupposed deep knowledge because he couldn't just say anything he wanted about the Holy Spirit. But he would present things with great normality, and everything he said was very easy to receive. This is what impressed me greatly about him.

The pitfalls of false faith

Father Archimandrite, how are we to understand St. Silouan the Athonite's word: "Keep thy mind in hell and despair not"?

Saint Silouan wrote a book which was commanded to him from above. He was commanded to write something about spiritual life. In it, he talks about grace, prayer, humility, and the Mother of God. They are extraordinary and beautiful things. I believe that it is a truly inspired book, of a spiritual height almost equal to Holy Scripture. Here, we also find this word about which you asked. It is a word that is difficult to understand.

I learned—and it is not at all a novelty—that hell is not somewhere outside of earth, but it is somewhere in the earth. And I learned this from the sixth katavasia of the Resurrection which says: "You descended into the deepest parts of the earth."

After the Savior was crucified on the Cross, His soul descended into hell and removed all of the righteous that were there, somewhere in the earth. He was lamented and His Body was buried, sealed in the tomb, but His soul descended into hell. There is a prayer that explains what happened after very beautifully: "In the grave with the body, but in hades with the soul, as God; in paradise with the thief, and on the throne with the Father and the Spirit were You, Christ, filling all things, but inscribed by none." That is, the Savior is present in these places after His death on the Cross.

However, hell is also on earth. It exists both in the earth and on the earth, to the point that we are used to it. Many of those who live in a worldly way create hell for themselves when they lead a life without the fear of God. Thus, hell becomes discouraging and destructive. Yet, it is very necessary for us to endure hell on earth with trust in God. We live with this trust—that hell will have an end, and thus we will be truly free and able to occupy ourselves with our inner life. We have this trust despite the discouragement that the devil brings—because he is in hell, but he is also in the world. He is the prince of this world who won many mortal beings for himself.

For all of us who are still in the world, the devil hunts us and tries to overcome us and draw us into his kingdom, the kingdom of darkness and death, so that he can have his fun with us by tormenting us. However, by asking God for help, we resist and defeat this insatiable tendency of the devil to conquer God's creation.

Father Sofian, for a young person who desires to become closer to the Church, there can appear different spiritual pitfalls, and I would like you to tell us a few words about three of these. The first would be pietism. Some define pietism as a mix of superstition with exaggerations of certain unimportant things. What can you tell us about pietism and how can we avoid it?

By pietism, we can also understand formal prayer. In life, however, we try to follow the path of Orthodoxy which is the light of our faith, the light of Christ, and which we know for certain leads us to the Kingdom of God. We disregard other surrogates of Orthodoxy, and for this reason, I recommend to young people that they don't slip into superstition and other movements like pietism. Piety, true devotion, is something completely different; it is the path that a young person who desires salvation must follow. I am not interested in pietism, and therefore I do not even talk about it.

Another temptation is intellectualism, in which faith appears more like an interesting cultural problem and not mainly as a living experience

And this culture, as superior as it may be, is often mixed with pride. Pride is thrown into the world by the spirit of lies, that is, the devil; he is very learned. The devil knows well philosophy and theology, and he impresses a person with his knowledge, but this knowledge always keeps a person cold toward God. His mind is frozen in his knowledge. The same thing happens with his friends, proud intellectuals, especially atheists. They know everything and remain further enclosed in their knowledge, with no opening toward the True Living God. They are dead to God and themselves. They remain enclosed in this knowledge and impress those who have the same preoccupations.

With all of their philosophy and all of this superior knowledge, they are like a trumpet that emits powerful sounds, but the world is not attracted to this kind of sound. It is not a specific melody that people would like, but it is a scream, oftentimes dry, so that many times this intellectualism—even when it comes in direct contact with the Christian faith and life—does not reconcile with the teachings of Christ, in general, and with Christian living, in particular; it refuses them. It finds it convenient to remain in intellectual dryness. Those who are used to it are happy to listen to this exhibition of knowledge and problems of the intellect, of the mind, but they remain barren in this form of dry knowledge about the soul and life in Christ. I have also known, of course, people who were learned from a cultural point of view and who were, at the same time, authentic people of prayer.

Intellectualism does not, however, have spiritual value, because those who suffer from this kind of insufficiency are always outside of communion with God, like the devil, who is very learned, but cannot ever be part of Christ's friends. The friends of Christ are saints who had great spiritual knowledge but at the same time experienced it and kept the divine joy of grace in their soul, which made them truly joyful.

Another pitfall for young people who wish to become closer to the Church—a more recent pitfall—is criticism. Some maintain that we must criticize as much as possible so that things can be more dynamic, otherwise they become hardened; if we criticize, something new appears, something living. How do you see this problem?

I see this problem more simply. For me, this repetitive criticism is often confused with judging others. That is, criticism goes against the commandment of the Gospel to not judge my neighbor (Matt. 7:1).

Under certain limits this criticism may be necessary, however, it must be objective, and honest. Usually, judging others is done in the absence of the one judged and it is wrong, false. People judge and condemn others in their absence, and this is a sin. Scripture tells us that only God has the power and right to judge each one of us (Deut. 1:17), and His judgment is indeed correct. God does not make mistakes and is the only one Who knows all that happens with each person and with all humankind.

When someone criticizes another person who is not present, he describes the sins that he knows about the other person. But he who is reckoned guilty and sinful also has a conscience and thus can come clean before God through repentance. He who judges cannot perceive more than what he sees or hears, and therefore he can remain in this error of condemning the other person, whereas that person can correct himself. God receives the latter, but he who judged is condemned for failing to keep the commandment of not judging in order to not be judged (Matt. 7:1).

However, the criticism that you mentioned at the beginning is also necessary, because a person cannot always see what is around him. Thus, sometimes many minds are needed to solve a problem, and an honest criticism, done with love, humility, and sincerity, can bring something useful. You can criticize what is not good, but you must bring something positive in place of that negative element. And then you can collaborate to arrive at a complete truth, not a twisted truth or a partial truth.

Discernment. How will it be under the Antichrist's dominion?

Since we must clarify for ourselves and others the different phenomena that are tangential to life in the Church, please tell us how to relate to some of them. For example, how should we relate to the Legionary movement?[33]

The Legionary movement appeared during the interwar period. To have an objective view of this movement, I think we need to understand the problems that Romanian society faced in the period between the two World Wars well. The Legionnaires showed a measure that they could express at the time, believing in God, defending the Christian faith, and doing Christian deeds as well. However, they made some mistakes: they were in a hurry to make people holy, and if others did not listen to their imperative, then they killed them. This is how they were, and this was a capital mistake.

A person needs time and especially a good example to return to a Christian life. If these two things do not exist, it is very difficult to convert someone who is an atheist or indifferent. And thus, the Legionnaires were not able to change many people spiritually. They converted some people who often had pure hearts—and who were apparently naive—and attracted them to the Legionary movement. However, they could not convince many people, the majority of which had a critical spirit and thought about things from different perspectives and truths.

Therefore, in this problem, you must have a special capacity which in the Church's language is called discernment. If we do not have a balance in our thinking and our life, we do things imperfectly, that is, we do not see a certain side to a problem that can even be its essential side. But if we have discernment, we see things in their totality. And then we go on a course that others can follow successfully because it is a complete course, which gratifies a person from every point of view, or the majority of points of view. Otherwise, when things are hurried, they do not last.

33 The Legionary movement, also called the Iron Guard or Order of Saint Michael, was a fascist political party in Romania that promoted Orthodox Christianity and attracted many young men who were opposed to Communism.

Although the Captain was a balanced man,[34] after his death there remained some principles that were poorly defined and understood. Afterward, the Legionnaires took control of the country for a very short time; however, some negative elements entered this movement—elements without sincerity who wanted to compromise the movement. The Legionary movement eventually failed politically and became what we now know it to be: a dangerous, terrorist movement.

Did you take part in the Legionary Movement or the Brotherhood of the Cross?

No! Those were different things. In general, the Legionnaires had a rash style and wanted to change society at its core; but we were in a spiritual frame of mind, and in the first place, we wanted to change ourselves. Our spirit did not fit with their spirit. I did not want to be close to the Legionary movement, neither when I was a student at the Cernica Monastery Seminary, nor when I was a college student or later.

The Legionary movement had some good aspects, but also questionable parts. From a Christian point of view, the principal mistake of the Legionnaires was, sadly, the crimes which they committed, some of them when the Captain was still alive. At that time, the leadership of the Legionary Movement did not express any distancing or public apology for these crimes. I believe that towards the end of his life, Codreanu realized this. He had become more thoughtful and spiritual. If he had not been killed, the Captain would have tried to reorient the movement in a more humble and Christian direction. Those who succeeded him did not truly understand the necessity of such changes; rather, they continued their violent actions and amplified them.

Father, some say that Prince Stephen the Great committed violence by defending the faith and nation. Yet, he was canonized by the Romanian Orthodox Church.

Some situations and times were different; the mentality was very different. First of all, St. Stephen had a very strong repentance for the sins he committed as any other human being. Such repentance can lead anyone to sanctity. It must not be forgotten that the Prince had a saint as his spiritual father (St. Daniel the Hesychast) to whom he confessed with

34 Corneliu Zelea Codreanu (1899-1938), known as the "Captain" of the Legionnaires.

fear of God. Saint Stephen also built many churches and monasteries that have lasted in large part to this day. A very important thing is that he succeeded in defending European Christianity from the Muslim threat with humility, faith, and much sacrifice. Stephen the Great was anointed by God as Prince of Moldavia so he could defend this ancestral land from pagans and traitors. Our Orthodox believers have considered Stephen the Great to be a saint for many centuries. The Church took this into consideration and officially proclaimed Stephen the Great a saint in 1992.

How should we relate to Ecumenism—to the Ecumenical movement?

I am not convinced about this issue. Ecumenism is a very difficult problem for Orthodoxy.

Many faithful people are not happy with the fact that in our country we are encouraged to have religious services with non-Orthodox, especially Protestant denominations. And the faithful ask us how can a Divine Liturgy, or another service, be celebrated with denominations that exclude the Mother of God from Christian worship! They reject the Holy Cross, which is the altar of the sacrifice of our Lord Jesus Christ, they reject icons, they reject saints and martyrs—all those who died for Christ, who served Christ in this life, and whom Christ Himself calls God's friends (John 15:14). How can you serve a Divine Liturgy without the Mother of God or the Holy Cross, the saints, or the Holy Eucharist? This is a negative aspect. They oblige us to participate in such services. I do not think that such prayers are received by God; on the contrary.

On the other hand, we are told that Ecumenism is beneficial in a way for other denominations to learn about Orthodoxy.

Orthodoxy is the integral life of Christianity. We have preserved and we try to respect all that the Savior, Holy Apostles, and Holy Fathers recommended from the beginning.

However, it is possible that the Orthodox faith can be discovered in other ways: through conferences, papers, or books, but not through common prayers. But to serve God sincerely and to see at the same time that others scratch their heads or look for a cigarette.

Thus, in regard to Ecumenism and the Ecumenical movement, I am in a state of perplexity, and I am waiting for things to become more clear to me over time.

How should we relate to the so-called entrance into Europe [the European Union], especially when the legalization of homosexuality is imposed as a condition for joining it?

Yes, this is a repulsive issue for me. And for all of Europe. Of course, we also have some truly beautiful things to learn from Western Europe, but not when it is at the expense of accepting certain sins. Especially when we are talking about certain passions that the Bible, from the very beginning, tells us are so perilous that to punish such sins, angels descend from Heaven to burn, to destroy, these towns together with their inhabitants, so that only fire and brimstone remain (Gen. 19:1-28).

I went to the Dead Sea, I put my finger in the water, and tasted it; the water was thick, bitter, and smelled of sulfur. This is all that remained from the civilization of the two towns (Sodom and Gomorrah) that the Old Testament tells us about. Thus, we see what contempt God shows toward such passions.

As we read in the Holy Scripture, for no other human passion does someone descend from Heaven to bring punishment. And "civilized," proud Europe wants to defile our nation with these very sins, which we have guarded ourselves against. People have made mistakes (because there have been and still are homosexuals in this country, without it being legalized by Parliament), but these are problems related to confession, to canons. However, if these sins are legalized, people commit them without a care under the protection of "Holy Parliament." Our politicians are free to do what they want, but forgetting the faith and sensitivity of this nation, they approve all kinds of transgressions in order to be friends with so-called Europe.

Therefore, I do not agree with receiving a divine punishment in exchange for earthly goods. If angels descended from Heaven and burned Sodom and Gomorrah, God will now send chastisements from Heaven to our country, through which the legislations of such sins will be punished. But our people are not convinced. They say with superficiality: "These are questions that only bother old priests!"

On the other hand, it must be said that a Christian is a two-fold personality that is part of the earthly state, but also part of the heavenly state; he is also God's citizen. He must emphasize what is essential. He must know that he is made up of two components: one is the material person, which will be devoured by worms in the grave; and the other is the spiritual part, the soul, which will go to the Judgement after finishing its life on earth. And the soul will await in some place for the body to be resurrected so that they can be united and continue their life in eternity. If a person falls into this sin which is against God, he disobeys an old commandment, from the creation of the world. When He creates man, God says: "Be fruitful and multiply."[35] With the legislation of homosexuality, this fundamental commandment is transgressed, because a man cannot give birth to children and cannot continue the human race as God decided from the beginning.

What attitude should we have toward Masonry?

We must do our Christian duty to the end! Masonry is a universal movement that has methods of forcing you to be silent. And since it I do not know what measures we can take against this movement, we must only preserve our faith and witness God until the final moment of our life.

Because the Antichrist will come and surely he will have the freedom to do certain kinds of miracles and tricks to deceive people. Many people will agree with him so that the majority of those who take measures against these movements will be suppressed. In the future, only those who live for life on earth will be left; because not all will be against Masonry when it will start to act.

Thus, I cannot fight with the world so that it agrees with me. I will do my duty as a Christian. Everyone knows how to do a good deed, but not everyone wants to because it obliges him to make sacrifices, and man is inclined to resolve life's problems as simply as possible. If Masons were to give you a number with which you could buy anything, so that you could eat, buy clothes, live well, and travel everywhere, then many people would agree with it: "Yes, dear, thank you!"

Then the world will be divided: each person will choose what interests him. Those who choose to suffer anything to be close to Christ will be a little flock, as Scripture says (Luke 12:32). There is a passage in the Gospel in which the Savior asks Himself if there will be faith left on earth.

35 Gen. 1:28

"When the Son of Man comes, will He really find faith on the earth?" (Luke 18:8)

Yes, yes—all these problems will come to be; but salvation, faith, and attachment to the Savior will remain as a choice for each person.

After 1990, two books written by Athonite monks were translated into Romanian: *The Twilight of Freedom* and *Apocalypse 13*. In essence, they claim that all these processes of creating a New World Order are in fact obvious signs of the gradual rise of a global dictatorship; and this dictatorship will result in the enthronement of the Antichrist. The authors bring this to our attention based on a pertinent argument that things are evolving towards total control of the entire populace through modern technology and sophisticated networks of surveillance. That is, we are moving towards the most total and subtle enslavement of humans that has ever existed in history. Do these claims seem exaggerated to you?

Maybe they are exaggerated a bit, but things are progressing toward that. I have not read these books, but humanity is moving towards its end through the way it behaves nowadays. The disorder in the world today angers the Good God. I am thinking, first of all, of unbelief, of the apostasy from God in which we find ourselves; and also about our actions, our increased sins—sins that the Bible completely condemns and that the government approves.

We do what He does not like. I am sure that God does not like it. For example, to name a sin that today is very widespread (and protected by laws) in many countries: homosexuality. I spoke before of the two cities in the Old Testament that were accused of this grave sin. They were burned, nothing remained of them. That is why I think that the world is moving, maybe inevitably, towards its end.

The end would possibly be postponed if great repentance and atonement occurred, but this is difficult. I do not know the ins and outs of politics, but without a doubt in the world today, which is heading on the broad way of pleasures and passions, there must be a person, a sort of leader, who is engaging people in this rush toward the destruction of the entire humankind. There are institutions who do not say outright that their political aim is the destruction of humanity, because then no one would listen to them. These institutions lead nations toward disaster,

but they say they are leading them toward freedom (as some understand freedom, not as it is in reality).

I will say it again: the world could be reinvigorated if we made an effort to truly be sorry about our sins; if we all repented, from the king to the lowest servant, as it happened in the city of Nineveh in the Old Testament (Jonah 3).

Are there other signs which show that these are the last days?

There is no need for other signs given the fact that this march towards evil exists today.

On other occasions, you responded to the same questions with more reservation...

In the meantime, many things have changed. I believe that the more we approach the end of the world, the more God will intervene on behalf of the few who remain with Him. God will spiritually fortify the Orthodox Christians who strive for a life lived in faith. In the beginning, there will be many fanatical people and young people close to Him, but in the end, very few will remain on the side of the Lord Christ.

Those who remain Christians until the end will be few, but they will be more determined and more steadfast in their faith. There will be many disputes, much confusion, uncertainty, and rejection of God. Many will give everything for one thing, that is, they will renounce their wealth, and their cars, to preserve their faith. They will have only what they need to survive so that they do not die of hunger, yet others will live in luxury.

At that time, the Antichrist will appear, and the persecutions will be merciless. Christians will be searched and interrogated, so that everything can be known about them. There will be much intimidation and much fear, but there will also be optimism and much courage among those who witness Christ to the end.

Humility and love—attributes of Orthodox life

How are we to understand the Savior's words: "I desire mercy and not sacrifice"? (Matt. 9:13)

Sacrifice is an act of giving from the best that you have. At that time [of Christ], animals or birds were sacrificed in the Temple. The Savior tells us, however, that love is the most precious thing to God.

It is very difficult to acquire this love, this mercy, all at once. God always seeks something living, something personal, in a sacrifice, and the sacrifice of animals was well-known and worn out. In many cases, these sacrifices were not done out of love, but only routinely. It was not something living; it was not something from the heart, from the soul of the believer. Sacrifice in itself is dry, it does not have much value. However, if sacrifice is united with mercy, then this is well received by God.

If you were to enumerate the principal attributes of Orthodoxy, which of them would you put in the first place?

Humility and love! Those that the Savior recommends: "Learn of Me, for I am gentle and lowly of heart and you will find rest for your souls" (Matt. 11:29). Here, our Lord Jesus Christ urges us to try to acquire humility and love, which are God's attributes, and they are also the fruits of Orthodox life. That is why I think we can begin to describe Orthodoxy through these two virtues

To what degree is monasticism a calling from God and to what degree is it an act of personal choice?

Of course, when it is a work from God, it is a calling: someone is called by God to monasticism so that he will lead a God-pleasing life through this way of life.

There are also cases when someone leaves for a monastery by his own will, without having a calling from God, saying that he likes the monastic life. Many years ago, I met such a case. A young lady wanted to become a nun, but I told her: "Miss, first finish your studies—she was a medical student—and then you will see what your thoughts will be." She would listen to me, but then she would still do whatever her heart told her. I know that she would dress in nun's clothing and look in the mirror to see how the clothes looked on her. I went abroad for some time, and when I returned, I learned that this girl visited some monasteries. She didn't like it there, so she returned to her ordinary life. She did not continue her medical studies because she didn't like the classes on Marxism that she was obliged to attend.

Later, I learned that she had gone somewhere in Africa. She got mixed up with someone there and married him. After a while, I heard she had returned to the country to be with her parents. Her father was a lawyer, and her mother was a housewife. She left afterward for a Nordic country, Sweden or Norway, with this young man and their daughter. This showed me that you must have a calling for monastic life to some degree. Otherwise, you get lost along the way, as she got lost, poor girl.

Even though sins are common to all people, if you are called by God to monastic life, even if you make mistakes, you have a chance to repent. With the church in the monastery courtyard, with the *simantron*, with the bells that wake you up every day to strengthen your longing for God, if you have patience, even with all the passions that war against you, you can conquer them at some point. Because God surely helps us, especially when we pray.

Whoever does not have any spiritual calling to the monastic life and his blood runs hot—this carnal passion hiding under different guises—must listen to the voice of his blood and follow the traditional path of the family and lead a family life. However, whoever has an inclination to prayer, to some higher spiritual ideals, to the Holy Fathers, whoever feels impressed by a word from St. John of Damascus, St. Gregory Palamas, St. Basil the Great, or St. John Chrysostom, and seeks good thoughts, God helps him, and he progresses in the monastic life.

Even when a thought for the monastic life occurs without a special calling, if the novice has somewhat of a good start, is preoccupied with monastic problems, and from time to time regresses, falls into some sins, God doesn't leave him. His guardian angel helps him, and he increases and deepens in his monastic life. He can become a very helpful person for other people who do not go to a monastery, for ordinary people.

But, if he is powerfully called by God to monastic life, then he is even more fulfilled; he has even more grace. Because grace likes to find clean ground. That is where the grace of God settles. Holiness is something very fine, very delicate, blueish, and very difficult to obtain in an ordinary life. Holiness has something heavenly in it. When grace envelops a human body, it lifts him and helps him grow spiritually, surprisingly beautifully, compared to other people.

What do you think is the main issue that needs to be corrected in Romanian monasticism today?

We should live monastically, like the young and old men of the past. There is a lot of knowledge around. It is better for us to live these three

vows: unconditional poverty, purity (virginity) of soul and body, as well as obedience.

It is good for the monk to listen to the head of the monastery. All abbots like order in the monastery; they want the monks to live a true monastic life and to be useful both to their own monastic brothers and to the faithful who come to the monastery to be invigorated spiritually.

Pilgrims, when they experience a monastic environment, when they participate in the services, when they confess or find strength from the example of a monk, are straightened spiritually and go home stronger. This is what matters greatly: a living example. This is the role of the monastery: the salvation of its inhabitants and of those who visit it.

The faith of young people

For many faithful young people who live or study in big cities, an important problem is that they cannot find inner peace, since they are scattered by many problems. What do you advise them to do?

They should make a program [prayer rule] for the soul. This emptiness and unhappiness are within them. They need to fill this void with something else. Therefore, they should make a program and fill this spiritual emptiness with prayer and a life in God.

How should a student interested in the Christian life act when he is with his friends who are not at all attracted to the Church?

You guide yourself with common sense. That is, you shouldn't talk a lot about Christianity, fasting, and other religious practices, which are usually not well-liked by young people, and discourage them. It is good for a Christian student to be humble, to be a true model. He should not affirm his Christian faith ostentatiously, but it should transpire from within himself in all that he does, says, and thinks.

And so, he needs common sense that will prompt him to be a good person, conscientious, and spiritually honest.

What do you think was the role of ASCOR [Association of Romanian Orthodox Christian Students] from 1990 until now, and what would you recommend that young people who are part of this organization continue to do?

ASCOR tried after 1990 to fulfill a very necessary work: to spread the teaching of God among students in colleges. They did beautiful things, yet insufficient in comparison with the spiritual needs of students. Maybe the members of ASCOR need more help to enrich their activities. I am happy that during these turbulent times in which we live, there are young people with Christian preoccupations who formed such an organization.

It is good that the young people of ASCOR were united and wanted to do something when the Church was confronted with certain problems. ASCOR was on the side of the Church and defended its position. In time, this organization has matured. ASCOR members have gained experience from one another. On the one hand, there are those who finish their studies and go about their lives and their jobs, but on the other hand, there are others who come and start on the same path. Still, young people benefit from the experience of older members and they can thus do something more daring. My advice is that members of ASCOR associate as much as they can with the life of the Church, and that they collaborate with the Church in its problems.

Also, we must realize that there are a lot of things that people do not know, and ASCOR members are educated people, having recently graduated from college. If a young person who has graduated from college talked, for example, with a peasant, he could convey much information to him, something that would be useful to him. But this information needs to be relayed in a friendly manner, and not haughtily as if it comes from some great learned person. Because ASCOR members are not only theologians, but they are also from other fields of study. There should be a dialogue between a young person and one or more simple citizens, because people are ignorant, not only in religious matters. On the other hand, a genuine peasant has, in his own way, a way of thinking and a faith that sometimes astonishes you by their profundity. We all have a lot to learn from these peasants, whom Fr. Staniloae considered the aristocrats of our people, and who are harder and harder to find.

Then, the students who take part in this organization need to have courage and be a bit more organized. There are grave social problems toward which it is good for them to take a position, for example, these ugly novelties—the effort to legalize homosexuality and prostitution. ASCOR students should not only be theologians but people with good sense, young people with diverse studies, psychology for example, who

could have something to say against these decisions, showing that it is not necessary to legalize such sins. There is an empire of evil and a prince of evil who is the devil; he already legislates evil by urging people, with great cunning, to do bad deeds, so that there is no need for the state authority to also associate itself with these malefic deeds.

How should the relationships between young people who are part of ASCOR be? How should the atmosphere of this association be?

It should be a Christian atmosphere—a familial atmosphere, that of an ideal family. A family in which all members respect one another and live under the grace of the Holy Spirit. Even if some stray from this heavenly path, the majority however should be like this. They should help each other, be modest, collaborate with good will, and, as much as possible, be united in eradicating evil—not to encourage and not to practice it.

Father, how can we convince young people to come to Church?

If young people are sincere and truly seek something, we call them to come and try out life in the Church. Because ordinary life, the life of pleasure that surrounds a young person, is not sufficient, and he often feels an emptiness within himself; he feels this without me telling him. How can he fill this inner void? He must seek something. If he is superficial, he will go with this emptiness into the emptiness of the grave. But if he is serious about what he is seeking, he will find something that will heal this spiritual infirmity. Thus, he needs sincerity in understanding and resolving this personal inadequacy.

Usually, we are interested in our soul's gratification, but not the gratification that you have after you eat and drink and party and delight in all kinds of sins. In reality, we long for the gratification of our soul which will accompany us in life permanently. We seek something which will help us to grow spiritually. For example, you can know all of the science that exists in the world and still not be content, and then you seek something else.

The Church is the place where this spiritual fulfillment can be found because here, we have truths spoken and chanted that have been left in the world precisely to fill our inner emptiness. We don't hear random ideas from the altar or the chant stand, but, through the text of the services, we hear Christians who have discovered this source, this wellspring of knowledge that fulfilled them, because it had an answer to their problems and helped them obtain this inner spiritual gratification.

And then, of course, the Church instructs you to read especially the New Testament. You read the Gospels, the writings of the Holy Apostles. You read that St. Paul was lost, that he had been an enemy of Christ, and he met Christ on the road to Damascus (Acts 9:1-7). And certain people who seek God with sincerity can meet Him not only by reading the New Testament, but also on a different road to Damascus.

Or the young person can meet a spiritual father and maybe God helps him confess and then—still in the Church—he finds a path by which he can find peace for his soul.

The Importance of a spiritual father

The relationship with a spiritual father is a very important issue upon which the transformation of our inner life depends. What are the criteria for choosing a priest to whom we confess?

I cannot tell you. This is a problem for the one who is seeking a confessor.

Let's say that he is just beginning and wants to find a priest to whom he can confess...

He can ask someone he knows: "Who is your spiritual father?", "So-and-so.", "Are you satisfied?" He asks another person who recommends someone else. He prays to God to help him find a spiritual father. It is not so easy to immediately find a spiritual father who will correspond to your spiritual state, to your problems. Therefore, we remain with the instruction of the Gospels: "Seek and you shall find" (Matt. 7:8). Asking from person to person—obviously you don't ask every person on the street, but only the ones preoccupied with life in the Church. In the beginning, you can confess once or twice to a few priests in order to decide on a single one.

I also sought a spiritual father, but I could not find one whom I could stay with my entire life. Father Ioan Kulighin was not suitable for me, because I did not know enough Russian to understand the advice of a Russian father confessor. I then looked for another spiritual father, using all the means possible to find one. That is why I advise you to ask from person to person, and in the end, you will find one.

In what circumstances can we change our spiritual father?

When you are not satisfied with him, pure and simple. When he is insufficient for you.

There are certain well-known situations in which you are allowed to change your spiritual father: when he is very sick and can no longer hear confessions, when you move to another place, or if he is a very busy confessor and you—because of work—can only confess to him very rarely.

There are also exceptions: it is possible for a person to increase spiritually and the spiritual father is no longer sufficient. And then he seeks another one. These, however, are rare cases that usually happen to those who wish to have a guide for the Prayer of the Heart. Especially in relation to the issue of the Jesus Prayer, it is difficult to have an instructor, it is difficult to find a spiritual father who lives this prayer and can say something true and gratifying.

However, we must first be careful not to have within us these severe problems of vanity or judging others, and then, instead of repenting, we blame our confessor. Therefore, it is good for us to cry to God with sincerity, insistence, and repentance, with all of our soul, and then God will bring us the spiritual father that we need.

We must also understand that all priests have the grace, coming from the Savior, to forgive sins. We do not need to be too demanding with the priest to whom we confess. If he is sincere and has the fear of God, then we can confess to him with complete openness. It is very beneficial for us to feel sorry for the sins we committed and which we confess. It is not good at all for us to confess formally!

Some intellectuals are very demanding when they look for a spiritual father...

Some people are demanding. You ask your spiritual father about your problem, and he answers you entirely or to the degree he can, and he satisfies you. The second time, you ask him again about problems that you encountered or confess your sins to him. He can pray for you; he can help you in this sense.

If an intellectual is demanding and seeks a special spiritual father, he will have a harder time finding one, because he wants to talk to a priest who is a philosopher like him. He expects an answer in a language he understands, but he might encounter a spiritual father who cannot understand all his questions but has great experience with the spiritual life that the intellectual or philosopher needs. They cannot understand each other because the intellectual is too demanding and often drunk with pride because of his knowledge. It is difficult for such a demanding person to find a "spiritual" father confessor. And he will seek one all his life, and often he will never find him.

How strictly should a spiritual father apply canons, knowing that in today's times, many people fall into grave sins out of ignorance?

The one who fell into grave sins out of ignorance must be taught. He shouldn't be left in ignorance. It is good to tell the person who confesses that the passion that dominates him can lead to the death of his soul, and maybe even to eternal death.

It is very important that the confessor think of the penitent with love and advise him in such a way that the penitent—if he really wants to change—is aware of the gravity of his sin and sincerely desires to escape all their passions.

On the other hand, if a father confessor recommends a canon with authority or anger, you must be sure from the start that no one will respect him. It is good for the spiritual father to be gentle, to be calm, and to try to convince the faithful with love that the canon he gives is of great benefit to them.

Before anything else, the penitent must be prepared to realize that the habit that is rooted in him is the greatest evil. Proceeding in this way, the believer will learn to fulfill any canon more easily, however difficult. If we directly impose a canon, people will not respect it, because usually, these people are not aware of the danger of a sin and the fact that they can lose eternity because of their passions. Neither do they have a clear understanding of what eternity means. Such things are foreign to them. So, it is very necessary to prepare them spiritually to understand that their passion is so great that they must escape it at any price, that it must be absolutely cast out.

We should be kind to the faithful who come to confession. If we command them and if the canon is heavy and surprises them, they will not do it. They leave you and go about their business; something like this does happen. That is why I said that the canon should not be imposed; because it may be a canon that they cannot do. Then the penitent will

wish to escape from it, and even if we tell him some useful things, he will not accept them within himself. We must pray to God to inspire us if it is good or not to give a canon to the penitent. If it is God's will to give a canon to the penitent, we must pray to the heavenly Father to inspire us as to what kind of canon we should recommend.

A spiritual father can be compared to a surgeon who needs to take care of a person who is gravely ill and whose illness has spread throughout his body, and a painful surgery is needed to heal that person. The canon given by the father confessor is such a surgery performed for spiritual illnesses. The canon is like a medicine given by a physician to a sick person.

To what point does obedience to a spiritual father go? Because there can be two extremes: one in which the spiritual father's function is to forgive sins endlessly, and another in which the confessor is idealized by his spiritual children and their minds do not accept anything other than what he says in general, not necessarily just during confession.

I think that there are some mistakes on both sides. What the spiritual father does not know, God knows. A man cannot know everything. That is why, when we do not know something, we tell the faithful to read St. John of the Ladder, St. John Chrysostom (who was a great spiritual father), St. Basil the Great, and others. Each person can pick what he needs from these Holy Fathers.

A spiritual father cannot say something definitive about all problems related to spiritual life. There are, however, certain things that he can say: how to guard yourself from passions, and what you can do to escape them—for example, from carnal sin, which is frequently encountered among young people. Or how to escape the passion of smoking (because this too is a frequent passion that brings many troubles and scandals in families). The spiritual father can give you some instructions which, if you put them in practice, can help you escape these passions. But we do not go too far and then we send such believers to certain books, to read, take notes, and understand more than they could understand from a man who is usually limited.

A contemporary priest said that there will come a time of persecution against the Church and then lay people will have a very important role, while priests will not be able to do too much. What do you think of this idea?

It will happen, probably, as it happened in the time of the Soviet revolution, right from its beginning, when the clergy, and especially spiritual fathers, were run through by the sword. And then you could not find spiritual fathers. There simply were no more priests to whom you could go confess.

Let us think about what is going on in America today. There are very few spiritual fathers there. However, there are psychiatrists. And great sinners go to psychiatrists for help. Psychiatrists there, in America—like the ones in the time of the persecutions that will come—can give advice in abundance, but they cannot loosen sins, because they do not have this grace. It is not us priests who forgive sins, but in confession, at all times and in any circumstance, Christ is also present and listens to the confession, and He is the One Who forgives. I, as a priest, only say the prayer of absolution.

When the time comes when there will be no more spiritual fathers but only lay people who will have very great importance, then people will be content with advice from these physicians (somewhat skilled regarding the soul), but they will remain weighed down by the same passions which they had until then.

Confessed sins are fully forgiven if the canon given by the spiritual father is respected. If you respect the canon with humility and with the conviction that your sins are forgiven, they are forgiven and you are gradually healed of your soul's illnesses. But if, while doing the canon, you do other foolish things, then neither the old sins nor the new ones are forgiven, and they always weigh on you.

Therefore, the spiritual father, with the help of the grace of the priesthood which he received through Apostolic succession (John 20:22-23), can forgive sins in the Name of Jesus Christ. A psychiatrist gives you only what he personally has, from human knowledge.

The psychiatrist, if he is not a zealous Christian (by this, I mean that when he investigates the human soul, he does not give priority to the inspired teachings of Scripture and of the Holy Fathers above other ideas), can offer you some instructions that are insufficient for the soul and that you can take seriously if you lack instructions that come from God, through a spiritual father. Later, you forget these instructions, and you go on living your bitter life.

Sin is a great obstacle to freedom

Freedom is a pressing problem for young people. We are taught from a young age that we should be free, and that we must demand our rights. In this context, we ask you to teach us how to convince our colleagues of the truth of the words in Scripture: "If the Son sets you free, you will be free indeed" (John 8:36).

It is difficult to give an answer. It is easier to ask, as children ask about certain things which are very difficult to answer. Let's also take the answer from the Savior: sin is that which makes us slaves (John 8:34) and we must fight against it to be truly free. For man was created free in the beginning.

We can advise young people to live a pure life. In what way? For example, there are many young adults who, before marriage, break a divine commandment, that very delicate commandment. They want to have trial marriages. For him to live this life with the girl he will marry; to fulfill his own desire, to satisfy his lust through this sin of fornication. If he does this from the beginning of his adult life, he becomes a slave, he loses his freedom, he becomes the friend of passions and the friend of the devil. And then, it is very difficult to convince someone who is living in sin to live a pure life.

A pure life means a luminous life—his mind is luminous, his thinking is correct, and often his whole life has integrity. A young man or woman who preserved their chastity are whole, honorable people: advice, a word from them can have power. A person who is corrupted in this fleshly life can be timid and unsure in what he says, and he is at odds with God (Who is the source of wisdom and holiness). Thus, a young person who wants to become someone must preserve this integrity, must guard it.

To speak today about what I am proposing, I think that many would laugh, would roll their eyes, and would say: "He is a fool!" To give such advice today, when a father tells his son: "Go, find a girl, and do this...Why are you thinking about marriage?" Sadly, I know of such cases. It is very difficult today to stop a young person from sinning. And so, I continue with this method of guiding the youth—who are on the threshold of their adult life—to preserve this state of purity for their body and soul, as God recommends.

There are, however, many young people today who want to listen to this spiritual advice, even without the approval or agreement of their parents. Their parents advise them to seek an open path, as they did in their youth. There are people, some of them old, who have not yet married and have not confessed in twenty or thirty years. And they die like this. And then what education can they give to the young person who wants to lead a Christian life? The young man (or girl) withdraws to his room and reads some evening prayers or psalms. His mother looks through the keyhole and when she sees him reading a prayer, opens the door with brutality and tells him: "Don't read anymore, don't pray like this anymore, because you will go crazy!" What can these young people choose when they feel joy while praying, but hear things like these from their mothers? The mother does not pray; she lives in sin, unmarried, with all kinds of abortions and sins that overwhelm her and darken her life; without realizing it, she is in agreement with the devil. And she urges her son or daughter to be like her. Then these young people choose to live a Christian life as they understand it now, at their age. Today, there are many cases like this that I learn of in confession.

Sadly, many old people and adults today are somewhat frozen; they have become hardened in all sorts of passions. In contrast, there are now also many young people who align themselves with the luminous path of faith. Regrettably, parents cannot give good advice to their children who could become saints.

Life is left for each one of us to strive to acquire a capital of good deeds and a Christian life which will be very useful in eternity, in the Light. All of us must live with this perspective of our future life. We should not live as animals, for earthly things only. You eat, drink, multiply, and have fun like animals do, in their own way! Our human life has another ideal and another much higher aim. We know from the Savior that sin is an obstacle to the freedom of each human being. We also know that human life has this perspective of eternity and of total freedom in Christ in the future (John 17:3).

What are the main reasons for arguments among young couples, and how can they be overcome?

It is very difficult to overcome them, because usually, attraction between a young man and woman is limited to anatomical forms and bodily pleasures. Rarely do young adults think before marrying to discuss how one or the other understands life—the purpose of life. It is important for them to know if both have a Christian aim in their life, that is, to not only think about getting rich. If he or she has a car (some think) it is an advantage and a reason for marriage! If they have some money saved in the bank, if they have some material possessions, they think everything is settled for their relationship and their marriage. However, if young people limit themselves to only this material aspect, then their marriage, this lifelong association, is often compromised.

Other than these material, earthly problems (car, land, possessions), there are also spiritual conditions—for example, if these young adults who want to start a family are interested in the Christian faith, if they find satisfaction in faith, or in religious problems. Because if one is Christian and the other is an atheist or mocks the faith, I recommend emphatically that they do not dare marry just because he or she is beautiful, or because of some other human aspects. All of these will deteriorate at some point, and the young people will be in a sad situation and will have a life with problems and pain. Therefore, faith and agreement in matters of faith are very important conditions for starting a family.

If the parents are faithful, then they raise their children in faith and wisdom, in a life of respect and communion with other people. If only one of the parents is faithful, for him life is truly an ordeal. She goes to church and he goes to parties, or the theater, or the cinema, or other forms of entertainment. He comes home drunk, but she comes from church. And then what association, what communion, what discussions will they have together?

Thus, faith is an essential element for a family. At least these two things should exist: an agreement in faith and sincerity. Because some promise much at the beginning, so that they achieve their goal of getting married, but then they turn the page and start a life of evil deeds, which leads to unhappiness and misfortune for both spouses for their whole life. I have met all kinds of families, and so I can say this with much conviction.

There are also other instances. For example, a young Orthodox marries a Catholic. I also encountered such cases. She, for example, has her Catholic circle—her friends, colleagues, classmates, their feast days, their Easter. On the other hand, the man, who is Orthodox, has his friends as well, church services, and all the other things. She goes to church for a celebration of Catholic Easter (when we celebrate Palm Sunday) and eats red eggs. He eats according to Great Lent and prepares for Holy Week. He fasts more severely, but she eats non-lenten meals. It seems as if this wouldn't be that important, but this kind of relationship is quite sad. It is good from the start for young people to be prudent and to arrange a climate which will be of benefit to them for their whole life.

Why can we not say the Prayer of the Heart?

We are approaching the end of this very useful interview. Father Staretz, for what reason are most of us not able to practice the Prayer of the Heart?

For what reason? Because the Prayer of the Heart presupposes persistence in calling on the Name of the Lord. Persistence with much attention and with a humble spirit! Those who commit to this prayer because they heard many things about it want to acquire it, but they don't possess the means that can help them.

That is, in the first place they don't have the patience to say it continuously. It is called unceasing prayer, as the Holy Apostle Paul commands us (1 Thess. 5:17). In our ordinary life, all sorts of preoccupations attract us. We are scattered and this prayer is interrupted very frequently. We don't have spiritual continuity; we can't keep ourselves in a spirit of prayer when we call on the Lord's Name. Our mind flies even in the moment when we say: "Lord Jesus Christ, Son of God, have mercy on me, a sinner." Our mind often wanders, it is preoccupied with all kinds of other problems, foreign to prayer. And, in fact, we do not pray continuously, and this harms us very much.

Then, when we pray, we usually have some remnants of hatred within ourselves. We argued with someone, but we didn't realize it. However, when we quarrel with someone, prayer doesn't take root; it doesn't stick, we pray as if to an object. It is idle talk. And, of course, in these conditions neither will we be able to acquire the Prayer of the Heart.

There is also this state of humility in which the prayer must be said. Humility! We are strangers to it! If the prayer catches a bit within us, we congratulate ourselves: "Look where I've arrived!" And then we start from the beginning again and don't make any progress. But in terms of the Prayer of the Heart, even if we don't reach its highest point, the fact that we call on the Name of the Lord is of great benefit to us. Where God is, all things calm down and become favorable for our inner life. Pride is

broken down and all evil things depart.

Our relationship with the Mother of God is very important as well. The Holy Virgin is the greatest mediator for this prayer and helps those who have total devotion to and veneration for her. Saint Silouan acquired the Prayer of the Heart after several weeks of praying ardently to the Mother of God. The Savior and the Most Holy Mother of God know our inner state exactly and respond exactly to this request. When God knows that humility will continue, devotion to the Mother of God will be preserved continually, and veneration of the Savior, of God—for He is the One called in prayer—will last, he gives this Prayer of the Heart more quickly. Other people receive this gift with great difficulty, or not at all. Because, in any case, this prayer is a gift. People seek to acquire the Prayer of the Heart and many say it with joy and benefit to themselves, however not as many as there should be, because of our instability.

Father Sofian, over a long period of time you met diverse Christians who practiced the Prayer of the Heart. Some were formed in the quiet of monasteries, others lived in the crowds of large cities. That is why we would like to ask you: what is the connection between the environment in which we live and the practice of unceasing prayer?

The "environment" for the Prayer of the Heart is the persistence with which we engage in this kind of work. This is the most favorable "environment." We must persevere in saying the Jesus Prayer with seriousness, that is, with attention and much repentance.

In closing, we ask you to explain the Holy Apostle Paul's words: "And now abide faith, hope, love, these three; but the greatest of these is love." (1 Cor. 13:13)

Love is the greatest because God Himself is love (1 John 4:8). Thus, true love is greater and for this reason, it abides in eternity.

Living with love, you live with God. Then you have everything, with God's help. But if you do not have love, neither faith nor hope have any steadfastness in you because they are missing the essence: God Himself. Let us strive to have this love and then we will talk more about it!

We thank you very much and may God continue to give you strength and health!

I responded to the questions you asked in my own way. However, if you want to acquire more gifts than you have imagined, make an effort, and strive to accomplish what the saints of our Church teach us! Nothing comes from only listening to words. Because we already know many things that are useful for our spiritual life. If we limit ourselves to what we know, and we don't accomplish any of the things we know, we will not reap any benefits.

Therefore, I urge you, the readers of my words (spoken with the infirmities that can be seen in them): if you want to benefit from a spiritual word, live it! Without living it, you cannot truly taste its essence, and you cannot bear fruit. For it to bear fruit, it must be lived! The Savior says these words, too: "Whoever does and teaches men so, he shall be called great in the Kingdom of Heaven" (Matt. 5:19). Do it, and God will help you so that all these teachings will grow in your soul! Amen.

"May God Grant that the Entire Country Be a Burning Bush of Prayer!"[36]

Recollections of the "Burning Bush" movement • Father Ioan truly prayed unceasingly • The union of mind and heart • "The entire cosmos that surrounds us gathers around the being of the person who prays"

At Antim Monastery in Bucharest, not during the time of the Babylonian or the Egyptian captivity, but during the time of the Communist captivity, a spiritual life was preserved without interruption with the help of God. The services were continuous, especially the Divine Liturgy—which is very beneficial for all of humanity. With all the threats hanging over our heads, the Divine Liturgy was performed daily.

As you know, the Communists came to power in 1945 and installed themselves with great boldness. They changed all of the rules that had existed up until then through a kind of societal "renewal," which in fact aimed to pervert our Romanian and Orthodox Christian identity, it aimed to change it into hatred toward God and into unbelief.

Moses once wanted to free his people from captivity in Egypt and for them to all go pray in the wilderness. But Pharaoh did not give them permission (Ex. 5:1-5). Once the Communists came to power, prayer was not really allowed here either. Many monasteries were greatly oppressed during that time of great disturbances and changes to the country's rules.

Recollections of the "Burning Bush" movement

In a similar atmosphere of pagan and atheist pressure on the Romanian soul, a Christian flame and a cry to God was born at Antim Monastery in Bucharest. I am talking about the conferences of the "Burning Bush" movement.

36 Talk addressed to a group of young people from Bucharest, after Vespers, on March 10, 1993. Transcription from an audio recording.

That is, after Vespers (especially Sunday evening, when a great number of people would come), we would enter the monastery library and there we would hold these conferences on the spiritual life, while outside the Communists' wrath raged. For example, one week we would interpret the Divine Liturgy in different ways. One day, someone talked about the Divine Liturgy in history. On another day (of the same week), we discussed the Divine Liturgy as a sacrifice. One person spoke about the Divine Liturgy in iconography; another about how it was expressed musically; another about the mystical understanding of the Divine Liturgy (what occurs in the Holy Chalice or on the Holy Paten). A great number of people would come to listen to these interpretations. Communist informers, who took notes to add to political dossiers, blended among the Christians. We did not discuss political problems. We knew there was no point in doing such a thing, since the country was occupied by a foreign army.

The speakers were priests who knew Orthodox teachings very well, and their words had great power and influence over the listeners, because such interpretations truly interested the entire audience. Notable speakers came from all over the capital. There was Fr. Benedict Ghius, a Doctor in Theology with superb studies in France. His very presence, gentleness, and spiritual depth brought a wealth of new understandings, which comforted everyone's soul. There was Alexandru Mironescu - a journalist and professor of physics, chemistry, and philosophy. When he explained a spiritual subject, he would not only fill our minds, but also our hearts with joy and spiritual comfort. Another was Paul Sterian, a well-known author; another, Ion Marin Sadoveanu (for a time he was the director of the theater in Bucharest); another, Vasile Voiculescu, a writer, doctor, and, especially, a man of profound Christian experience. Similarly, Alexandru Elian, a Byzantine Studies professor and a man of great spiritual depth, also participated.

They all brought treasures from their wealth of true knowledge to those who thirstily listened to the conferences. All spoke about the soul, about the spiritual life of man.

An invisible flame burned, lit on the Holy Altar Table, from the heart of the Divine Liturgy, and it encompassed all the speakers with its light, as well as the listeners who gathered in the monastery library. This group of preachers took the name "Burning Bush." The principal problem that

we discussed - from the practical, historical, and mystical point of view - was the Divine Liturgy and the liturgical service in the Holy Altar, as well as the Jesus Prayer. Thus, from the Holy Altar to the altar of the heart. Because the heart is the true liturgical celebrant! That is, an inner liturgy can exist and be continually served in each of us. This is the ideal. An ideal that is easy to fulfill if there is a zeal for the Jesus Prayer in our hearts.

Father Ioan truly prayed unceasingly

In 1945, Fr. Ioan Kulighin arrived in Bucharest, as a gift sent from God. He had grown up in Russia. He had been a novice at Optina Monastery. From Cernica Monastery, where he was hosted, Fr. Ioan would come to us at Antim every week and participate in these meetings.

I will tell you something very important. From a very young age, Fr. Ioan had mastered the Jesus Prayer. Father Ioan prayed unceasingly. Optina, where he was raised, was a very spiritual place with elders who practiced this Prayer of the Heart.

And I will tell you that until I met Fr. Ioan, I had not met a priest or a Christian who truly had unceasing prayer. For example, Fr. Ioan was asked about different things about his country, about Communist Russia, about his life (he had suffered greatly in the Communist prisons). And when he was engaged in his replies, I put my hand on his shoulder and asked him: "Father Ioan, are you praying now?" "Yes, Father, I am praying," he replied. Even though he was speaking with others, amid explanations, his heart was praying. And this did not only occur during the day but also at night, all the time. His heart prayed with this short prayer. For many years, Fr. Ioan's calling on the Lord had descended from the mind into the heart. He prayed when he talked, when he ate, and when he walked. Prayer was like breathing for him. He prayed in his sleep, too. I know this from him, actually. I would host him in my cell from Saturday to Monday and speak with him about many things that were truly beneficial for me.

He was a very luminous man, both in mind and countenance. When you saw him, you wouldn't think much about him; you didn't realize what spiritual value he had. He was small; he had a thin beard, glasses, long hair, blonde; he wore a poor cassock and was very modest. But when you became closer to him and asked him about spiritual things, he responded masterfully, since he was filled with this great grace of unceasing prayer.

He contributed very much to the strengthening of the "Burning Bush." The Russian Communists took him from Cernica in January 1947. They condemned him to prison for life, considering him a traitor to their country and a war criminal. He was taken to Odessa. He was with brother Leontie, a Basarabian, Fr. Ioan's translator. Brother Leontie sent me a postcard that ended with the prayer "Lord Jesus." This postcard passed through all the Communist censures and arrived at Antim. Father Ioan died in Odessa, but they sent brother Leontie to Siberia. Metropolitan Nicolae is buried at Cernica Monastery.

I spoke to you about Fr. Ioan since he was a great spiritual treasure for us all. He was both a great man of prayer and a very good advisor. He knew the *Philokalia* and the Holy Fathers, similar to how Fr. Cleopa knows and recites entire pages of St. Maximos the Confessor from memory. He also had this unceasing prayer, which, said for much time and with great attention, fixes itself somewhere in our heart; and there can be no greater joy for someone than the joy he feels when this prayer works in his heart.

The meetings at Antim existed for a long time, without being called the "Burning Bush." It was natural for the faithful to receive advice, comfort, and spiritual guidance at Antim Monastery, despite all the informants who came to Church and were afraid about who knows what we were saying against the Communist regime.

When the "Burning Bush" movement took shape, its author was Sandu Tudor, who at Antim became Hiermonk Agathon (in Greek, "agathon" means improved). Later, he became Hieroschemamonk Daniil Teodorescu. He was an erudite man and a true practitioner of the Jesus Prayer. If Fr. Daniil had not registered this movement with the court, maybe we wouldn't have been imprisoned. All of us were taken, seventeen monks and novices, and sent to prison in the name of the "Burning Bush."

I remember that during the interrogations, I was asked something like this: "Oh, you're the ones who light fields on fire outside the city, and you threaten those of us from the leadership?" I responded: "No, sir. I never set a field on fire..."; and I told them about this page in Scripture which talks about Moses and the bush which was not consumed. They, poor people, were not informed at all, but were thinking about who knows what we could be up to, a few fathers and novices from Antim. Even though this movement, like Moses' movement in Egypt, truly was against the spirit of Pharaoh. We, however, were against the spiritual works of the Communists who sought the de-Christianization of souls.

The union of mind and heart

I will tell you a few things about the Jesus Prayer, or the Prayer of the Heart, as it is also known. Its content is very short: "Lord Jesus Christ, Son of God, have mercy on me, a sinner." Some seek to practice this prayer, but with influences foreign to its spirit - a mix of yoga and other currents of Eastern spirituality, which are very harmful and falsify prayer. To correctly learn this prayer, I recommend three books: *The Way of a Pilgrim*, *The Art of Prayer*, and Volume 8 [(Vol. 5 in the English edition)] of the *Philokalia*, which especially focuses on the Prayer of the Heart. Whoever practices the Jesus Prayer and follows the instructions in these books will walk on a sure and good path. Whoever follows other instructions may make mistakes.

This prayer is very simple, but it must be said as often as possible, day and night if possible. You can read in the *Way of a Pilgrim* that at a given moment, the elder tells this pilgrim to say the prayer 3,000 times a day, then 6,000 times, then 12,000 times, and this pilgrim did as he was told and progressed very much. Read this book; it is very engaging. You feel the spirit of prayer in it, and when you read it, it seems like you have acquired the prayer. I could not put it down.

This prayer can be said in a whisper or silently, but with an effort that each word of the prayer falls on the place of the spiritual heart. In the left part of the chest, two fingers higher than the nipple, is the center of our spiritual being. The words of the prayer must fall on this place, and then it is said calmly, with very much benefit, until, with the help of the Good God, the mind descends into the heart.

For this is the aim of the Jesus Prayer: to unite the mind and heart, these two centers of our inner being which work separately nearly all our life. That is why so many falsities, flatteries, and lies are uttered. You can speak very convincingly, with beautiful words, but your heart remains very far from what your mouth is saying. However, when this union takes place, when the mind descends into the heart, a person becomes unified in all that he thinks, in all that he says, in all that he does.

After a long time of repeating the Jesus Prayer with attention, this inner settling takes place, and an extraordinary peace is born in the spiritual heart, a kind of warmth around this center, and one feels great joy, serenity, and an increase of faith, of trust in God. You feel the presence of the God of our fathers. You feel God and you love Him very much.

Additionally, you feel a very pure and holy love for all human beings and all creation (a love that is very different from cold, intellectual love).

"The entire cosmos that surrounds us gathers around the being of the person who prays"

The Jesus Prayer is not only for those in monasteries or for hermits, but it is very possible for anyone. There is so much dead time in our lives. For example, when we stay in line or wait for the bus. Don't let your mind wander everywhere! Pray with "Lord Jesus" and, slowly but surely, a passageway, a path of light, will appear between the mind and heart, and you will feel this great inner peace and joy. The Prayer of the Heart will greatly help you say other prayers (the Psalms, the Paraklesis) with much concentration and collected thoughts. But thoughts of blasphemy, debauchery, or pornography do not have a place in the environment of this prayer. Even children ages eight, nine, and ten can catch onto this prayer and the benefit is unimaginable.

Therefore, this prayer can be practiced by anyone, on the condition that the person is honest in his soul, that he says it with much attention, and that he unceasingly works towards dispassion. However, if someone is filled with passions, cunning, prone to anger, a drunkard, or creates a lot of commotion around himself, then the prayer will not take root in him. But, to the measure that you fight with the passions within yourself, its force grows, and it descends into the heart of the one who prays. I urge each one of you to try this prayer, and after you try it, not to interrupt it. If, after a time of practicing it, you forget to pray, then the prayer itself reminds you that you have not been praying. The benefit of this prayer is indeed very great. The entire cosmos that surrounds us gathers around the being of the person who prays, and people regard this person with goodness, with calmness, and with love. Practice it, and you will feel its benefits!

Since the time this movement took shape, the "Burning Bush" has continued to grow, because very many people began practicing this prayer. With us, it was only the beginning. But look, I see a face here that practices the prayer; I see another, and even another one. May God grant that the entire country be a "Burning Bush" of prayer!

Very much prayer is needed because there are many who blaspheme God, and this blasphemy removes God's mercy from us. For me, it is a very great joy to see young people preoccupied with the Jesus Prayer.

Try to draw near to this prayer as much as possible. Don't become

discouraged! Prayer is not acquired that easily, you must actually practice it to your measure. By persevering, with the help of God, you will truly grow in prayer.

And do not forget that this great enemy of prayer, the devil, exactly at the moment when we pray, attacks us with thoughts, with passions, with bad memories; he does anything so that you do not see any progress in prayer. But stubbornly call on the Name of the Lord, and you will see the results! That is all!

Maybe you were expecting more from me. Do not expect me to be an orator, I never liked to give speeches. I spoke to you about some things from my heart, as I felt them and understood them. May God help us!

THIRTY TESTIMONIES ON LOVE[37]

Fill my soul with greater love for You. Make me understand Your humility, in which You lived on earth.

1 Whoever does not fulfill the commandment to love others cannot consider himself a Christian. No state is more pitiful than not being able to forgive your brother even in the most difficult moments of life. Whoever cannot forgive cannot love. Whoever cannot love others can neither love God. And in order to love God, we must be reconciled with those around us.

2. Only what comes from love, from the heart, can go to the heart. Whoever does not pray from the heart can neither open his way to the hearts of those around him nor to the heart of God.

3. Lover of man, Lord, Your mercy is great and unmatched, for You patiently endured with forbearance.

4. Struck across the cheek by the Jews.

5. Sold by an apostle.

6. Denied by an apostle.

7. Prodded with unbelief by another apostle.

8. And greatly tempted by those who renounce You.

9. Lord, You Who became incarnate, was crucified, rose from the dead, and is without sin, grant us understanding as You did Thomas (John 20:28), so that we may know and love You, and cry out: "My Lord and my God," glory to You!

10. There is a spiritual love. Just as there is nourishment for the body and for the soul, a drink for the body and another for the spirit, so too there is a love of the flesh that comes from Satan, and another love of the Spirit, with God as its origin. No one can be ruled by both loves. If you are a lover of the body, you cannot contain the love of the Spirit.

37 In this chapter, diverse notes left by Elder Sofian on pieces of paper, as well as transcripts of audio recordings taken by the editor of this edition between 1998-2001, have been gathered.

11. If you have despised all bodily things in your spirit (I am not only talking about flesh and blood, silver and wealth, but also the earth itself and even the sky, because all these things will pass away) and if your soul is not attached to any one of these, if you are not enslaved by any passionate love, then you can understand spiritual love.

12. He who abstains from idle talk and from each kind of passion, from passing pleasures (not out of disdain for people and life, but from the fire of an overwhelming love for God) if such a person does not chase after people, they will chase after him. Where there is a great flame in the soul, there people gather to warm their cold souls.

13. Instead of condemning people, we should try to love them, in order to understand them. To know, cherish, and help a person, you must feel his soul, his inner world. Lord, help me not to criticize anyone! I want to say every good thing that I know about everyone.

14. The grace of God is very delicate. When we stray from the humble path, from obedience or love, on different occasions in our life, grace withdraws. And—Lord forbid!—we can remain without grace! We are like the dead.

15. Whoever commits evil against another, especially without a reason, but only out of the pleasure of doing evil, has a sick soul. He is an impassioned person, darkened in mind and heart, who has become a tool of the evil spirit. The devil, the spirit whom the Savior tells us was a murderer of men from the beginning (John 8:44), works through him. If we respond to such a person with the same degree of evil, it means that we too allow ourselves to be caught in the net of the same evil spirit who controls him and whom he serves. Allowing ourselves to be defeated by evil, we give the victory to the devil; we let him enter us too and help him increase his destructive work in the world. In this way, we support and encourage evil and sin around us.

16. With this attitude, we cause great evil to ourselves too, because fulfilling the will of the demons, we separate ourselves from God, remaining troubled and scattered. Furthermore, what is even worse, we can no longer pray to God as we should.

17. Think about the prayer "Our Father." If you have quarreled with someone, if you hate someone, then this invocation of the Holy Father turns into a curse: "Don't forgive me, Lord, as I too cannot forgive!" The contradiction between what we say and what we do nullifies our prayers.

18. God's forgiveness of us depends on the forgiveness we show others. These are not empty words, it is a great calamity. Whoever does not forgive does not love! Whoever does not forgive and does not love others, does not love God either! Saint Maximos the Confessor says this too: "If we detect any trace of hatred in our hearts against any man whatsoever for committing any fault, we are utterly estranged from love for God, since love for God absolutely precludes us from hating any man."[38]

19. In daily life, we sting one another with our words, we grieve one another, and without a doubt we trouble ourselves, we retaliate. People come to our monastery who have some enemies and begin to pray: "May God strike them! May He turn them to dust and ash!" We forget that we must fulfill certain divine commandments, that we must pray for our enemies.

20. Possibly, the greatest virtue is love for enemies; or at least to pray for them or not take revenge. Let God do justice. Do not judge! "Vengeance is Mine" says the Lord (Deut. 32:35). Divine Providence exists, and nothing happens in this world without God's knowledge.

21. Love your enemies! Forget persecutions! Lay aside evil, reconcile with your enemies, and do good to them! Overwhelm them with goodness! Reconcile this very day with them so that the sun does not set on your anger![39]

22. The most important weapon against the evil that comes upon us is humble-mindedness. Let us ask God with contrition to calm this evil and to cover us with His grace and love.

23. In the Church, each person has a personal relationship with God. There is no formula by which all people can be saved.

38 St. Maximos the Confessor, "First Century on Love," in the *Philokalia Vol. 2* (New York: Faber and Faber, Ltd., 1981), 54.

39 Eph. 4:26

24. It is necessary from time to time to return to ourselves, because we are all lacking in comparison to what we should be. Let us repent with the sincere awareness that we are unworthy. And God, Who does not put us on trial as people do, will receive us with all of His love. God's love surpasses any human love. In any state we may be, let us ask for forgiveness in a profound way, with tears and repentance.

25. The Spirit of God guided St. Parascheva's steps, her entire being, throughout her brief life on earth. The Spirit of God now rests in her earthly tent—her body, in her holy relics. By God's grace, inner peace, help in difficulties, and healing pour forth upon the faithful from [her relics] like an undying spring. Venerating her holy relics, we venerate God Who works miracles through them. Holy relics are a clear proof of the truth that whoever serves God faithfully, with love, even if he dies bodily, remains alive in Christ.

26. We are never alone; we are always with God. The more you call on Him, the more present He is in your life.

27. There is a prayer that a monk has to say, a prayer invoking the Name of God: "Lord Jesus Christ, Son of God, have mercy on me, a sinner." We are indebted—according to the monastic rule—to always say this prayer. And little by little, this duty transforms into a calling of love.

28. If this prayer is done persistently, for a long time, its results are extraordinary. A spiritual warmth is produced in the heart of the one who prays; his faith and love for God, for people, and for all creation increases; he is penetrated by this sentiment of living in God. Just as a fish lives in water, so does the monk live in God, in this atmosphere in which you feel fully in God.

29. I am referring to monks who strive to live according to the ordinance of God. Because all kinds of currents of earthly life flood us, too. Practically speaking, we are not at all heavenly beings, even though we would like to be. We strive, through calling on God in our life, to become beings who are not alone. If we succeed in making space for God within us, all the better for us, but also for others.

30. The Jesus Prayer requires much patience, sacrifice, and especially suffering love.

31. Grant us, Lord, the persistence that the saints had on the path of salvation! Grant us, Lord, the strength of their faith, the humble spirit in which they lived, and the zeal of their love!

32. Sometimes we act as if God is obligated to help us by trespassing His first commandment: love. We cannot progress spiritually if we do not struggle to fulfill the commandment of loving one another. You do not approach God by commanding Him with anger, as to a slave, but you approach with humility and tears.

33. It is just as difficult to forgive the one who greatly wronged us as it is necessary and beautiful. We meet all kinds of people in everyday life. Some are bad, rude, egotistical, envious, unjust, proud, greedy, and irritated. There are people who take pleasure in insulting and upsetting others. They either harm our natural rights and interests, or they speak badly of us behind our backs, or they mock and wound us by unjust, harmful words. In such cases, our human nature urges us to respond with the same degree of evil. It urges us to remember wrongs and to take revenge; it urges us to hit back when we are attacked. This is how the sinful person within us urges us. Not only do such impulses seem natural and permitted, but also many people praise and recommend them.

34. A Christian, however, is not permitted to act in such a way, but on the contrary. In every upsetting circumstance, a Christian must resist the first impulse of anger. When we are struck and mocked, when our enemies treat us unjustly and our own brothers hate us rightly or wrongfully, we must control ourselves, patiently bear it, be victorious over hate through love, and forgive.

35. Holiness or perfection does not necessarily presuppose signs and miracles, as we are used to believing. Not all the saints worked miracles in this life.

36. The Savior told us these words that should make many people ponder: "Many will say to Me in that day, 'Lord, Lord, have we not

prophesied in Your name, cast out demons in Your name, and done many wonders in Your name?' And then I will declare to them, 'I never knew you; depart from Me, you who practice lawlessness!'" (Matt. 7:22-23). Sorcerers, aided by the powers of darkness, can work miracles that amaze people. But holiness can only be acquired by the gentle and lowly of heart, who are full of love for God and their neighbor.

37. Some people are born with a greater power to receive and give love. When they give an answer, they speak from a place of love. They can grow in this love by co-working with God. Other people cannot have love. They are dry and die like this if they do not ask God to help change their lives. They talk about love, but they do not have it, they do not speak from its core. I met many people without love. People can appear cordial and polite; they speak nicely, respectfully, and sweetly to you, but it is artificial. It is not authentic love. It does not pour from the heart. Certainly, if we ask God to grant us love, this love is given to us. Some Christians receive the gift of love after they struggle for a long time to live a life of humility, a life fully in God. In time, humility turns into love, and then these believers can receive the gift of love from the heart, the flood of love about which the Holy Apostle Paul speaks in 1 Corinthians 13.

38. The Holy Virgin's motherly love urges her to immediately help where the Most Holy Name of Her Only Born Son is called and honored, and where Her children by grace—zealous believers—honor Her as a true Mother of God.

39. Therefore, when we are troubled by difficulties, stricken and burned by passions, let us especially turn with faith to the Mother of God, who is also the Mother of us on earth, knowing that the prayers of a mother before Her Son can do much. Let us pray with contrition, saying to Her:

40. "Most Holy Birthgiver of God, who brought to earth the Light of the whole world, enlighten the darkness of our minds and hearts, so that we may know our sins, repent for them, and no longer serve them.

41. You, who with your body gave birth to the King of peace, plant in us the peace of your Son and chase away the storms of passions from our souls.

42. You, who are the unquenchable spring of healings, heal our infirmities and ease our pain, because all that You will, You can do, as the Mother of the All-Powerful One. Amen."

43. The Savior teaches us to name God: Father. The love of a father is vast and profound! God, Whom we address, is a Father Who bears with us and awaits us. It is as if we fear His great patience and goodness. He is always good! He is the God of love and waits calmly, as the father in the Gospel waits, shielding his eyes with his hands, looking into the distance: "Is my son coming by any chance? Is he by any chance returning with all his heart to his Father?"

44. The young man in the parable mocks not only his possessions, but also his father. Did the father reproach or rebuke him in any way? Not at all! He washes him, clothes him in new garments, gives him a ring, prepares a feast for him; this extreme gentleness of God is extraordinary. God is as noble, tender, full of love, gentleness, and goodness as can be—He is love. You must believe in His love!

45. If there is no love and mercy in your soul, this means your heart is unfit for grace. You can even be a Doctor of Theology. We have so many doctors of theology, and some of them are so dry, the poor people! They ask you: "What would you like me to tell you about? About kenosis? Kenosis is God's free and voluntary self-emptying out of His love for man." And they talk to you about kenosis all day long. They have theology in their back pocket, but they do not have it in their soul.

46. Many times, human "wisdom" can be summarized like this: to see the speck in your brother's eye. But divine wisdom is to see the plank in your own eye, and to have mercy on your brother; to heal him, as much as you can, with your love. If you persevere with a little love and you do not judge him, you deliver his soul from hell.

47. I do not know a sweeter word coming from the Lord's mouth than the one He addresses to His people through the mouth of the Prophet:

48. "I have loved you" (Mal. 1:2).

49. And at the same time I do not know a harsher and more unjust word than the people's response:

50. "In what way have You loved us?" (Mal. 1:2)

51. The God of Abraham, Isaac, and Jacob had freed them from slavery in Egypt, had brought them to a rich country flowing with milk and honey, had guided them through His Prophets; and He was summarizing all of this with: "I have loved you."

52. Do not measure yourself with those who are weaker, but rather with those who are further ahead in love, that is, in virtue. Obedience and submission to God help zealous Christians to enter the joy of divine love.

53. Our salvation depends on us. What punishment do we make ourselves worthy of if, after reading all the teachings of the Holy Gospels, we not only do not forgive our enemies, but also pray to God to punish them? And we transgress the commandment to forgive, as if we want to spite the Heavenly Father. However, God does everything so that we do not hate one another. He does everything for us to wake up and realize that the root of all good things is love. God Himself is love (1 John 4:8).

54. Let us behave in such a way so that we do not offend others by our forgiveness. It is possible that our forgiveness may cause greater pain to the other than the trouble we have from him. Let us recognize our part of the blame and draw near to him with gentleness and humility. Then he will be overcome by contrition, and reconciliation will be a true joy for both of us.

55. Do not expect others to love you! You know the saying: do unto others as you would have them do unto you. The Lord Jesus Christ says to not only to do good to our enemies, but also to love them! Do all that is good to them, not in any which way, but out of love, and this love must be sincere!

56. Do not forget! As much as we love people, that much we love God. Father Veniamin, a very wise, cultured man from the countryside, was here at our monastery. Once, he was admitted to the hospital. There was another person in his room, an immobilized, sick person who, each time he saw Fr. Veniamin, spat on him and said all kinds of bad things—that he cannot stand him and that he hates him. But Fr. Veniamin pretended not to hear him. He was only interested in that the other person was weak,

bedridden, and that he could not help himself, such that, without saying anything, without asking him anything, he helped him with everything he needed: he took his chamber pot to the bathroom, he put a glass of water by his bed, he washed his clothes. When Fr. Veniamin left [from the hospital], the man cried and said: "Forgive me, father, I beg you to forgive me."

57. This is the work of love!

58. Marriage is the sacrament of love because God, Who is love, is at its foundation. In a true marriage, there is sacrificial love especially, the love the Holy Apostle Paul speaks of in 1 Corinthians 13. Sacrificial love is the only kind that is not extinguished after death.

59. There is no obstacle between obedience and love in family life. Love shatters all obstacles, and then spouses listen to one another, but the head of the family is the man, who in turn must listen to the Lord Jesus Christ. The wife is the heart of the family. She listens to the husband out of love. It is good for two young married people to have the same spiritual father to whom they can confess.

60. In monastic life as well, when there is love, you open up and listen, and what you do out of obedience is readily received by God. If a monk feels that he does not have love for his abbot, or in general for people, then he must persistently ask God to grant him humility and love, as St. Silouan the Athonite prayed.[40]

61. One year, on Easter, when I was in prison, I felt the joy of the Resurrection more profoundly than in freedom, and a deeper connection to love in prayer.

62. During the Feast of the Resurrection, time almost stops and the faithful have different faces, they are brighter. At that time, you can feel this flood of God's love more richly, and we have more love. All of creation is full of the grace of the Resurrection. If we are truly prepared for this Feast of Feasts, our being opens and we feel how God is completely open to us, through His love.

40 "O Lord, grant me Thy humility, that I may be filled with Thy love, and Thy holy fear may dwell in me"; Archimandrite Sophrony, *Saint Silouan the Athonite,* Trans. Rosemary Edmonds (SVS Press, Crestwood: 1991), 278.

63. This is, possibly, the great benefit of the Prayer of the Heart: you feel that you are no longer in the world as in a desert. Someone is protecting you, accompanying you continually; you are in His arms, you feel His love. Everything depends on our diligence. And you will see that by praying more, a desire, a love for prayer fills your soul. If a day passes and you have not prayed, something weighs on you painfully, consumes you, and hurts you.

64. In order to progress in this prayer, you need to confess as often as possible. You must continually examine your conscience to see if you are in any way proud, prone to anger, hard-hearted, or who knows what else. It is essential! Confess as often as possible.

65. When you have God, you will see how easily you can bear everything! There will be sorrows. But with God in your heart, you bear everything much more easily. You know that you are in God's hand, and you no longer fear anything or get troubled by anything. You know how to act around an enemy, in a mishap, or disaster. When you choose prayer above all else, what you were not able to do in a year seems to resolve itself in five minutes. Everything is resolved if God is in your heart, if we acquire Love.

66. In our daily life, we encounter Orthodoxy as a powerful calling to love that God addresses to people. If man is nothing other than the image and likeness of God, it is clear that man, in the secret depths of his being, is or must be only love, just like God.

67. Orthodoxy means the full experience of Christian love; the full experience of the Savior's teachings. And our Lord Jesus Christ Himself, through Orthodoxy, lives invisibly among us, living and acting upon us ceaselessly, helping us and always encouraging us to transform our lives and convert to God, always conveying to us the divine knowledge of life, and always helping us raise ourselves to the wonder that is the act of love.

THE MONK BEFORE THE FINAL JUDGMENT[41]

Are we truly aware of Judgment Day? • Overstepping the limits placed by God, we become our own executioners • How does the monk appear before the Final Judgment? • Monasticism is the spiritual center of the world • Living according to the image of God • "Now is the judgment of this world!"

I say these words this evening with a sense of concern. I think we all realize the power with which our own words, whether spoken or written, engage us, as well as our responsibility for them. This is so true that the Word of God Himself, taking on flesh, wanted to make it perfectly clear when He said: "But I say to you that for every idle word men may speak, they will give account of it in the day of judgment. For by your words you will be justified, and by your words you will be condemned" (Matt. 12:36-37).

Reflecting on these words of the Savior, we realize that he who dares to talk about what he knows well is above all words—that is to say, about the Final Judgment of God—is greatly exposed to a double judgment: from God and from his listeners. We will find ourselves before Him at some point so that we can gain our right to eternity, depending also on how we handled our words in our earthly lives.

Let us realize, then, that every word we have said about the Universal Judgment will be scrutinized. How carefully do we need to approach the meaning of this fearsome, mysterious moment that will forever seal our life, which is mysterious enough! In this case, a certain difficulty of the topic announced for this evening is augmented by an evident personal unworthiness.

Talking about "The Monk Before the Final Judgment" is less about solving a problem than about expressing it justly. Because the complete revelation of the true spiritual disposition that the monk had toward the reality of the Final Judgment will only happen at the end of this age.

41 A summary of a conference held by Elder Sofian at one of the "Burning Bush" meetings. The summary was done with the Elder's blessing, based on the conference's manuscript. Elder Sofian approved the content of this summary in 2001.

Until then, the sensing of the true, vivid presence of the Day of Judgment is given to only a few chosen ones, to those giants of the Spirit who, even within the confines of this age, are worthy to see the Kingdom of God coming with power in the secret of their inner heart, according to the very promise of the Lord (Mark 9:1; Luke 17:21).

Returning, then, to our announced topic, we can discern three essential ideas. First, it is natural to dwell for a moment on the meaning of the notion of "Final Judgment" and its purpose in our lives. Second, we will need to examine the particular position that the monk will have in front of this supreme court. Finally, in the third part, we will try to draw some practical conclusions that reveal to us that we already have an effective—and most of the time, unsuspected—connection with God's final judgment.

Are we truly aware of Judgment Day?

We find ourselves, then, facing this first question: what meaning and purpose should we discern for ourselves in the notion of the "Final Judgment" of God? We do not intend to analyze here the dogmatic teachings of the Church, but, based on the unwavering revelations of the Gospel and of the Holy Fathers, we will try to clarify the significance that the thought and the reality of the Final Judgment should have on us, who still live in our present age.

We have to admit from the beginning that the thought of the Final Judgment attracts little of our serious attention.

As beings conceived in sin, it is our habit to think almost continually about the immediate purpose of our lives. We all try to order our existence in short but safe (we think) intervals, and to this end, we struggle with all our strength to acquire a livelihood that becomes itself—by turning the truth upside-down—the purpose of our life on earth. This way, we become tied to our small goals. Imperceptibly, we bow lower and lower, and we fall, without realizing it, away from our authentic life; we utterly forget that the true worth of this life is beyond it and not within it. In such a situation, the thought of our ending is erased from our minds. At most, it abides as a vague and weak memory, when, in fact, it is meant to be one of the main levers of a continuous renewal within ourselves.

When we lose sight of the finality, of the authentic aim that our entire existence is directed toward, then we arrange for ourselves a flat, gray life—a two-dimensional life, I would say. We no longer know how

to look at heights or depths, but are interested only in our immediate surroundings, just like creatures that move only along a length and a width. Whereas, spiritual life demands of us, according to the words of the Holy Apostle Paul, to "comprehend with all the saints what is the width and length and depth and height" (Eph. 3:18).

This is when the value of the Final Judgment comes about. Since there is an ending to our life on earth and a judgment that will measure, weigh, and appraise even our smallest deeds from our life in this age, our whole existence acquires an unfathomably deep meaning.

For those who enlighten their life with the thought of the summits of the Final Judgment, the world is transfigured. It is not accidental anymore, it is not subject to eternal destruction, nor to our whims and pleasure, but through it are manifested God's intentions and decisions, which will be revealed at an appointed time.

From the moment our thoughts are set on the Final Judgment, the world is transformed into a holy place. The fact that the Master of all creation will demand an account from you of how you have behaved in the world forces you to realize better the value of everything that comes from God's hands. The reality of the Final Judgment thus becomes the most solid ground for revaluing the world by transcending it with the perspective of a new dimension—the dimension of eternity.

Overstepping the limits placed by God, we become our own executioners

The thought of the Universal Judgment bears fruit in our life in a different way as well. To understand this, let us meditate on the following biblical fact: the fall of humankind took place under the tree of the knowledge of good and evil, when our proto-parents forgot that not everything was permitted to them (Gen. 3). Today as well, the greatest temptation, a terrible danger, the root of sin, continues to reside in the same thought we have: "Could it be that everything is permitted to us? Could it be that we are allowed everything? Even if the human laws from the outside set some limits to me, couldn't I, known only to myself, do whatever I want?"

If we think only for a moment about our own lives, we need to admit that all our spiritual falls stem from the fact that we transform ourselves into our own judges, and, of course, judges who are very lenient to ourselves. However, the undeniable reality of judgment comes and tells us: "No, not everything is permitted to us!"

There are limits to what is allowed to a human being, limits set not by God's whim but through the profound laws of life. Overstepping these limits, we become our own executioners.

The fact that all of us will pass through a Final Judgment helps us understand from this moment that humankind exists within a well-arranged, ordered frame, and it is responsible for keeping it. I have to behave with those around me not according to my will, which is often led astray by my sins, but according to an order above us that protects both myself and others.

The Final Judgment thus becomes—for those who understand its meaning—a genuine basis for social communion. In its name, we are called to realize, even from now, a truthful living together, a communal living in a spirit of love and tolerance. At the time of the Judgment, humankind will appear as a single communal body, and we will each be called to account for what we have done with our brother, who is a member of the same communal body. That is why the fear and trembling that should be naturally awakened in us by the thought of the Final Judgment are not at all base and blind feelings but, on the contrary, they are born from a sentiment of responsibility—maybe the highest sentiment of a human person.

Because we will be called to give an account for ourselves in front of God, I become convinced that I have a mission to fulfill on this earth, that I am responsible for myself—that I represent, therefore, something of value in God's eyes, and because of this, I need to behave with much spiritual care for myself. Besides the basis for social communion, the Final Judgment is thus revealed as a factor for inner personal growth.

Finally, the vigilant expectation of the Future Judgment can contribute to our self-fulfillment in this age by prompting us to avoid premature judgment, that is, the slander and condemnation of our neighbor. Only at the final confrontation of the world with God will the distinction between good and evil be truly revealed. Good in itself and evil in itself are not clearly differentiated except in the eyes of the All-knowing One. Therefore, He alone is worthy of performing the absolute and final distinction between them at the end of this age. Because only God knows the overall plan and the ultimate purpose of His whole creation.

We, His finite creatures, who live a limited existence with restricted possibilities of knowledge, cannot fathom the true meaning and consequences of the actions of our fellow human beings. Therefore, all who judge their neighbors substitute themselves, knowingly or not, for God and place themselves under the condemnation of the Judgment which is merciless for the ones who judge (Matt. 7:1-2). In light of the great question posed to us at the end of this age, our life needs to be lived in a spirit of self-condemnation and not of condemnation of our neighbor. This is the only way by which we have nothing to lose and everything to gain.

How does the monk appear before the Final Judgment?

We said before that whether we know it or not, the true meaning of this world resides beyond it, namely at its end, on Judgment Day. That will be the time of complete and surprising revelations of ourselves and one another in front of the entire creation that is gathered together. Until then, none of us appears as we really are. We can cheat others in this life, we can cheat ourselves, but we will not be able to cheat the Final Judgment of God. We will each present ourselves before it according to the foundation of our soul that we have strived for.

What will then be the specific posture of the monk at the Final Judgment? What will he be asked for, and what will he answer at that time, different from his fellow human beings? And indeed, the condition of the monk at that threshold of eternity will be entirely different from that of other people.

Others are allowed to occupy themselves, decently, of course, with the matters of this world and to indirectly prepare their answer at the Final Judgment according to the way they administer their earthly lives. The monk, however, is expected to place his whole life, consciously and in an organized manner, under the light of the Final Judgment.

It is natural for people in the world to care about the different aspects and problems posed by this life. For the monk, however, as one who has died to this world, it is natural to first be concerned about the problems of the next world, and to avoid the temptations of this world. In other words, to the degree that a person in the world needs to remember that he lives in it and needs to behave decently, according to the laws of the world, to that same degree, a monk is required to remember that he is called to live, even now, the life of the age to come, that he is called to behave according to its laws. Here is the mystery and unutterable value of monastic life!

The monastic order was placed by God in the midst of this age like a harbinger, a proclaimer of the Heavenly Kingdom to come. This is how the Holy Fathers understood and lived monastic life: like a lever to transform the world according to the image of the incorrupt life after the Universal Judgment, so that people—according to the Savior's words—should not come into judgment but should pass from death into life (John 5:24).

The monk lives, moves, and always breathes in the atmosphere of the dread moment of the Final Judgment, which becomes the strongest ground for his striving for perfection and victory over himself. Saint Gregory the Theologian tells us that he who has lost himself in God and is concerned about His Judgment becomes a Church of grace. But how is the one who has lost himself in God? And what does concern about the Judgment mean? What else but to always seek His rest, and to always mourn and be concerned that you cannot reach perfection because of the weakness of your nature? And, thus, God always dwells in your soul because the remembrance of God causes you to always have Him present in you. In the depths of his conscience, the monk is obliged to see himself always facing the Judgment, knowing that only this way—according to St. Isaac the Syrian—can he set out for the Kingdom of Heaven.

Monasticism is the spiritual center of the world

The fact that the monk achieves through his life an anticipation, a foreshadowing of the Final Judgment, has an incomparable spiritual value for all humankind. Monasticism becomes the spiritual center of the world, regardless of the conscientiousness or worthiness of monastics. As people who live in the world but are already beyond it, monastics set in front of humankind the icon, the model that needs to be followed to live an authentic Christian life. Doubtless, not everyone is called to be a monk. But precisely because of this, monastic life gives a criterion to all who live outside of it—an eternal and unmovable sign of Christian perfection. The three monastic vows, says St. John of the Ladder, are the signs of victory for monastics, and the world cannot encompass them. Because if it could encompass them, there would be no need for monasticism and separation from the world.

In this way, the monk becomes a judge of the world. The monk's responsibility before the Final Judgment is incomparably greater than that of any other human being. "He who is spiritual judges all things, yet he himself is rightly judged by no one," teaches the Holy Apostle Paul (1 Cor. 2:15). And he also asks: "Do you not know that the saints will judge the world?" (1 Cor. 6:2). Before the Final Judgment of God, the monk appears as a judge who is judged. He who had been surpassed by nothing on earth, because the monk is an angel in the body, is now called to give an account before the All-Knowing One about the way he spent his life so he could be an example for those around him.

A great burden weighs on the shoulders of the monk who presents himself before the Righteous Judge. Saint John of the Ladder tells us: "Angels are a lamp for monks, and the life of the monk is a lamp for everyone. So may monks struggle to be a good example in all things, giving no opportunity for falling, either with deeds or words."[42]

Before the Final Judgment, the monk will discover something that is perhaps often unsuspected in this life: even though he renounced and left the world, or, better said, precisely because of that, the monk will not be set apart from the spiritual destiny of humankind. On the contrary, we might say that only then will he form a more profound connection with his fellow human beings.

The most humble of monks carries around his neck, through the manner in which he understands and strives to carry the redeeming cross of his vows, the burden of the salvation of some of his fellow human beings. Before the Final Judgment, the monk will realize how closely his life should have resembled the life of the Apostles and even that of our Savior Jesus Christ, Who exemplarily carried the yoke of the sins of humankind. There can be no more difficult calling for man, it is true, but there can also be no higher calling than monasticism.

"An impoverished monk is a king of the world. He has given over his concerns to God and through his trust has received all men as his servants," Saint John of the Ladder tells us again.[43] The monk renounces the cares of this world and of his own person, not from a denial of life, but, on the contrary, from a love for life. He does not flee the world but the worldly, that is to say, the sinful and corrupt aspect of the world that prevents him from drawing closer spiritually to it. Setting himself apart from the world and from himself (that is to say, from the "old man"), the monk becomes free to serve God and His vicar, meaning our neighbor.

42 *The Ladder of Divine Ascent,* Step 26: "On Discrimination of thoughts, passions and virtues".

43 *The Ladder of Divine Ascent,* Step 17: "On Poverty"

Because our neighbor is the permanent presence of God in our life.

Living according to the image of God

And thus, when, on the Day of the Final Judgment, the Son of Man will divide humankind into two groups, depending on whether they served with love the least of His brethren (Matt. 25:3—46), the monk will be specially called to give an account of the way he cared—through deeds, prayers, and his whole life—for the spiritually poor of this world, under whose guise Christ Himself was hidden.

Because the monk is a spiritual master in this life, he will be asked if he fed the hungry with the word of God, and if he gave the thirsty to drink from the living water of the gifts of the Holy Spirit. He will be asked if he welcomed those who were strangers to Christ with love, if he clothed those who were naked and barren of it with the power of faith, if he visited those who were spiritually sick with the medicine of love, and if he went to see those who were in the prison of sin with patience. All these duties are included for the monk in what constitutes the primary meaning of his life.

To the degree that the monk earnestly seeks his own salvation, to the same degree he will be put into the situation to care, in one way or another, for the salvation of his neighbor. The Final Judgment will weigh on both the monk's personal spiritual condition and that of his community—because they are intertwined in his life.

It is indeed a frightful thing to be called to give an account before God, as one who willingly and wholly embraced His cross and promised to live a life according to His image amid this world. To live according to the image of God means to live first of all for the other and not for yourself. It means living for the great and essential things in life and not for the small and insignificant ones. It means to live for understanding that which is eternal and incorruptible, and not for having dominion over what is earthly and corruptible.

No one is more justified than the monk in understanding the holy—not blind—fear we must have before the Judgment. Human beings are more or less prepared for any great sorrow that might befall them. Earthquakes, fires, floods, wars—they have been part of the memory of humankind for long, and we can easily represent them to ourselves. But for that which will take place at the Final Judgment, and for the spiritual states we will experience, we do not have such elements in our conscience;

we cannot imagine them simply by gathering data from this world. Only the monastic life demands from those who embrace it to have as one of their main preoccupations the creation of a sensibility, of an ability to sense within themselves, even now, the supernatural fear that will master us then.

In the history of the Church, there have been monks who spent their whole lives meditating on the Judgment, as seen also from their sighs: "What will it be? What will it be?" This spiritual state helped them avoid sin and kept them pure for the final hour, which, in a way, had become familiar to them.

This very intimacy with the Final Judgment will make the zealous monk realize the terrible gravity of that moment and feel his soul divided between fear and joy, between spiritual despair and hope, between terror and happiness. Before the Final Judgment, the monk—even the most holy and able—will appear with his being torn by these spiritual states, as if eternally crucified on the cross of his thoughts. And maybe this spiritual state will be a not insignificant reason for his victorious resurrection into eternal life by the One Who destroyed the power of death through His Crucifixion on the Cross.

"Now is the judgment of this world!"

Having reached this point, it is time to try to discern, from everything we have said so far, some meanings that are as close as possible to our concrete lives and thus to harvest some possible guidance for our practical existence.

A thought that guided us from the start of tonight's presentation was the evidence of the truth that we are, even now, in a real and live connection to the Final Judgment. We only need to be aware of this fact. Of course, in the *oikonomia* of the history of the world, Judgment Day has a special purpose, a unique meaning that nothing can replace. But this does not mean that, until then, our deeds are not always present before the Judgment Seat of the Eternal Judge and that they are not weighed justly by Him. The Word of God Himself, He Who became man, tells us these words that always resound in our ears: "Now is the judgment of this world; now the ruler of this world will be cast out" (John 12:31).

At every moment, the Orthodox Christian believer—and all the more the monk—needs to truly feel he is under the penetrating and correct Judgment of the Lord, and needs to cast out the ruler of this world from his heart. Knowing that we are constantly being judged and waiting with respectful fear for the words that will condemn or absolve us, we will understand, at the time of the Final Judgment, that, in fact, we have always been before the Judgment Seat of God, hidden in the depth of our heart. We will understand that, by forgetting this fact, we have condemned ourselves throughout our earthly life. Becoming aware of all this, we are worthy of those beautiful words of our Holy Fathers: "Do not be afraid of death because, behold, God can raise you above it!"

If everything we have said so far is still insufficient to leave an impression on our minds, the Church herself reminds us of the Final Judgment through the order of the liturgical year. We are now in the week before Great Lent. We feel, however inattentive we might be, that we are entering into a more holy, spiritual time than the regular one. This crucial week for the Church year sits between the Sunday of the Dread Judgment and the Sunday of the Expulsion of Adam and Eve from Paradise. A spiritual meaning is hidden in this order, which we should reflect on for a moment.

The Final Judgment will be the last and greatest spiritual feast of our world. It will truly and justly be the Feast of God, the Day of the Son of God, with which history will end. On the contrary, next Sunday, we will commemorate the Expulsion of Adam and Eve from Paradise, the first day of humanity living under sin, the start of the history we are still part of.

We are first presented with the end of the world because it is in the nature of spiritual life to be more concerned with this end of the ages, from where the eternal rest in God starts. Then, we are reminded of our beginning, of the sin and the disobedience that caused our expulsion from Paradise, so that we keep in mind that everything we see is passing, and that the purpose of humankind is to redeem the sin of our nature and to fight for the re-establishment of creation to its initial, paradisiacal state.

Between these two spiritual states, the punishment by expulsion from Paradise and the appearance before the Dread Judgment, the whole drama of our redeeming unfolds. The time between them was given to us so that we can get up again from where we fell, obtain the price of our salvation, and return to God, from where we broke away. The guarantee of these truths is the Lord's Resurrection, which awaits us at the end of the Lenten period.

The time of Holy and Great Lent is thus revealed to us as a supernatural abbreviation of the highest spiritual meanings and actions. The thought of the Final Judgment, as well as the significance of the following Sundays of the Triodion, remind us of the only way possible for our salvation: from the fall of the first Adam, we need to raise ourselves to the Resurrection of the second Adam, Christ our God.

And if every Christian needs to follow the Savior all his life, even more the monk, especially in this time of Great Lent, must understand and take upon himself the saving action of our Lord Jesus Christ. That is to say, he must understand that the entire meaning of Christianity and the entire service of monasticism consists in these three deeds: to take upon yourself the evil that is in the world, to die with this evil through shunning of passions, and to resurrect in purity. The time of repentance and self-knowledge during Great Lent is particularly favorable for this understanding.

As the Holy Fathers say, he who knows his sins is better than he who brings people back from the dead by his prayer. He who sighs for an hour for his soul is better than he who shows himself to be useful to the whole world. And he who is worthy to see himself as he really is, is better than he who is worthy to see angels.

The zealous monk presents himself humbly before the Final Judgment as one who is victorious, and he can appropriate even now the fearsome, salvific, fiery appeal with which the Son of Thunder seals both the Holy Scripture and our hearts: "Amen. Even so, come, Lord Jesus!" (Rev. 22:20).

"Jesus Christ has Risen for the Joy of the Entire World!"[44]

"Everything has its source in the Resurrection of the Lord"
• *"I am the resurrection and the life"*

Christian brothers and sisters, today is the third day that we have been bearing within our hearts the joy of the Holy Resurrection, of this Feast of Feasts. This joy is all the greater because it comes immediately after the sorrow of Good Friday.

Let us imagine for a moment, brothers and sisters, that the Lord Jesus Christ had not risen. That His life had ended pitifully there under the tombstone in the garden of Joseph of Arimathea. What would have remained of Him for us except a memory? Jesus Christ would surely have occupied a central place in human history. They would have spoken about Him with admiration, like He was a great man, like He was a great prophet and reformer. If He had remained defeated by His murderers, Jesus would have had the same significance to us as Moses, Buddha, Confucius, Muhammad, or other founders of religions.

But Jesus Christ has risen for the joy of the entire world! He did what no one else had been able to do before Him or after Him; He rose from the dead by the power of His will. But, from what we understand, only God can command the living and the dead, as an All-Powerful Master. Therefore, the Resurrection of the Lord is the greatest evidence of the divinity hidden in the Son of the Virgin. His human body was killed by men and sealed in a tomb, but His divinity remained almighty and free, and from it resurrected His Holy Body. He is the living Word of God, Who took flesh and dwelt among us, and "we beheld His glory, the glory as of the only begotten of the Father, full of grace and truth," as the Holy Gospel tells us (John 1:14).

"Everything has its source in the Resurrection of the Lord"

Christian brothers and sisters, the Resurrection of the Lord, which fills our hearts with joy, is a real event that actually occurred in history.

44 Transcription from an undated audio recording.

The Resurrection of the Lord is an event verified by eyewitnesses worthy of complete trust, honest and sincere witnesses who, at the cost of their lives, confirmed what they saw with their eyes, what they touched with their hands, and what they lived with their entire being.

When they are dragged before the Sanhedrin to give an account, the Holy Apostles, these witnesses of Jesus Who rose from the dead, declared: "Let it be known to you all, and to all the people of Israel, that by the name of Jesus Christ of Nazareth, whom you crucified, whom God raised from the dead, by Him this man stands here before you whole... Whether it is right in the sight of God to listen to you more than to God, you judge. For we cannot but speak the things which we have seen and heard" (Acts 4:10, 19-20).

Christian brothers and sisters, through this unshakeable confession of the Holy Apostles, which has deep roots in Holy Scripture, through the surprising collaboration between God and men, and through much shedding of blood, the word of the Gospel spread in the world, arriving to us today.

Everything has its source in the Resurrection of the Lord. Biographies of great men, even of founders of religions, usually end at the grave; whereas the life and death of Jesus Christ is followed by the Resurrection and His Ascension to Heaven. After His Ascension in divine glory, He does not abandon us and does not forget us, but being present everywhere, He is continually present in people's lives, as He Himself assured us, saying: "I am with you always, even to the end of the ages" (Matt. 28:20). In another place in Scripture, God tells us this: "Behold, I stand at the door and knock"—the door of each one of our hearts. "If anyone hears My voice and opens the door"—the door of the heart—"I will come into him and dine with him, and he with Me." (Rev. 3:20).

"I am the resurrection and the life"

Brothers and sisters, if Jesus Christ is God, then all that He did and taught is of overwhelming importance for each one of us. Then, His life is not like any other person's in history, but it is a living example that must be followed by each of us. Then, His commandments and teachings are not like those of the philosophers of this world, which you follow when you feel like it and abandon them when they do not work for you. The words of the Lord must always be fulfilled, in any circumstance, without wavering, as difficult as it may be sometimes.

And if Jesus Christ is truly God, as He is, then in Him we always find a support and a comfort without limits throughout our life. That is why, when the sky of life is darkened by clouds of trials, when sorrows surround us, we must go to Him, like St. Peter when he was caught by large waves and prayed full of trust, saying: "Lord, help us!" And He will help us, because He is All Powerful and Good.

When we are overwhelmed by the weight of sins, let us call out to Him from the depths of our hearts with tears: "Lord, forgive us our trespasses!" And He will forgive us, because He is All Good.

When the day of our life turns to night, let us not be sad like those who do not have hope. But, resting our weary heads on His fatherly arms, let us wait for the eternal rest and Jesus will give us rest, remembering that He once told us: "I am the resurrection and the life" (John 11:25).

And He comforts us another time as well, saying: Come to Me, all you who labor and are heavy laden, and I will give you rest" (Matt 11:28). And we know that we will not be forgotten forever in the darkness of the grave, but, just as Jesus Christ rose from the dead, so too will we be resurrected with our body at some point, meeting our soul. And after the Great Judgment, if we attain salvation, we will continue the unending life in His Kingdom.

These, Christian brothers and sisters, are the comforts and joys which are tied to this great feast of the Resurrection of the Lord, for all who receive with love His holy teachings and fulfill His holy commandments according to their power. This is the day which the Lord has made, let us rejoice and truly be glad in it, for Christ is Risen!

Christ has Ascended! This means that Heaven is open to humankind![45]

On the Mount of Eleon, or the Mount of Olives, the Mother of God and the Holy Apostles accompany the Lord with tears of joy. He ascends while blessing them, and they look at Him with eyes directed at the blue sky until a cloud takes Him away from their gaze.

Christ has ascended with His body to heaven! This means that our fallen nature is raised again to its initial glory and is sitting at the right hand of God the Father through Jesus Christ, the God-Man.

Christ has ascended! This means that we all have a Friend and a Brother in Heaven because this is how our Good Savior and Intercessor named Himself (Luke 12:4, Matt. 12:50).

Christ has ascended! This means that Heaven is open to humankind, that the Lord Jesus prepares a place in Heaven for all those who fulfill His commandments, as He promised us (John 14:2).

Christ has ascended into Heaven! This means that we are not alone in the world, that we are not wanderers without purpose and ideals anymore, but we have a lasting homeland there; while here, in the world, we are protected and comforted by the grace of the Holy Spirit, the Comforter. We are fed with the divine nourishment of Holy Communion, and Jesus Christ Himself is with each of us every day of our life, because this is what He promised before His Ascension: *And lo, I am with you always, even to the end of the age* (Matt. 28:20).

Our Lord Jesus ascended into Heaven, to the bosom of the Holy Trinity, as the High Priest interceding for all of us. He has within Himself the same redeeming will and suffering love that He had at His sacrifice on Golgotha. This disposition manifests the supreme love and closeness of Jesus Christ to humankind and to the heavenly Father. Through this love, the Lord draws humankind closer to God; through this love, He shows Himself to be the great and eternal Intercessor and High Priest.

45 Undated hand-written notes.

Of course, the Lord Jesus Christ is in Heaven in all His glory, at the right hand of the Father. There, nobody strikes Him as on earth; nobody insults Him. And yet, He still bears, entirely of His own will, a certain suffering, different from that on earth.

Glory to Jesus Christ, Who resurrected and ascended to the right hand of God the Father! Amen.

The Presence of the Holy Spirit in Our Life[46]

Confession for Christ • The trial conducted against the Savior

In chapter two of the Acts of the Apostles we are told that the Descent of the Holy Spirit was preceded by a "rush" of wind and the appearance of "tongues of fire" which rested on each of the Apostles. These signs do not constitute the Descent of the Holy Spirit itself, but they are only symbols. The moment of Pentecost is a mystery, like all that is divine. God is the greatest Mystery and His actions are also mysterious.

Based on how they view this biblical event, believers can be divided into three categories. Some "Christians" doubt such historical events and consider them inventions or myths. Others are religious formalists who reduce the entire faith to forms and who affirm that they have never felt once in their life how the Holy Spirit descends. And others believe and affirm with conviction the truth related in Holy Scripture, yet not all of them know the teachings of the Holy Fathers, which help us very much in understanding the Bible.

From the beginning we must say a great truth: it is not possible to have a Christian life completely lacking the Holy Spirit. Each Christian received the Holy Spirit at least once, at Baptism.

It must also be said that many of the miracles and signs seen at the beginning of Christianity happened and were necessary for those times. Some sects, such as Pentecostals, still try to reproduce such material manifestations today—exactly like at that time. The way they act is a blasphemy, distorting the truth because the material signs of Pentecost happened only once in history.

The essence of the event of Pentecost—that is, the Descent of the Holy Spirit into human beings—always exists in the Church, but Christians must seek and preserve the Holy Spirit, and yet not all succeed in this.

46 Written in 1958, before Fr. Sofian was arrested. The text was handed over to us by Fr. Sofian at the end of the 1990s, so it could be published in this book.

There have been periods in the history of the Church when the Holy Spirit has poured into people's lives in greater or lesser amounts. In our days, a crisis of the Holy Spirit in Christians' lives is felt. To have the Holy Spirit means to live in God, to be united with God, and to love God as much as possible.

Confession for Christ

The question is: what attitude should we have toward the Holy Spirit? Are we filled with His power, or are we not? To answer these questions correctly, it is worth examining carefully what happened with the Holy Apostle Peter ten days after the Ascension of the Lord (Acts 2).

After the event of the Pentecost, the Apostle Peter gave his first sermon. We know St. Peter in different hypostases: brave, sometimes enlightened, uttering fundamental confessions, and other times wavering, filled with human thoughts, fearful, denying Christ in the courtyard of the high priest (Luke 22:54-62).

After the Descent of the Holy Spirit, the Apostle Peter is a wholly new man, with an infinite courage; he is like a granite monolith, with a forceful interior light. He preaches the Gospel simply, with no oratorical talent, he only reprimands people with the goal of correcting sinners. However, his sermon has a formidable effect because three thousand souls convert to Christianity at that moment. That is when the Church is founded visibly!

Because of the work of the Holy Spirit in his soul, the Apostle Peter is ready for any sacrifice. And all the saints were the same way, because the presence of the Holy Spirit is manifested in His fruits. Saint Peter's sermon awakened people's consciences and brought to life the powerful faith that stems from repentance. In reality, it is not a simple sermon, but it is most of all a living confession for our Lord Jesus Christ.

The trial conducted against the Savior

For two thousand years, there has been a trial in this world conducted by Satan against Christ, our Savior. The ruler of this world (John 12:31) does not want to be left without his subjects.

For two thousand years, the Church has been persecuted on earth, sometimes even by those inside it. Every generation and every member of the Church must testify in this trial that surpasses time and space. Those who confess Christ will be confessed by Christ before His Father (Matt.

10:32). At the end of this trial, it will be demonstrated to all of us how we have known the Lord and how much we have felt the power of the Holy Spirit in our lives, how much we have repented for our sins, and how much the Holy Spirit has pierced our hearts. Therefore, we absolutely need repentance, confession, the fulfillment of the commandments of the Church, and then, as a result, a new life in this world, a life lived in God.

The truth that God exists, that God is Love, does not need to be confessed through volumes of sermons, but through the life of those who believe. Faith is life!

We should not complain about evil, but about the lack of good. Christ's witnesses in the world are absent! There is no Holy Spirit in our lives! We should not be terrified of the atomic bomb, but of the bomb of God's wrath that appears for our grave sins and for our lack of repentance!

Let us return to life in God, which depends only on us! Let us call on the Holy Spirit in all circumstances, in every thought or deed, and then, when He will be present in our life, we will be worthy to be called Christians!

LETTERS[47]

YOUR EMINENCE, METROPOLITAN BARTHOLOMEW,

For the holy Feast Days of the Lord's Nativity and Baptism, please accept my best and most sincere wish for your complete health and renewal of strength, by divine grace, so that you may continue your holy work as archbishop and the labor of great value and responsibility entrusted to you to translate the Holy Books of the Old and New Testament.

With the new year of 1999, I wish you many years blessed by God, for the benefit of our Holy Church and to the glory of God.

Many years, full of peace, spiritual fruits, and holy joy.

With holy love,
Archimandrite Sofian

MOST VENERABLE AND BELOVED FATHER PETRONIUS,

Truly the Lord Jesus Christ is Risen!

I thank you from all my heart for the words that you sent me regarding the luminous celebration of this year's Pascha, as well as the consolation for the trial from God sent on April 6 during Holy Week. I am speaking of a herniated disc, after which my right leg does not allow me to leave my cell—beginning on April 6 and continuing until today, April 15, when I am writing these lines. I patiently wait until I have fulfilled the canon arranged by God.

I pray that the Good God and Mother of God protect your brotherhood of Prodromos [Skete] unceasingly and that the joy of the Holy Resurrection accompanies each of you throughout this life.

I am glad that the restoration of the mural paintings in this great and beautiful monastery church is nearly finished. It is an important and difficult work that requires knowledge, conscientiousness, and patience. Glory to God that it is being done.

47 In this chapter, we have published the text of copies of seven of Father Sofian's letters, as well as the facsimile of a greeting card sent by Father Sofian to the students of ASCOR (Association of Romanian Orthodox Christian Students) Cluj.

May God help you serve in it as much as possible with holy devotion and much benefit for your soul.

With love in Christ,
Archimandrite Sofian Boghiu, 1999

Venerable Mother A.,

I received your letter a while ago, as well as the long list of holy relics at E. Monastery. There are very many. Thank you. Thank you also for the well wishes for the New Year.

I read your entire letter, with all your spiritual and physical turmoil. All this turmoil and the flood of passions come upon you because you pray little and maybe with a scattered mind. If your obedience is at the gate, during the night, where you must be awake all night as the gatekeeper, that is a very good time for your prayer rule. Time passes more easily and with much benefit. The Psalter, Paraklesis to the Mother of God, Akathists—they are very beneficial if they are read with attention and humility. There, at the gate, the night is the most fitting time for "Lord Jesus..." [the Jesus Prayer]. At the beginning, for a week, strive each night to say it 500 times, following the knots on the prayer rope, and see how long it takes you to say 500 "Lord Jesus Christ's."

Do not use the prayer rope the days after; only look at what time you begin and end. During the following weeks, use the clock too and say a thousand [Jesus] prayers. You must reach 3,000 prayers each night.

Do not be discouraged because you do not feel anything; continue to say it with humility and contrition, and the Lord will give you the feeling of prayer; however, do not get discouraged. Say it with patience and trust that God knows, sees, and hears you.

Additionally, be careful not to speak much and especially strive not to condemn anyone, but as sinful as the other may be, pray to God to forgive him or her and you as well.

With the new year of 1999, I wish you many years blessed by God and spiritual zeal.

With holy love,
Archimandrite Sofian

Most Venerable Father Iustin Pârvu,

Thank you for the spiritual greeting card you sent me for the Nativity of the Lord. I pray that the Good God pours drops of grace upon us, too, for the renewal of our souls at this time between millennia. With the new year, we entreat the All-Merciful God for peace and goodwill among people.

With holy love,
Archimandrite Sofian, 1999

Most Respected Professor Ioan Alexandru,

I have had the joy of knowing you for a long time, especially when you would come to Vespers at Antim Monastery, holding a child by the hand and another in your arms, which impressed many of the faithful who admired your devotion.

I followed your teaching work at the University, where I learned from your students how convincingly you spoke to them about the incarnate Logos; I also learned about the Christian advice you gave young people who admired your courage to speak in such a way under the Communist regime.

Reading your *Hymns of Transylvania*, *Hymns of Putna*, and *Hymns of Romania*—works that will never die—my admiration for their author grew without end for the magisterial way in which they combine our holy Orthodox faith with the best qualities of the Romanian nation.

All of this grew until one day, not long ago, in the "The Free Romania" newspaper from May 14, 1994, a conversation between you, Mr. Ioan Alexandru and Răzvan Bucuroiu appeared on the respective page created by the Anastasia Foundation.

There, you maintain that for the Romanian Orthodox Church after the Communist period, American preachers would have benefited us greatly so that they could evangelize our country.

Our Patriarch Teoctist did not and cannot agree with this idea of yours, knowing that these preachers are Protestants, thus the heads of sectarian denominations, and we cannot be indifferent to their teachings. In their worship, they do not accept the veneration of the Holy Cross—the Altar upon which Jesus Christ sacrificed Himself for the salvation of the world; they do not honor the Mother of God—the mother of our Savior; they do not have the seven Holy Sacraments, etc.

In response to the question posed to you in the conversation: "Why did the Patriarch oppose the propaganda films that were going to be shown on screens in the Capital during the final week of Great Lent?", you responded to His Beatitude in a very hostile manner. Here is the response:

"Even then, before '89, when churches were being destroyed, I knew that this poor man sat like an owl on the Metropolitan Hill, and no one went to him to tell him the truth and difficulties."

I did not expect the author of the *Hymns*, the instructor of students who carried Orthodoxy on his shoulders for half a century, I did not expect such a harsh word, such an undignified, unjust blame from you.

"This poor man," as you say, is nonetheless the Patriarch of Romania, a country where Orthodoxy is predominant.

I ask myself, and I ask you:

How is it that he stays alone and no one goes to tell him the truth when he is visited by dozens of important people every day? Cultured people, professors, ambassadors, learned men, politicians, writers, foreign prelates from the West and East, like the Ecumenical Patriarch of Constantinople, different delegates from the country and foreign ones, with problems of all kinds. From what I know, even you, Mr. Professor, visited His Beatitude multiple times, alone or in a group of five or six people.

His Beatitude often serves with other priests and bishops, preaches openly, visits exhibitions, as he recently went to the exhibition on *The Icon in the Child's Soul,* where he gave awards to child painters from the entire country. His Beatitude puts much time and effort into the issue of religious education in schools, spending many millions on textbooks alone; he is present in disputes with Greek Catholics, is involved in religious aid in hospitals and prisons in collaboration with the government, to which are added issues of the internal organization of the Church and relations with the Romanian churches abroad.

Therefore, His Beatitude Patriarch Teoctist is neither alone, uninformed, nor isolated. He works together with the Holy Synod of the Romanian Orthodox Church and is present in all aspects of our Holy Church's life.

Yet, because he was blamed in public, he should be rehabilitated publicly as well, showing the truth regarding the effort exerted by His Beatitude for the protection of our Holy Orthodoxy, as it has been given to us by the Holy Apostles, Holy Fathers, and Ecumenical and Local Councils, throughout the two millennia of Christianity in this Romanian land.

With the same appreciation as always,
Archim. Sofian Boghiu
Hegumen of Holy Antim Monastery
June 10, 1994

MOST VENERABLE MOTHER B.,

With the arrival of the holy celebrations of the Nativity and Baptism of the Lord, please accept my wish for your well-being, full, deep health, and peace of soul that only God can give through a long time spent calling upon the Name of Jesus in our heart. I know that you do this without ceasing, and it is good that you do it.

There is no greater wealth and comfort in heaven and earth than the presence of Jesus in our heart. With the new year of 1999, I wish you as many years as the Good God wills, but, in these years, I wish that you feel Him present in your heart, comforting and guiding all the thoughts and feelings of your heart.

Here, there is good peace, and we rejoice in these holy feast days that come with their grace and all the beautiful customs and traditions, which the difficult times experienced until recently did not harm. May the Good God protect you for many years, with much holy joy.

December, 1998

Christ is Risen!

I wish with all my heart that my two good, old friends, Felix and Roman, who are across the great and deep ocean, may rejoice in the deep peace of the Risen One, in full health, and love unwaning on this Holy Pascha of the year 2000, as well as many more to come.

I thank the Good God that after a year of not serving at the Holy Altar, I was able to serve the Divine Liturgy three times for Holy Pascha, with good hope for the future.

His Eminence Nestor, Metropolitan of Oltenia, died peacefully in May 2000.

Here, there is good peace and hope for the better.

I am glad that we experienced these days of Pascha in the year 2000 together, in this life on earth.

With holy love,
Archimandrite Sofian
May 20, 2000

PRAYER TO THE LORD JESUS CHRIST, WHO WAS TRANSFIGURED ON MOUNT TABOR[48]

Lord, enlighten our mind so that we can know Your Law, guard all our senses so that we only do Your will, and help us travel all our life with propriety, staying on the path of Your commandments, so that we can reach the Kingdom of Your unapproachable Light, and so that we too can then say: *Lord, it is good for us to be here, in the Kingdom of Your Glory*. Amen.

48 Undated manuscript

PRAYER TO SAINT JOHN THE BAPTIST[49]

✝ Saint John the Baptist and Forerunner, pray to the Most Holy Trinity for all of the people of this earth. Intercede before our Savior Jesus Christ for all who believe in Him and wait on Him with hope in His mercy. Pray to God, with your boldness as a Prophet, Martyr, Apostle, Baptizer, and Forerunner, for the Church and our Romanian nation, that we may be freed from all evil and all danger.

Pray to Christ, St. John the Baptist, for our bishops and flocks, for our leaders and citizens, for priests and monks, for the healthy and the sick, for the poor and the wealthy, for the courageous and the fearful, for the pure and the impure, for those who fast and those who do not fast, for those who pray and those who do not pray, for the good and the bad; that He save some according to righteousness, and that He show His mercy to others.

Pray to God for parents who do not have children and for children without parents; for mothers who wish to have children and those who hate their children; for those who do not know how to raise children in the fear of God and those who curse their children; for parents who destroy their children through their ugly life and for mothers who kill their children.

Pray, St. John the Baptist, for widows and orphans—and pray, O Saint, for our souls, too.

Saint John, pray to our Savior to forgive our trespasses, to comfort our hearts, to increase our faith, hope, and love, to multiply our courage, to banish fear from us, and to pour in our souls more light, love, wisdom, and joy of a holy life, desire for God, mercy towards others and care for our salvation.

Teach us, O Saint, to forgive more, to pray more, to fast and to endure patiently, to humble ourselves more and to witness Christ, with all of our heart, in all our life.

Saint John the Baptist, help us with your prayers that are well received by the Most Good God. Amen.

49 Undated manuscript.

TESTIMONIALS ABOUT FATHER SOFIAN

Father Sofian and I have been very close spiritually. I saw Fr. Sofian for the first time at the Cernica Monastic Seminary. He was six years ahead of me. I used to see him now and then. I knew him as Br. Serghie Boghiu. He was very well-behaved, quiet, and joyful; he was never sad. That was his nature; this is the nature of a spiritual man. People used to call him "the old child." In 1927, when he was a monk at Rughi-Soroca Skete, he was sent to be a disciple of Metropolitan Visarion Puiu, the Bishop of Balti at that time. Father Sofian had a bicycle and would ride it to run errands in town or wherever he was sent. He was always joyful and quiet, he would only say what was needed; some people thought he was mute. Some people would make bad jokes, but Fr. Sofian smiled and kept silent. That is how he was until the end of his life. If you went to the Antim Monastery, even when he was old, he would sit there looking at the ground, smiling and listening to you. Father Sofian never contradicted himself; he was equal to himself from his childhood, in the sense that in matters of faith, he would do exactly what he preached. This is the proof of an innate spiritual maturity which he didn't acquire through effort, as we do, but he received as a gift from God through the Holy Spirit—it was an inspiration.

Polite and serious in everything, Fr. Sofian was admired, even from the 1940s, by intellectuals from the University of Bucharest. Antim Monastery used to have an elite of faithful Orthodox—people like General Tetrat, Professor Anton Dumitriu, and Alexandru Mironescu—who would serve as readers. And they were all intellectuals from the University of Bucharest who came to Antim because of Fr. Sofian.

Father Sofian served the Divine Liturgy with faith, joy, and seriousness. I remember how once, after 1989, he reprimanded a priest who talked in the Holy Altar. "This is the Divine Liturgy! You have time to talk afterward. The Holy Spirit is here!" He was very serious, and, at the same time, kind, very kind.

I met Fr. Sofian in prison, too. If an old man was unable to do something, Fr. Sofian was the first to help him. This was Fr. Sofian's motto: help someone! Because he was convinced that we only exist as long as we help others.

Another characteristic, in my opinion, of Fr. Sofian's spirituality, is that he was a practical spiritual father, not a meditative one. Don't imagine Fr. Sofian just sitting on a low stool and saying the Prayer of the Heart. Of course, he loved this prayer very much. But Fr. Sofian was also practical. He would take money out of his pocket and give it away. There were crowds of beggars surrounding him. He had a list of people in need, and he would talk to people who got rich after the revolution of 1989 and would tell them: "Good for you that you opened a new store; now take this list of poor people and go to apartment X on street Y. Don't forget this list! They have nothing to eat. God gave you much, but He didn't give it to you in vain." And they were all impressed and won over by him. This was his practical spirituality. He was not one to sit and do nothing; that is why both Patriarch Justinian and Patriarch Teoctist loved him enormously. Father Sofian had a good influence on both these patriarchs and other hierarchs. Patriarch Teoctist used to confess to Fr. Sofian. Especially after 1990, Fr. Sofian didn't have time to stay somewhere secluded and say the Prayer of the Heart. He was always in a state of prayer, even though he didn't even have time to finish his regular prayers. He hosted me in his cell for a few days when I visited him from America. During the day, he would come by rapidly, pass through the room, and say: "I won't bother you for too long, I don't have time. The Patriarch has sent for me, I don't have time!" Then, he would quickly go back to church. And apart from this, he would make time to hear confessions until 2 AM.

Archimandrite Roman Braga († 2015)

†

Father Sofian was hospitalized at Christiana Hospital in 1994 or 1995; I don't remember the year precisely. I was working there as a nurse. Even though I used to go to Antim Monastery very often, Fr. Sofian didn't know my name. Many people were going to Antim during that time, so Father couldn't have known me. I was going through a lot of psychological pain during that time, and I had nobody to confess it to since my spiritual father, Fr. Adrian Fageteanu, was hospitalized (he had heart problems). After the Divine Liturgy one Sunday, I walked from Antim Monastery to

the hospital. I cried on the way there, and I told God I had great pain in my soul and I had nobody to confess it to because I couldn't be open to just anybody, and I also had nobody to ask advice from.

When I reached the hospital, the guard told me to go quickly to Fr. Sofian. My colleagues also told me to go to Father quickly, without changing into my nurse uniform, because he had already asked for me three times. I want to add that only the chief nurse was allowed to go into Fr. Sofian's room and give him his medication. I thought to myself with astonishment: "How does Fr. Sofian know my name? How does he know I work here? How does he know it was my shift? Why does he call me and not the chief nurse?" I knocked timidly on the door; I can hear his gentle voice even now: "Come in, Julieta, have courage! Forgive me for lying on the bed; my shoulder is badly hurting because I have a wound there." Then he continued: "There is a little stool under the bed; take it and sit on it." Then he used the same words I had spoken to God on my way there and told me: "If you have a bit of trust in me and you can open up to me, tell me about the pain you have in your soul that you cannot tell anyone, and then we will see what we can do, with God's help!"

From that moment, the pain in my soul totally vanished, and in its place, I felt peace and joy in my heart. I didn't know what to tell Fr. Sofian anymore. Then, Father taught me how to say the Prayer of the Heart, which he had truly acquired.

Julieta

†

I confessed to Fr. Sofian for eighteen years and don't remember hearing anything untrue from his mouth. Once, I went with three other girls to receive a blessing from him to go to Jerusalem for Easter. Father Sofian told the other girls to rejoice in the blessing of the Holy Light, but he didn't tell me anything. And it happened exactly like this: the three girls went to the Holy Sepulcher for Pascha, but I could not go.

Some other time, a group of Romanian friends who lived in London came to Bucharest. There was also a Japanese man with them who was not a Christian. We all went to see Fr. Sofian. The Japanese man watched us talk to Fr. Sofian for half an hour. He could not understand a word, and we forgot to translate to him what we were saying. But I think he felt something from the power of the Holy Spirit in Fr. Sofian's person, in his way of being, in the light of his face, in his words, and beyond his words. When we were ready to leave, the Japanese man suddenly said, to our astonishment, that he wanted to be baptized in the Orthodox faith by Fr. Sofian. Unfortunately, Fr. Sofian had to leave abroad the next day, so he couldn't perform the baptism. I don't know what happened to that Japanese man anymore, but I was impressed by how Fr. Sofian's spirit could move the heart of a non-believer who could not understand a word that was spoken.

Father Sofian had infinite patience and extraordinary strength. I usually went last for confession because Father would hear confessions until 3 AM or 4 AM, especially when there was a feast day with many people in attendance, and I didn't want anyone to be in line behind me. One day, Fr. Sofian finished hearing confessions at 7 AM, went to his cell for a few minutes, and then came back to serve the Divine Liturgy!

I also want to confess that, after Fr. Sofian's passing, the last day when his body was laid in the church at Antim Monastery, I was there all morning. Someone said out loud that we shouldn't get too close to the coffin because it might start to smell. I felt very hurt by these words. And Fr. Sofian smelled...of myrrh! Before taking the coffin out of the church, it smelled of myrrh so strongly, as if someone had poured a bucket of myrrh over his body.

Maria Curticăpeanu, artist, painter

†

I sat next to Fr. Sofian for eight years when we were both students at the Monastic Seminary at Cernica Monastery, between 1932 and 1940. Father Sofian was always at the top of his class. He received A's in everything. He was the best in each subject because he quickly understood everything and memorized everything he read and studied. His eyesight was not so good; he suffered from conjunctivitis, so I would read the lesson to him sometimes. Of course, Father would always get an A, and I would get a lower grade. Father Sofian was very peaceful and quiet, and he liked solitude at the same time. He could be communicative, but not excessively, and only when it was needed; if he was asked for help in any subject, he would get involved and try to help his classmates. He was honest and fair; he was an example to all of us.

After many years, Fr. Sofian became the Abbot of Antim Monastery, where he was also a living example of seriousness, dignity, honesty, and moral rectitude in everything related to monastic life.

We have several recordings left from Fr. Sofian, and some books. They are extremely interesting, and they deserve to be known by all Christians.

Archimandrite Grigorie Băbuș († 2008)

†

I confessed to Fr. Sofian for a short period of time because he became sick, and he told everyone in church to seek other father confessors. Every time I confessed to Fr. Sofian, I felt as if I was at the Final Judgment. Father was able to read my thoughts each time. After hearing my confession, he would go to the altar, and I would feel how he was praying for me. Sometimes, when he blessed me, I would feel a power overflowing my entire being.

After Fr. Sofian became sick, I went to Fr. Iulian Stoicescu (at Flaminda church) for confession; Fr. Iulian had also been imprisoned during the Communist regime. Once, after I confessed, Fr. Iulian insisted that I go and take Holy Communion at Antim Monastery on Holy Thursday. I don't remember the exact year; it must have been between 1998 and 2000. When I reached the monastery, I felt as if I entered into a different world, an angelic world. Father Sofian was feeling better and was quietly serving in the church, alone in the altar. There was a divine peace in the whole church. It was the most wonderful and full-of-mystery Divine Liturgy that I ever attended.

When I, the unworthy one, went to partake of Holy Communion, Fr. Sofian looked at me insistently, and I felt he was praying for me. After communing, I was filled with an energy, a force that cannot be described in words. I communed many times in my life, but I never felt the same power as when Fr. Sofian communed me on that Holy Thursday.

Emilia Popescu, engineer

†

Father Sofian would hear confessions all night until morning, and he would never tell anyone to leave. He would tell us: "I sit here quietly, but how will you get home?" And nobody would leave without confessing. He was so kind; he would warm you like the sun. You felt he had immense mercy for all people. However troubled you were, you became peaceful in his presence. I was told the same thing by the nuns at Dealu Monastery, where Fr. Sofian painted icons for a few years. When they were troubled, they would go to the church and watch Fr. Sofian paint calmly, absorbed in the presence of God. It was enough for them to watch Fr. Sofian, and all their troubles subsided, and they would go back peacefully to their work.

When Fr. Sofian would go abroad, Antim Monastery felt lifeless and empty. When Fr. would come back to Antim, everything became alive again; even the birds sang more beautifully. There was more peace, more grace. I saw demonized people who respected Fr. Sofian, because they would become still through his prayers and blessings. Some of them would come and kiss Father's hand with respect and devotion.

Ileana

†

A French actor, Roger, visited Romania a few years after the fall of Communism. He told us that he would play, together with Alain Delon, in a movie about the beginnings of Christianity. Roger had a blessing from some Roman Catholic priests to play the role of Jesus Christ. He also wanted a blessing for this work from an Orthodox priest. And so, we brought him to Fr. Sofian.

Father Sofian listened to him very attentively and told him, very naturally, that he agreed that Roger should play this role. We were astonished that Roger had obtained this permission, so we asked Fr. Sofian after Roger had left, "How is it possible that Roger has your blessing for such work?" Father Sofian was calm and replied quietly: "Yes, yes... It is good for him to play this role." We didn't say anything more but were almost upset with Father.

After this meeting, Roger started to visit Romania more and more often. He was increasingly interested in Orthodoxy, and he was no longer thinking of playing the role of the Savior. He went to Putna Monastery in 1992 when Prince Stephen the Great was canonized. After the canonization, Roger came to Bucharest full of enthusiasm and asked to be baptized by Fr. Sofian. We were there for the baptism. Out of love for St. Stephen the Great, Roger asked to have Etienne (Stephen in French) as his baptismal name. During the service, he wore a mantle that was black on one side and white on the other, a mantle that he had received from his sponsor in baptism, Fr. Mihail from Râşca Monastery. Once he was baptized, he wore the mantle with the white part on the outside. Those were wonderful moments! From this beautiful conversion, we understood more deeply how mysterious and full of love the work of the saints is!

Roxana Cristian, Doctor of Hematology, Bucharest
Corina Gheorghiu, Psychologist, Los Angeles, USA

†

I confessed for several years to Fr. Sofian, whom I consider a saint because I have powerfully felt the help I received through his prayers. He greatly helped me both when he was alive and after he left us. I would like to recount two wonderful stories that show us how the saints intervene from the world beyond so they can quickly help us.

There was a time when I was going through a severe psychological crisis, and thoughts of despair weighed on me to a degree that I had never felt before. I went to the grave of Fr. Sofian at Căldăruşani Monastery in a state of spirit that had the imprint of hell. I prayed to Fr. Sofian and showed him all the pain I had at that time. In a short while, the power of grace chased away the dark cloud covering me. From hell, I suddenly found myself in heaven. Everything was simple, warm, bright, full of life and meaning. It was as in the days of Pascha. I couldn't tear myself away from that grave, which was indeed a giver of life. Father Sofian was spiritually fully present there for me. I felt this very clearly. That moment is, for me, a living testimony to the fact that Fr. Sofian is a saint.

The second story relates to an important decision I had to make. I struggled for several years to understand what God's will was in that matter. I prayed, went to relics and wonderworking icons, and asked spiritual people for advice, but I could not find a solution. One night, I dreamt about Fr. Sofian. I was confessing to him, and then, still in my dream, he showed me the Book of Hours and told me to read it in its entirety. At the end, he said: "Once you read the whole Book of Hours, come back to me again for confession." When I woke up, my first thought was: "That confession was exactly like the ones I had at Antim Monastery! There was no difference." I immediately started to do the canon I had just received from Fr. Sofian; I felt peace, safety, and stillness. I am not one to believe in dreams. To this day, it is the only time in my life when I have had such a dream. My father confessor told me that what happened to me with that dream shows the care that true spiritual fathers have for their spiritual children, even after these fathers leave this world.

After a while, I finished the whole Book of Hours and didn't know what to do anymore. God enlightened me to go to the only confessor where Fr. Sofian had told me to go when he would fall asleep in the Lord. I had not seen this father in a long time because he lived far from me. When I arrived there, I noticed two things. In front of the room where he was hearing confessions, there was a self-portrait drawn by Fr. Sofian on a wall. Also, when I entered the room to confess, father was holding a wooden cross in his hand, a cross that had been Fr. Sofian's for a long time. After confessing, I saw little by little how God wanted me to solve the problems I had struggled with for the last five or six years.

Father Sofian, pray to God for us, sinners!

Ioan

†

My first confession, when I was a college student, was in 1985, with a priest-professor from the School of Theology in Bucharest. He was a distinguished professor. However, perhaps because of my faults, it was not a good match for me. It seemed to me that he was too severe and sometimes moralistic. I then looked for another confessor. I would go to Antim for Vespers; I loved the vigils there. That is how I met Fr. Sofian, who impressed me from the first moment with his simplicity. I asked him to hear my confession, and Fr. Sofian, as we know him, with much love and gentleness, agreed. I did not know at that time that he used to be a

part of the "Burning Bush" movement and that he had been imprisoned. During my college years, I was always moved by the state of peace, calm, and grace I acquired from Avva Sofian every time I confessed. Father Sofian would not ask a lot of questions during confession, and he would not give much advice. He would strengthen and embrace you with all his being. Father Sofian had a healing gentleness. I had a vital need for this gentleness. Around him, I truly felt that my soul was healed of all illness.

After the fall of the Communist regime, I discovered that Fr. Sofian was one of the exceptional spiritual fathers who had participated in the spiritual movement of the "Burning Bush." Father Sofian has brought the balanced and luminous spirit of this movement to our present time. Father Sofian was not a simple painter of churches and icons, but especially a painter of souls. How can I put it? In Fr. Sofian, you could feel the naturalness of God's closeness to your heart. I felt the same naturalness in Fr. Dumitru Stăniloae. Both of them were part of the same spiritual family. You could find the same disarming simplicity in Fr. Stăniloae as well. Both would encourage you and make you understand that you are an important, worthy person in front of God. I thank God for my providential meetings with these two great Fathers.

I find Fr. Sofian to be in the same spirit as St. Silouan the Athonite, St. Sophrony of Essex, St. Seraphim of Sarov, and St. Isaac the Syrian—the same spirit full of burning love and peace, with no harsh outbursts. I am convinced that our Church is still alive today because of the testimony and sacrifice of these great Orthodox confessors the Romanian people gave to the world in the 20th century.

Priest Professor Gheorghe Viorel Holbea

†

Many people would write and ask Fr. Sofian for help. Here are some examples:

"Most Venerable Father Abbot, I had surgery on my arm, and my cast was taken off yesterday. I want to return to Budapest, but I have no money. Please help me, and I promise this is the last time I ask!"—writes "Daniel the sinner, a Christian because of you" (that is, he had been baptized by Fr. Sofian).

"I have no food to set on the table for my children. The electrical power has been cut, and we sit in darkness. My children are wearing the shoes you gave them. Do not abandon me now, as you have never abandoned me!"—Mariana from Turda.

"I finished high school, and I have no money to go to college. My mother lives on a medical pension, and I have no father. I am asking you as a father, please help me!"—Cătălin from Chișinău.

Father Sofian used to send out envelopes and packages almost every day. He would respond to every single person asking for help, with more than they asked for. He would never judge anyone and would not try to find out if what they were saying was true or not. He would cover all of them with the same wings of the love that believes everything, covers everything, and forgives everything—even though he knew that some people were trying to lie, cheat, and take advantage of him. At some point, I asked him, "Father Sofian, why do you give them what they ask you in that case?" And he answered: "Because that is what the Savior said: *Give to the one who asks you*" (Matt 5:42). Period. No other comments. Father Sofian's motto was: "Everything is a giving, everywhere is a fulfilling, a beauty like no other; everyone is my twin brother."

One of the people coming to see Fr. Sofian was Old Anton, born in 1899. Father Sofian said he had known him for forty years. I knew him, too. He would come to Antim Monastery from the almshouse every Saturday. Father Sofian would receive him every time and see to it that he was given a bath, a haircut, and new clothes, and then he would hear his confession. Old Anton had a long list of sins to confess, and he would spend more than an hour confessing every Saturday. Father Sofian would hold a lit candle over the piece of paper with the list, so he could see better. Father Sofian was like an angel bowing over a sinner, lighting his way to the Resurrection.

S.

†

Father Sofian was my spiritual father for almost twenty years. Father served at my wedding service, baptized my children, and was by my side, always guiding me on the path to salvation. There was a deep spiritual connection between us.

I was at Antim Monastery for confession one evening. In the church, by the light of candles, in front of the icon of the Theotokos, Fr. Sofian listened patiently, full of faith and love, to each person's confession. Nobody left without being comforted, without order, without clarifying their problems. You could feel Fr. Sofian as a burning bush that set your heart alight with divine love, burning up your sins. I would draw near for confession with nervousness and timidity. I knew I had strong support there, and Father would listen to me with attention, respect, and love, but also show my transgressions with directness. My turn came late, close to midnight. When I left the monastery, it was as if I was not stepping on the ground; it was a completely special sensation, as if I was stepping on a cloud, as if I was floating, as if I was extremely light. My heart and soul were light, and I felt an extraordinary peace! Father Sofian resurrected the souls of many people!

I knew a person who had received a severe diagnosis and was desperate. She had cancer. She hurried to Fr. Sofian crying (she was to be hospitalized the next day). Father listened attentively and calmly and told her that she didn't need to be hospitalized, but she needed to change her lifestyle and follow a diet based on fruit and vegetable juice, with no sugar, white flour, and coffee. Of course, Father started to carry her in his prayers. He told her to go as often as possible to the Holy Unction service, to confess with repentance, to take Holy Communion more often, and to venerate holy relics. This woman, the daughter of a Jewish man who had converted to Orthodoxy, lived twenty more years, even though the doctors had told her she only had a short time to live. She knew other faithful Orthodox women in the same situation who had been helped by Fr. Sofian in the same manner, so that they not only lived but also had very successful careers.

Right after Fr. Sofian fell asleep in the Lord, when his body lay in the chapel of the Monastery at Antim, there was an extraordinary atmosphere at the monastery. Father Sofian had not been embalmed, and he exuded a strong fragrance of myrrh inside the chapel and even more outside. You could feel a special peace by the coffin. Father looked as if he was asleep. It was just like during the Easter service!

When you meet a man of God, a true spiritual father, you keep him in your heart and feel his presence even after he leaves this world, because of the strong connection of spiritual love. That is how I dreamt about

Fr. Sofian in the first forty days after his passing to eternal life. In my dream, he was around thirty years old, dressed in monastic clothes, with a black epitrachelion adorned with red and white embroideries, holding a prayer rope and a cross. Father Sofian was standing in front of the episcopal house at Antim. There were many people in the courtyard of the monastery. I could see Father through an open door. I could not believe I could see him, so I asked: "Father, are you alive?" Father smiled at me and said that, yes, he was alive. In my dream, I thought, "What am I going to do now?" because I had started to confess to someone else. Father Sofian was looking at me peacefully, with gentleness. I had not seen any photos of Fr. Sofian from his youth. Only after several years, when I bought a book, did I see a picture of Fr. Sofian when he was younger, and he looked like I had seen him in my dream.

Dumitra Costea, Professor, University of Bucharest

†

Do not be surprised by what I am telling you, but I could not forget the gentle gaze with which you welcomed me in the courtyard of Antim Monastery fifty-five years ago. My name is T.G., and I live in Paris. I am an architect and served as a Colonel in the military; I fought on two fronts, eastern and western...I could not forget that gaze, Fr. Sofian, even though I turned ninety-one years old on March 7. Ever since you have been present and a living presence for me. Here and at all times. I know and I feel that you pray for me, too. And I need it, maybe more than ever.

Fragment from a letter to Fr. Sofian

†

Approximately two weeks before Fr. Sofian fell asleep in the Lord, I visited him at the Military Hospital, where he was hospitalized. At that time, I was serving as a priest at Christiana Monastery. I went there with Nun Mina from that monastery and Eugenia, an icon painter. Father Sofian was in a room with two beds. The other bed was occupied by Fr. Irineu from Ponor, who was caring for Fr. Sofian. As soon as I entered the room, I saw a very special light, if I can say so. I asked myself: "What is this light?" I looked out the window. The light from the outside, the

daylight, was different from the light that was bringing so much peace inside the room. I looked then at Fr. Sofian and saw that this special light was emanating from his face. I sat down next to Father; even though he was in pain, he started to tell us some words of advice. Father's face was calm and luminous; I deeply felt this state of peace, but that special ray of light disappeared when we started to talk. I think Fr. Sofian was praying intensely when we entered the room. I think Father had the Prayer of the Heart. Other Christians told me they saw this light coming from Fr. Sofian. And I also know many believers who feel very clearly that they acquire a state of peace when they pray at Fr. Sofian's grave at Căldărușani Monastery.

Protosyngellos Ghelasie Iorga, Nucet Monastery

†

When I went to see Fr. Sofian for the first time, I told him, proud of myself: "I like taking care of other people, helping them!" And then, looking at me with gentle understanding, Father told me: "First, take care of yourself because you need it; set everything in order for yourself, and then you'll be able to take care of others!" I understood what he meant, and I was ashamed. After 1989, most of us were "revolutionaries" criticizing everyone, even the Patriarch of the Romanian Orthodox Church, of whom we didn't know much. I told Fr. Sofian about our attitude, and he replied: "And you think that by noticing other people's mistakes, you help them?"

It has been twenty years since Fr. Sofian left this world, but I carry him vividly in my mind, soul, and thoughts as someone who brought us light, gentleness, and peace, enveloping everything in his love. A merciful love that healed and nourished the soul with a gentleness that brought grace and zeal for continuing on the path, filled with temptations, leading to our becoming, or better said, to our coming back to the Church that receives and calls all of us. I see him grieving or rejoicing, surrounded by a golden light that is a harbinger of sainthood. His voice was like honey, and I cannot forget his unique way of saying: "Let us lift up our hearts!" during Divine Liturgy. In my opinion, nobody has ever said these words, or will ever say them, with as much spiritual power as Fr. Sofian. There was so much need for holiness, so much joy in these words that were so encompassing. I see him and I hear him. He had so much dedication, a dedication that he transmitted, that brought fruit, and that he turned into deeds for all of us who were around him.

When you try to depict Fr. Sofian in words, all you can do is let your tears flow. Father had the gift of tears, which is so necessary. He loved all of us so much. The love that emanated from him became almost material; it enveloped us. Father loved my husband, the sculptor Vasile Gorduz, very much. He always told me, "You need to take care of Mr. Vasile!" Or, "Mr. Vasile needs to always have the chisel in his hands!" The connection between them was profound and not at all accidental. Father Sofian was born in Basarabia on October 7th, while Vasile was born on October 8th in the village of Trifești, next to Dobrușa Monastery, where Fr. Sofian started his monastic life. For Fr. Sofian, his native land had remained an open wound. The drama of Vasile Gorduz, who was born as a great artist through the pain of losing the paradise of his childhood, Basarabia, drew him closer to Fr. Sofian, who had assumed this pain through the power of faith.[50]

Father Sofian had a robust sense of humor and was not afraid to use it. There was an astonishing combination of sternness and gentleness in him, which did not exclude one another. Father Sofian was beautiful, kind, and filled with a thoughtfulness that enveloped and captivated you. The unique warmth of his voice nourished your soul. He was not generous with his words—I can say that he avoided wasting them—and from this was born the extraordinary weight of these words that were not scattered but given as a gift.

An excruciating yearning fills me when I wish he were here with us! I saw him twice drenched in tears, which became a true treasure for those who witnessed them. Approximately two weeks before he fell asleep in the Lord, when he was hospitalized at the Military Hospital, I asked him: "Father, how should I pray?" Father Sofian was lying in bed. Suddenly, tears started to pour down his face, and he said slowly: "Lord Jesus Christ, son of God, have mercy on me, a sinner!" Witnessing Fr. Sofian saying the Jesus Prayer and crying was a gift. Generally speaking, it was a great gift from God for Vasile Gorduz and me that He allowed us to be around Fr. Sofian for a while. Our life became different—better, more

50 *Translator's note*: Basarabia, an ancient Romanian territory, was annexed by the Soviet Union in 1940 and is currently the independent Republic of Moldova.

luminous. I can say that I genuinely feel like his daughter. For us, meeting Fr. Sofian was for our salvation. Our work also changed because of our inner transformation. After meeting Fr. Sofian, we created our essential works. Vasile Gorduz sculpted the statue of the Roman Emperor Trajan, which was placed on the shore of the Guadalquivir River, close to the birthplace of the emperor, and also the statue of the Romanian poet Eminescu, displayed in Montreal, Canada. I sculpted the statue of St. George, which is displayed in St. George Square in Timişoara, and made a series of reliefs. All these works of art had the same source: the light coming from Fr. Sofian's soul. Father Sofian gave us a treasure that has no end. Without him, my husband and I would have been miserable.

Father Sofian's prayers eased our difficulties and trials. He told me once, "Only your zeal has helped you!" But this zeal was there because of the gentleness, wisdom, and great love that Fr. Sofian always offered to us. It is something completely wondrous: I feel with all my being that the help Fr. Sofian gave me continues to this day.

Silvia Radu, artist, sculptor

†

For almost two years, I helped Fr. Sofian with different things he needed, especially in his monastic cell. One could powerfully feel the presence of the Holy Spirit in this cell. Father told me once: "Tomorrow, a certain person will come; bring that person in." Later, I found out that it was an ex-agent of the Secret Police who had tormented Fr. Sofian in prison and caused him great harm. Now, he wanted to come to Fr. Sofian to ask for forgiveness. Father Sofian had already forgiven him anyway. The next day, the person arrived. I opened the door, and before entering the room, he stopped and said softly: "Oh, there is something here!" I think he felt something of the presence of grace. He entered and stayed there for a few hours. Believe me, when he left, he was a different man! A totally different man! One man entered, and another left. The Holy Spirit had worked with power and had changed his soul, which now was luminous. I don't know how else to express this.

Once, a faithful Orthodox woman came to see Fr. Sofian; she was a seamstress. We called her "the Doe." She came to make an overcoat for Fr. Sofian, who was going to leave for Syria and "bandage" some of the saints he had painted. That is how he said it, and he was referring to the fact that some Muslim people had profaned some of the icons Father had painted in a church in Syria. Father Sofian told the seamstress: "The Mother of God just left, and she told me you need to make me a light-colored overcoat..." And that is the overcoat that is seen in some of Fr. Sofian's photos.

Father Sofian experienced so much severe suffering in those two years! I was astonished at this patience.

M.S.

†

When I received the obedience of caring for Fr. Sofian, because he was very ill, I considered myself unworthy to serve such a Father Staretz. The whole time I was with Fr. Sofian was filled with happy moments, special moments, unique moments of my life. I had never spent time before with an Elder, an Avva.

Father Sofian had a special calling from the moment of his birth, not from people, but from the Holy Spirit, from above. From a young, innocent age, he was called to serve, sacrifice himself, spend himself, and consume himself like a candle. Father Sofian left his parents' house for good at the age of fourteen years. And of course, he did not do this from childish thoughts, but he was called by the Holy Spirit. On December 25, 1937, he took the yoke of monasticism; he took the cross, crucifying himself forever to this passing and changing life and becoming a true, invincible soldier fighting the arrows of the enemy.

When he was close to leaving this world, Fr. Sofian confessed to me, starting with his childhood. That is why I said he was an invincible soldier. He never gave in, never bowed even for a second to this passing life, to the cravings of youth, to the riches that people often set before him—either houses, apartments, or land... Fr. Sofian would say: "I am a monk, I crucified myself, I took the vow of poverty; I would sink under the weight of these things."

Because of his illness, Fr. Sofian would often miss the meals in the monastery's dining hall, and so the faithful Orthodox would bring him all kinds of dishes; he didn't even know what they were called or how to eat them... But he would eat like a bird, a little bit from here and a little

bit from there. We were upset seeing how little he ate, but he would tell us: "This is enough for me. If I eat more, I lose what I have always wanted: the Prayer of the Heart!" Even more, he respected the meal hours. He could be very hungry, he could talk to people for a long time, but he never ate anything except at the regular meal time. Because he had never forgotten what he promised: the monk must never eat between meals; he must learn to cut his will.

Father Sofian suffered a lot, starting from his childhood. His soul suffered for this world that strayed away from the path leading to God. Later, as he got older, he suffered physically, too. But what wore him out was the pain in his soul. He would often sigh when I recalled life's sorrows, and he would tell me: "Father, this is the fruit of my sins!" He wouldn't say "our sins" but "my sins." Father truly carried the others' pain in his soul. This is what it means to fulfill the words of the Gospel: to give your life for your neighbor.

Toward the end of his life, Fr. Sofian heard all kinds of things said about him, but he remained unmoved and untroubled. He knew that the enemy targets the end of a monk's life the most. And then, since he knew this so well, he humbled himself to such a degree that I wondered and asked myself how he could endure so many things and not defend himself. He never defended himself! He only prayed. And I remembered the words that Fr. Sofian would tell us, which were fulfilled now: "When someone confronts you, don't defend yourself. Receive it for your sins, and you thus obtain a little bit of medicine for your humility."

As for the Church services conducted by Fr. Sofian, I am ashamed to talk about them, because we do not do what he used to do. We strive to do them, but because we don't have his zeal because we care too much for our mortal bodies, we are deceived. I remember that when there was time for Fr. Sofian to say the blessing for the Divine Liturgy, he would stop for a few moments, and we would tremble seeing his countenance before us. He would be deep in his thoughts, then he would look around as if he needed to be careful not to be consumed by the divine fire. He would see that he was surrounded not only by angels but by all those who had ever served in that monastery founded by St. Antim Ivireanul, and he would become contrite... on the verge of tears. That is why, when he was saying the blessing for the Divine Liturgy, his voice was more powerful, so that he could keep what he experienced in those moments hidden from the Orthodox faithful gathered there.

Protosyngellos Irineu Curtescu, Abbot of Ponor Monastery

†

I remember when Fr. Sofian was freed from prison, some guards started to tell each other: "Look at that, the saint is getting out of prison!" Father Sofian was full of light, a person upon which grace seemed to have poured. Father Sofian had such an aura that even the guards said that the saint was freed.

Marcel Petrișor (†2021),
writer who was also imprisoned
during the Communist regime

†

In 1987, we decided to establish a Romanian monastery close to Detroit.[51] Some people tried to discourage us by saying: "Three nuns by themselves; what would they be able to do?" With God's help, we found a suitable place for a monastery the following year, but it was very hard in the beginning. During those hard times, we received a gift from God: Fr. Sofian came to America to take care of a health problem. He spent three months in the United States. It was God's plan for us to receive a blessing from Avva Sofian to establish the monastery. Father Sofian was good friends with Fr. Roman Braga, the brother of Mother Benedicta, who was the founder of our monastery and its first abbess. I need to mention that Fr. Roman Braga, Fr. Felix Dubneac (both had already been in America for several years), and Fr. Sofian were all from Basarabia. They had all been classmates in seminary and were good friends before the Communist regime took power in Romania.

Father Sofian's visit to America right at that moment of beginning our monastery was providential and had great significance for us. Always smiling, always joyful, Father encouraged us and told us that the Mother of God wants this little corner of paradise; he told us how beautiful that place was, how suitable for a monastery, how good it was, but most of

51 *Translator's note*: the Holy Dormition Monastery in Rives Junction, Michigan.

all, he told us that we needed to proceed, that good things are done with hard work and patience. Father's encouragement helped us very much at that time, and we thus had the conviction that it was God's will for us to continue on that path.

Father Sofian visited the United States two more times, and each time, he stayed at our monastery, which had slowly started to take root. He felt very attached to this monastery. Some of us would confess to him, and he also tonsured Mother Benedicta into the Great Schema. All the Orthodox faithful coming to our monastery were also very happy to see Fr. Sofian there. Some of them did not understand what Father was saying because they did not know Romanian, but they would feel the state of peace, grace, and blessing surrounding Fr. Sofian, and this was indeed helpful to them.

Even though he left this world, Fr. Sofian continues to be with us; he is part of our lives!

Mother Gabriella Ursache,
Abbess of Holy Dormition Monastery,
Rives Junction, Michigan

†

I am a physician, and when I met Fr. Sofian, I was a student in medical school. I had a fairly serious health issue at that time, and so each Friday, I would attend the Vespers services that Fr. Sofian had at Antim, and thus, I got healed. After many years, I had another health issue that could have become very threatening, and I needed to have surgery. I didn't know what to do; I had no moral support. I went to Fr. Sofian's grave and prayed to him for support. When I left there, my soul was light and peaceful. I had surgery, and everything went well; I regained my health. Whenever I have a problem or something weighing on my soul, I go to Father's grave and feel how he takes away all the gravity of the situation. I feel that Fr. Sofian is a permanent support for me.

Mihaela Teodoru

†

What impressed and attracted people's hearts was, first of all, the light that radiated from Fr. Sofian's whole being and that filled all the surrounding space. It was the light of the grace of the Holy Spirit, which Christ gives to those who, through long asceticism, have purified their soul and body of passions and have become vessels of the work of divine energies.

I remember when I first entered Fr. Sofian's monastic cell. He was sitting on a chair, with his head bowed in deep prayer. There was a grace there that overwhelmed you. A profound peace and a spirit of repentance filled your soul. Father was silent. There was no need for words! His mere presence revealed God to us. Then, Fr. Sofian started to talk. His gentleness and love resurrected your soul. You understood that this is the love that Christ pours into the hearts of those who love Him with all their being and who gave themselves wholly to Him.

When it came to sins, however, Fr. Sofian became a rock! His sternness was deeply purifying and healing. But you could feel the same love beyond this severity. Father Sofian encompassed all of us in his wide heart.

How did Father Sofian serve in Church? There was a majesty in the way he served, which went beyond the limits of what was natural and that only grace could give. Father's grave voice, the concentrated and attentive way he prayed and chanted—everything would deeply move your heart. There was no fragmentation in Fr. Sofian! His entire being was one. What he expressed through words had passed through his heart first, and I think that was the reason his words were so powerful! In private conversations, Father didn't use many words. There was nothing superfluous in what he said; he always directly reached the essential. He had an extraordinary sense for what is essential.

I was very impressed by Fr. Sofian's love for the Jesus Prayer, a love that he was able to transmit to his spiritual sons and daughters, especially to young people. He was happy when someone expressed an interest or wanted to practice this prayer, even in the world. And the fruits of the prayer would not be slow to appear. Father himself used to say: "There are quite a few people in the world who have this prayer, who pray continuously, and their prayer is very fruitful!"

You had complete trust in Fr. Sofian, with no shadow of a doubt—I would say more than a child trusts his father. You received his words as an indisputable truth; with two or three words, the soul would clearly feel that it was the truth! Father would say these words from his long experience and, most of all, from what God enlightened him! He never tried to impose himself. I have never felt this absolute trust, with no shadow of a doubt in no matter what word he would tell me, after Fr. Sofian passed away. He was the Father of my life!

I was young, and I fell in love with a young man who had graduated from the School of Theology, but he was already divorced, and he had a child from his first marriage. I wanted to marry him. My "love" was mostly a passionate attachment that had enslaved all the powers of my soul. I was not sure what God's will was! It so happened that I met Elder Arsenie Papacioc and asked him for some advice. He told me that the relationship between spouses is in Christ and that a second marriage is out of the question. He asked me to forget that young man. And, still... I felt I couldn't forget him and be separated from him. I then went to Fr. Sofian. He told me gently to read the Paraklesis of the Mother of God, and I did it. A few days later, I was walking on the street, and I suddenly felt a gentle breeze—yes, exactly like a gentle breeze—entering my soul. Immediately, my heart was freed. And my first thought was that Fr. Sofian's spirit was also in that gentle breeze. He had prayed for me; he had prayed how only he knew how to pray, and he had freed me.

D.

†

One time, Fr. Sofian served in our monastery. When he started serving the Divine Liturgy, I felt that the entire church had caught fire spiritually. I cannot explain it any more than that. Many priests from different places have served in our monastery throughout the years, but I have never felt anything like it any other time.

A hieromonk

†

We often went to see Schemanun Paisia, who had a blessed life and fell asleep in the Lord when she was 104 years old. She is buried at Pasărea Monastery. She confessed to Fr. Sofian a few times when she was young and respected him very much. She used to speak very well of Fr. Sofian; she said he was a saint. She would tell us that Father has the power of words and that you were spiritually nourished when you listened to him. His words were comforting, like a balm; they penetrated your soul; they had power even over atheists. Mother Paisia used to tell us about an unbelieving person, an atheist, who said that the only church he could go to was Antim Monastery when Fr. Sofian would give a homily there. He was the only priest that person was drawn to, the only one around whom that person could feel something from the power of faith.

Schemanun Paisia kept hundreds of icons and photographs showing renowned Elders in her monastic cell—most of them received as gifts from priests, monks, and Orthodox faithful who came to see her. The walls were covered with holy images from top to bottom. One day, in 2010-2011, when we were all saying the evening prayers in Mother Paisia's cell (she was lying in bed because of the severe health problems she had in the last years of her life; she was practically paralyzed), we saw how myrrh started to stream from a photograph of Fr. Sofian which was right next to Mother Paisia's bed, above her head. It was a small photograph from a calendar, and you could see beads of myrrh full of fragrance. All of us who were there anointed our foreheads with that myrrh. That was the only time this happened; at other times, no myrrh streamed from Father's photo.

Maria Olaru
Richard Constantin Popa, Engineer

†

I was a student in the School of Economic Studies in Bucharest in 1989, and I had started to get closer to the Church; I had started to go to Fr. Galeriu and listen to his sermons. After the sermon, I would leave without understanding why Fr. Galeriu said: "With the fear of God, with faith and love, draw near!" I did not think it was inappropriate to leave

until I understood what the Divine Liturgy really is, and ever since, I have stayed until the end of the Divine Liturgy.

During that time, I went on a pilgrimage to Northern Moldavia. While we were visiting the museum of a monastery, I cannot exactly remember if it was Sucevița or Moldovița, we started to talk to a nun and told her we were college students in Bucharest and that we had started to go to Fr. Galeriu. She asked us: "But did you go to Fr. Sofian?" We didn't know who he was. Then she told us about Fr. Sofian being the father confessor of Bucharest and about the work he was doing.

After returning to Bucharest, I looked for Fr. Sofian at Antim Monastery, and he became my spiritual father during the time I was a college student in Bucharest. Even more, it so happened that I started to attend the School of Theology and became involved in the activity of the Romanian Orthodox Christian Students Association [ASCOR in Romanian]. I was the President of ASCOR for two years, between 1992 and 1994, during the association's early years. We were all very zealous and wanted to do more. There was something special at that time; we had a spirit of prayer and sound disposition, and we were unaware that this state of spirit was primarily due to our relationship with Fr. Sofian, who was the spiritual father of many of those involved in ASCOR. As many people have often said, Father had a discrete, delicate, but very alive presence. He was not the type of person to coordinate things, to tell us to do this or that, but he transmitted a spiritual state to us and carried us in his prayers.

At the same time, Father had an overwhelming humility and gentleness. He was unique because he was close to what a human should be. He liked to say that when the mind unites with the heart, the person becomes one, and what he thinks, he also feels and says. And I think we could clearly see this in Fr. Sofian. And this is the great mystery of Fr. Sofian: the union of the mind with the heart, keeping them unceasingly with God. It is the hesychast ideal, without considering hesychasm to be something reserved for certain initiated people. The Church assumed the hesychast teaching as its own in the fourteenth century, when St. Gregory Palamas set the foundation of hesychasm, but this attitude, seeking the union of the mind with the heart and keeping them unceasingly with God, had existed from the beginning of Christianity.

Father Sofian was, first of all, a person of presence, of discrete action, and less so a person of rhetorical discourse. He was a complete person with spiritual integrity. I think this is the only way we can explain the unearthly beauty of his luminous face and the peace he brought. Let us not forget that there were people who became convinced of the presence and action of God in the world and even became Orthodox by simply looking at Fr. Sofian's countenance.

Priest Professor Florin Botezan, Alba Iulia

†

Those who used to go to Antim Monastery in the 1980s and 1990s can attest to the fact that there was a unique atmosphere there, a richness of grace. Father Sofian, Fr. Paisie Prelipceanu, and Fr. Adrian Făgețeanu were truly begetting spiritual children; they nourished us with a state of grace that cannot be described because words are too weak.

Father Sofian was a very profound, mysterious person. It is very hard to talk about him. At Antim, during the second night of vigil around the coffin of Fr. Sofian, there was a priest professor who went into the altar, put on his epitrachelion, and censed around the coffin. He then said a few words that moved me very much: "The greatest liturgical servant of the Romanian nation has left to the Lord! The priest who served at least once during a Divine Liturgy with Fr. Sofian—that priest graduated from Theology School at that time!" Through these words, the priest professor conveyed everything I had felt at Antim Monastery during those years.

I think Fr. Sofian suffered the most when he could not serve in the altar anymore. Serving God, especially during the Divine Liturgy, represented the meaning of life for Fr. Sofian.

Dumitru Apalaghiei

†

Father Sofian often told me: "Get used to humility, sister! It is truly good for you! It brings peace to your soul. It is good not to be out in front at all, not to stand out at all. If there is no humility in the heart, it is in vain that you are wearing the monastic habit. God gave us freedom to do what we want, but we are corrupted by pride."

Another time, Father told me: "You always say, 'I can't do it anymore!' This is not good! Pray with repentance! When I was in prison, I was working at the Canal,[52] and I was carrying a load with a wheelbarrow. It was raining, there was a lot of mud, and the wheel got stuck in the mud. Some inmates were younger and stronger, but I got left far behind them and couldn't move the wheelbarrow anymore. Then, I cried out in my heart: 'Lord, help me, Lord!' At that moment, the soldier walking beside me told me: 'Go on the dry side!' Usually, you weren't allowed to separate yourself from your group because you were considered a deserter, and the soldiers had orders to shoot. But God answered me immediately in this way."

After confessing to Fr. Sofian, I was walking on the street lined with fir trees that led to the People's House, and I felt like I was in heaven. I didn't hear any noise or the hustle and bustle of the world; everything was quiet in my heart, and I could look at the world in a different light, with great mercy.

In the early 1990s, I asked Fr. Sofian for a blessing to enroll in the Department of Psaltic Music of the Conservatory. Father sent me a letter in which he wrote: "I do not like the thought of you enrolling in the Conservatory. Do not go back to that thought. What can you do with this Conservatory other than become proud that you can sing more beautifully than the other nuns? (...) I am not stopping you, but I am not encouraging you either." The next day, I went to see Fr. Sofian. He immediately rose from his study desk and welcomed me with a smile. "You did not get upset with me?" He asked me with humor, inviting me to sit down. Then he added: "I do not think that the Conservatory can help enrich in any way the life you have chosen. Slowly, you will become more like a layperson; you will not have time to pray either, and, who knows, maybe you will give up this life altogether. You will end up despising those who wear the same habit as you. I pray to the Mother of God to keep you as you are now, at this moment. Because you have joined the monastery out of your zeal, and you have some good qualities, by God's mercy, and it would pain me to see you lose them. This is my opinion: renounce all your worldly plans and fight to draw near to God with all your being because it is for Him that you joined the monastery. If

52 *Translator's note*: The Danube-Black Sea Canal was a forced labor camp in Romania in the 1950s and 1960s.

you want to study music, do as I told you: try to decipher some Byzantine music by yourself, and you will see what great joy you will have when you manage to do it yourself!"

Father Sofian was talking... I was listening to him and feeling my whole heart changing, becoming light as a feather. I suddenly felt so much peace and joy and a great need to pray, to say the Jesus Prayer. The Conservatory, which I had dreamt of my whole life, had dissipated instantly, like smoke. Only those who met Fr. Sofian can fully understand what I am saying. I kneeled, asked Father for a blessing, and promised obedience with God's help. I saw Fr. Sofian rejoicing like a child. His serene face and eyes reflected his heart's purity and joy. He got up slowly, made the sign of the cross, bowed deeply in front of the icon of the Savior, thanked God, and then blessed me.

One time, when I was confessing, Fr. Sofian showed me how he was saying the Prayer of the Heart. He explained it to me this way: "Look at me. I hold my right hand with two fingers on my chest and rest my left hand on my knee. The two fingers are here, above the heart of flesh. When we pray, however, we do not consider the heart of flesh but this spiritual center of our being—this is what we must seek. Look at me now..." I looked. Father started to say the Prayer of the Heart right then and there, during the Mystery of Confession. God is my witness! Father's face shone like the face of a man through whom Light was passing.

During the last period of his life, I saw him cry often. I think God wants you to be a saint even from your time on earth, especially before death, but this holiness demands an even greater sacrifice from those who are holy, through forgiveness and through patiently bearing their cross.

When Father Sofian fell asleep in the Lord, when his body was in the church at Antim, I noticed how the old Orthodox faithful would pray to him as if his coffin was a reliquary holding holy relics. I heard them say: "Father Sofian, forgive me for everything and help me with your prayers!"; or, "Father, pray for us!"...I remember a young boy, strong and handsome, in primary school, who was leaning against the coffin. He took Father's hands in his own small hands, caressing them. I then heard the most beautiful words from that child's lips: "The good Father!"

I would add that, during the first vigil night for Father Sofian, I was very moved by the presence of so many poor people there, and by a wreath of white carnations brought there by a group of beggars. I heard them say: "He was a saint... who will be merciful to us now?" An old white-haired man sighed: "Father Sofian, you taught us to love each other, not to be egotistical!" What a beautiful sermon!

Saint Seraphim of Sarov, whom Fr. Sofian loved so much, left this hope as consolation to the nuns at his monastery: "Every time you have a sorrow, come to my grave, and I will help you!" I think this is the case for Fr.Sofian's spiritual children and not only for them. I know with certainty that many people received help and support when they prayed at Fr. Sofian's grave. I am one of them.

Nun Mina, Christiana Monastery

†

One year, shortly after the fall of the Communist regime, I participated in a Divine Liturgy at Antim Monastery. His Grace Nifon, Bishop Vicar at the Patriarchate, was serving there. During the Divine Liturgy, when Fr. Sofian prayed for His Grace, Father mistakenly said, "Nifon of Târgoviște." We were all surprised that Father called His Grace that way. But in seven or eight years, His Grace Nifon became Archbishop of Târgoviște.

One time, I made a prayer list, and in the middle I wrote the name of a woman who was ill, but I didn't write "ill" next to her name. I gave the list to Fr. Sofian during a church service. Father read the list out loud, and when he reached that woman's name, he said only for that name: "Teodora, for her health!"

One of my granddaughters went to be anointed with myrrh by Fr. Sofian. I told her to pay attention to what Father said when he anointed her. Even though Father had never seen her, he called her by her name: "Rodica, make sure you say your prayers!"

Another time, when I was confessing, Fr. Sofian pointed to the altar and told me: "The Mother of God showed herself here, in the Holy Altar!"

A woman who was very ill came to some services at Antim Monastery and said she didn't like how the choir chanted. When she went to be anointed with myrrh, Fr. Sofian told her: "May God give you health, sister, because you are very ill!" After leaving the church, she told us: "May God forgive me for saying I didn't like the choir. Look at what Father Sofian told me! How did he know I was gravely ill?" And indeed, she was very ill; she had just had surgery for cancer.

Traian Brancioc

†

I saw in Avva Sofian not only a true Father but also a true human being who lived every moment of his life testifying, in Spirit and in Truth, that the Holy Gospel is true, that it can be experienced and followed here, in our earthly life, as each of us, being followers of Christ, is called and urged by Him to do, as a Commandment. Father Sofian practiced wholly, in minute detail, what he advised others to do; he wouldn't ask anything of others that he hadn't already practiced himself.

Father Sofian glorified God at all times and revealed his feelings especially when he smiled. His luminous countenance was like a sunrise. An innocent child's smile flooded his whole being with an unearthly brightness. You could feel from a great distance that he had the Prayer of the Heart.

When my brother, the poet Daniel Turcea, fell asleep in the Lord in 1979, Avva Sofian mourned him and said he was sorry for not doing more for him. At some point, Father told me: "What can we say about the humility of brother Daniel, since we are not worthy of it?" Daniel confessed to Fr. Sofian and loved him very much. He went to Avva Sofian and asked him for a blessing to write about God. Father blessed him and told him to write as simply as possible, without hard-to-understand metaphors, because the Savior spoke plainly. Then, Daniel wrote his beautiful verses in the volume "Epiphany"—verses of which Fr. Stăniloae said that they would be appreciated in the whole world at some point.

Daniel knew that Fr. Sofian was a saint. One day, a professor of Russian language came to the Writers' Union in Bucharest—he was a good Christian and was suffering from cancer. He told Daniel something unexpected. When Fr. Sofian was imprisoned at the Salcia forced labor camp, a guard had drowned, and this professor replaced him. The man was working there because he had a family and could not get any other work. The first night, he inspected the barrack at midnight to see if everything was in order. He saw Fr. Sofian kneeling, sitting on his heels so that he wouldn't draw attention to himself, and praying with the head bowed down on his bed. The guard was very impressed by what he saw, and the next day, he gave Fr. Sofian a prayer list so that he could pray for all his close ones, living and dead.

Father Sofian told me once about the heroic faith of the Great Martyrs Hieromonk Daniil Sandu Tudor (beaten to death at Aiud prison) and Costache Oprișan (killed at Pitești prison by Țurcanu, the torturer). Tears were pouring down Father's face as he was speaking. He told me: "The common graves are filled with the remains of martyrs. But many also have apostasized, have lost their coherent mind, or committed suicide more or less willingly on account of their troubled minds—because of the torture they had suffered."

I remember how, one time, Fr. Sofian returned from the Holy Land and gave an extraordinary homily during the Vespers service. He cried bitterly that whole time, presenting us in vivid images the places where God-Man had lived, suffered, wept, resurrected, and ascended into Heaven on the throne that, as God Himself, He had never left. Father's grave voice, shaken by the tears pouring down his face, could have caused the walls of Antim Monastery to cry—not to mention all of us who were there and who felt moved to the bottom of our souls.

Not long before Fr. Sofian fell asleep in the Lord, I went to see him at the hospital on August 29, 2002, the feast of the Beheading of St. John the Baptist. I am sure that Father's prayers called me there. Many students from ASCOR filled the hallway, so you couldn't even pass through. We all wanted a word of spiritual advice or a blessing to accompany us all our lives. I was at the top of the staircase and had no hope of seeing Father. My heart was trembling in my chest as a bird in a cage. I yearned to see Father; I didn't need anything else. I am small in stature and there were taller people in front of me, so nobody could even see where I was. Still, even without hope, I was praying! Suddenly, I felt a great peace, and I said: "Lord, for the prayers of Fr. Sofian, it is impossible that I will not be able to see him today!" I think Father saw me by the work of the Holy Spirit, and even more, he wanted to receive me "in the flesh." All of a sudden, Fr. Irineu drew near to me—as if he came down from heaven—and told me: "Let's go, Lucia, because the Most Venerable Fr. Sofian wants to see only his older spiritual children, and he will give a blessing to the newer ones at the end." Because Fr. Irineu took me by the hand, we quickly passed through the people in front, who allowed us to go to the door, so that, unexpectedly soon, we were next to Fr. Sofian.

Avva Sofian looked at me very seriously and, with great warmth of soul, told me: "Lucia, you worked on church paintings at my advice. Have you ever thought truly, not just theoretically, that our Savior is alive, here and everywhere? You should know without doubts, unequivocally, that there will come a day when you will see Him face to face, and nothing will remain hidden from everything that you have ever done, or said, or thought, or whispered in the dark, or if you avenged yourself, or thought poorly of someone, or blasphemed, or cursed, or talked ambiguously, or were filled with pride and vainglory—nothing will remain hidden! All your life, have the Gospel of Matthew in front of you daily—the second part of the twenty-fifth chapter. Pay attention always to those verses and their profound meaning. And you should know that only almsgiving, for soul and body, will save you! Nothing else! Almsgiving has love, kindness, humility, gentleness, compassion, and forgiveness—it encompasses all of these. Be merciful to poor people, and do not stay far from those who strive to live in Spirit and Truth!"

Father Sofian's life was a heavy cross for him, and he left us on the Day of the Elevation of the Cross. That is how God wanted it! I think that Father now has joy to the measure of the suffering he had in his earthly life. Thank You, Lord, for giving me such a Spiritual Father!

Lucia Turcea

†

One year, on the third day of Pascha, at Antim Monastery, the Venerable Staretz Archimandrite Sofian caused a severe pain I was experiencing to cease immediately by praying intensely after the Divine Liturgy when he was full of the grace of the Holy Spirit. I felt at that time how the power of grace penetrated me, an energy separated from my being, like an electrical current. Later, Fr. Sofian helped me continuously through his gentleness, kindness, patience, humility, generosity, and the wisdom he had as a true saint.

A faithful Orthodox woman

†

I saw Fr. Sofian for the first time in the early 1980s. An acquaintance of mine told me he wants to bring me to the place where "the Bible is read the most beautifully in all of Bucharest." I was almost forty years old and had a solid materialistic scientific education. I reached Antim Monastery during the Divine Liturgy, shortly before the reading of the Holy Gospel. When Father started to read, I immediately felt that something was happening there that was very different from what I had expected. God wanted to bring me to the faith by looking at Fr. Sofian and listening to his voice. Later, I found out that many people had the same experience. I started to confess to Father—I who until then was untrusting and almost contemptuous toward confession.

After some time, I had the great joy of driving Fr. Sofian to Dealu Monastery, where he needed to work on repainting the church. We made several trips there. He would leave there on Monday and return on Saturday so he could serve the Divine Liturgy at Antim on Sunday. I was alone with Fr. Sofian, an hour and a half each way—I couldn't believe it! He had so much gentleness, kindness, and joy in everything he said that I never wanted the trip to end. I can say I spent a long time with Father. I never saw him hurried, unsure of himself, impatient, angry, or proud. Any question I would ask him—about life, religion, or culture—he would answer serenely and naturally, with no doubt or hesitation. He had much knowledge, culture, and life experience, but I felt that everything he said was from a form of superior wisdom that he could access differently than a regular person. I have always felt his presence after he fell asleep in the Lord. We have his books; we are comforted when we listen to his recordings of the Psalms; we have photographs and even an icon of him. When we pray to him, we truly receive help.

A few years ago, I met a Church hierarch who had spent several years at Antim Monastery and knew and loved Fr. Sofian. He recognized me when he saw me, but I could tell he didn't know where he had met me. I told him: "I used to go to Fr. Sofian." He brightened up and said: "Yes, yes... Fr. Sofian. I count him among the saints, with no hesitation!" Amen!

A disciple of Father Sofian

†

I was born in Bucharest, and I lived close to Antim Monastery. I confessed to Elder Sofian from the time I was a child. With his blessing, I went to become a monk at Sihastria Monastery, where Father Cleopa was, whom Fr. Sofian respected very much. Elder Cleopa fell asleep in the Lord in 1998. In 2001, I went to Antim Monastery to receive a blessing from Fr. Sofian one year before his passing. Even though we had not seen each other or talked for seven years, Fr. Sofian immediately recognized me and told me: "Welcome, Brother Stefan!" Then he added: "Father Cleopa showed himself to me! I had a vision with Fr. Cleopa!" And, while he was telling me this, his face filled with light. I had a photo of Fr. Cleopa with me. I showed it to Fr. Sofian, and he joyfully kissed it. Holy Confessors Sofian and Cleopa, pray for us!

Monk Stelian,
St. Mina Skete (county Neamt)

†

Dear Father Teofan,

I confess I am very happy to write down a few thoughts related to Father Sofian. I will never forget his presence—very quiet, warm, seraphic—which used to draw my attention ever since I was a child. I was very impressed by Antim Monastery, surrounded by tall walls that helped that blessed place offer me a calming sensation of being sheltered and protected right in the middle of the city. Antim Monastery witnessed that all I read in history books about our past was real, not simple children's tales or legends. Once inside the monastery, I would see a large group of people waiting patiently. They came to confess to Father Sofian. From time to time, Father Sofian would come outside, smile at everyone, and promise he would see all of them. His promise was sacred, and he would always keep it. At that time, I did not go to Antim Monastery to confess to Father Sofian. My grandparents would take me with them to walk around there. Sometimes, my mother would come, too. They would tell me that the area around Antim was representative of how Bucharest traditionally used to be and how it developed under King Carol the First. Then, we would stay for the Vespers service. Father Sofian would talk to my grandparents, happy to see them. And I think that, for my grandparents, the real reason for these walks was to meet Father Sofian again. It was a special connection because Father Sofian painted the icons on the church iconostasis from Gusterita in Sibiu, where the parish priest was my grandmother's brother. Father Sofian had a wonderful smile; he talked slowly, but his words resounded beautifully. Nothing he said was unnecessary or only polite. He had an implicit sincerity, with no trace of doubt or dishonesty. You would immediately feel that you were close to a special man.

I do not believe that that generation of great personalities of the Romanian Church will enter into eternity just because they suffered in Communist prisons. Of course, their sacrifice is an undeniable reality, an existential testimonial, dramatical but also realistic, of those dark times. At the same time, we must emphasize that God always cares for His Church. This axiom is a reality of overwhelming importance. And Father Sofian was one of those whom God chose to be in church when they were absolutely needed. This way, Archimandrite Sofian was, through everything he did—through the icons he painted, through the people he helped as a spiritual father, through serving in the altar of Antim Monastery—the divine help we needed at that time. This thought gives me much courage because it represents the clear, infallible proof of God's care for all of us at all times and in all our trials.

I told you, dear Father Teofan, that Father Sofian was my mother's spiritual father starting at a particular time. More than this, he advised and supported her when she had to make difficult decisions. Because of all these reasons, I am happy that you keep alive the memory of this remarkable monk who was a model and source of strength for all who sought the truth of our faith in God. He was a person who truly sanctified his place through his blessed presence.

Thank you!

(These words were read on July 6, 2024, at the last memorial service organized at Father Sofian's grave at Caldarusani Monastery before his canonization on July 11-12, 2024.)

"The person who feels the need to paint icons
must strive to become an icon himself!"
(Father Sofian)

Jesus Christ Pantocrator
The dome of the Dealu Monastery - painted in 1989 by Father Sofian Boghiu

Church Nave, South

Holy Archangels Michael and Gabriel- Holy Altar
Saint George Church in Deir El Har, Mount of Lebanon

Church of Hama, Syria

The Baptism of the Lord- Nave
St. George Church, Mount of Lebanon

The Ascension of the Lord - Nave

Holy Hierarchs - Holy Altar
Radu-Voda Monastery, Bucharest

Holy Hierarch Nicholas Calming the Storm - Dealu Monastery

St. Antim Ivireanul - Icon painted by Fr. Sofian Boghiu for the canonization of St. Antim Ivireanul (St. Anthimos the Iberian) in 1992

Antim Monastery, 1992
The day of proclamation of the canonization of St. Antim Ivireanul

Photo of Fr. Sofian on a train pass

21 Iunie 1977
În fața bisericii Radu-Vodă – Buc.
cu Păr. Director al Seminarului Pr. Ion Larm
și un grup de elevi seminariști
Arhim. Sofian

August 1986
Funeral Procession for His Beatitude Justin, Patriarch of Romania

"Standing in the Temple of Thy Glory, We Think Ourselves to Stand in Heaven, O Theotokos!"

Serving next to His Eminence Teofan Sinaitul, Bishop Vicar of the Romanian Patriarchate, currently the Metropolitan of Moldavia and Bukovina

“Rejoice always, pray without ceasing!” (1 Thessalonians 5:16-17)

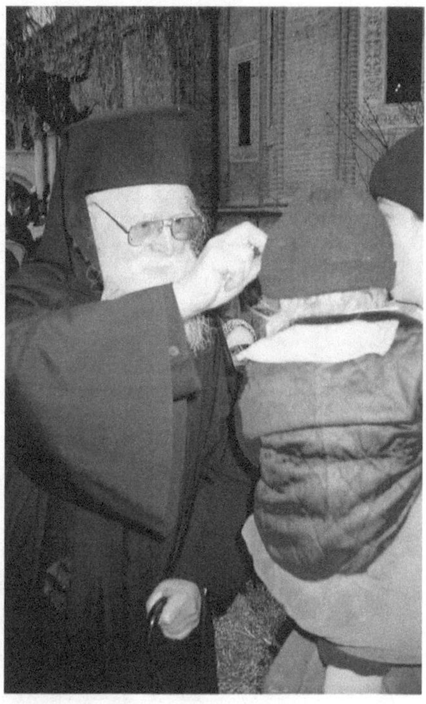

In the courtyard of Antim Monastery

In the old monastic cell

In the garden of Antim Monastery

In Bethlehem

Visiting the Holy Mountain

By Prodromu Skete, in the Garden of the Theotokos (Mt. Athos)
In the first row, from left to right: Fr. Petroniu Tanase, Fr. Sofian Boghiu, Fr. Grigorie Babus, Bp. Epifanie Norocel

With Elder Cleopa at Sihastria Monastery, 1998

Reading the prayers to the Holy Spirit on Pentecost, together with Fr. Roman Braga, at the Dormition of the Theotokos Monastery, Rives Junction, Michigan, USA

In the United States, with one of Fr. Sofian's best friends: Fr. Roman Braga

Damascus, Syria, 1992. In the house of painter George Jannoura, with Archim. Qais (Sadiq), currently Bishop of Erzurum

In Syria, together with Met. Athanasios Skaf of Hama

On Oct. 7th 1996, on Fr. Sofian's birthday, representatives of ASCOR wished him Many Blessed Years

Bright Week, 1997. A group of young people from ASCOR sang Pascal Carols to Fr. Sofian and Fr. Adrian at Antim Monastery

Speaking to young people on prayer, at a conference organized by ASCOR Bucharest on Nov. 14th, 1996

"Assuredly, I say to you, unless you are converted and become as little children, you will by no means enter the kingdom of heaven." (Matthew 18:3)

"Sacrificial love is the only kind that is not extinguished after death."
(Fr. Sofian)

"Y oung people who want to become someone and have a luminous life must preserve the purity of their bodies." (Fr. Sofian)

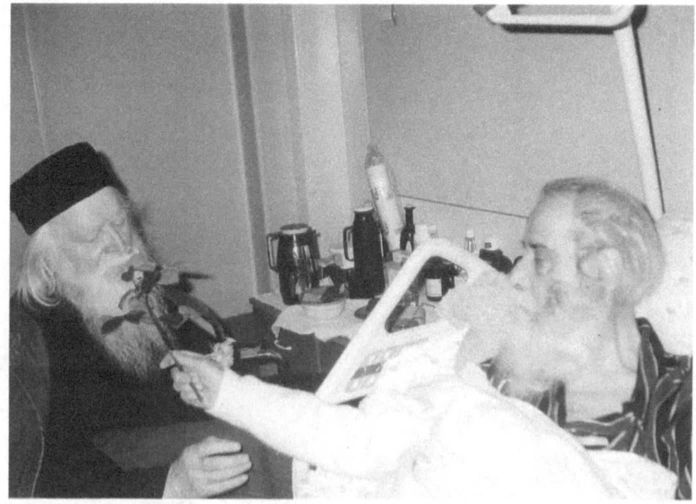

"I remember dearly to this day when Fr. Sofian met Fr. Galeriu in the hospital. There was so much light in Fr. Sofian's soul. There was so much kindness in his words and deeds that you felt it flooded and enveloped you."
(Fr. Nicolae Bordasiu)

"I have seen all the works that are done under the sun; and indeed, all is vanity and grasping for the wind." (Ecclesiastes 1:14)

"My life is in Thy hands, Lord! I am Thine, save me!"

Christ is Risen!

Rugăciune către Sf. Ioan Botezătorul (1)

Sfinte Ioane Botezătorule şi Înainte-Mergătorule, roagă-te Prea Sfintei Treimi pentru toate popoarele pământului. Roagă-te înaintea Mântuitorului nostru Iisus Hristos, pentru toţi cei cred în El şi aşteaptă cu nădejde mila Lui. Roagă-te lui Dumnezeu, cu îndrăzneala ta de proroc, de mucenic, de apostol, de botezător şi înainte-mergător, pentru Biserica şi neamul nostru românesc, să fie izbăviţi de tot răul şi primejdia.

Roagă-te lui Hristos, Sfinte Ioane Botezătorule, pentru păstori şi turmă, pentru conducători şi supuşi, pentru preoţi şi călugări; pentru tineri şi bătrâni, pentru sănătoşi şi bolnavi, pentru săraci şi îndestulaţi, pentru cei curajoşi, ca şi pentru cei fricoşi, pentru cei curaţi ca şi pentru cei desfrânaţi; pentru cei ce

The handwritten notes of St. Sofian for the chapter Prayer to St. John the Baptist.

(2)

postesc, ca și pentru cei ce nu postesc;
pentru cei ce se roagă, ca și pentru cei ce nu
se roagă; pentru cei buni, ca și pentru cei
răi; Ca pe unii după dreptate să-i
mântuiască, iar pe alții să-i miluiască.

Roagă-te lui Dumnezeu pentru părinții
care nu au copii și pentru copiii fără părinți,
pentru mamele doritoare de copii, și pentru cele
care își urăsc copiii; pentru cele care nu
știu să-și crească copiii în frica de
Dumnezeu și pentru cele care își blestemă
copiii; pentru părinții care își smintesc
copiii ~~pentru~~ prin viața lor urâtă, și pentru
mamele care-și ucid copiii.

Roagă-te Sfinte Ioane Botezătorule
și pentru văduve și pentru orfani —
roagă-te sfinte și pentru sufletele
noastre..

(3)

Sfinte Ioane, roagă-te Mântuitorul nostru să ierte nedreptățile noastre, să mângâie inimile noastre, să sporească credința, nădejdea și dragostea noastră, să înmulțească curajul nostru, să alunge frica de la noi și să pună în sufletele noastre mai multă lumină, dragoste, înțelepciune, lumină de viață sfântă, dor de Dumnezeu, milă față de oameni și grijă pentru mântuire!

Învață-ne sfinte, a ierta mai mult, a ne ruga mai mult, a posti și a răbda, a ne smeri mai mult și a mărturisi pe Hristos, din toată inima, toată viața noastră.

Sfinte Ioane Botezătorule, ajută-ne cu rugăciunile tale cele bune primite de prea bunul Dumnezeu — Amin.

din anii 1927-1940
Amintiri despre I.P.S. Mitropolit Visarion Puiu
când era episcop la Bălți - Basarabia, având în episcopie 3 județe:
Hotin, Bălți și Soroca - de Pr. Serghie - Sofian Boghiu

L-am cunoscut prima dată în viața mea pe Prea Sfințitul Visarion Puiu, în primăvara anului 1927, ca episcop la Bălți - Basarabia.
Aveam atunci 15 ani. Acum am 85 de ani. Cei 70 de ani care mă despart de Prea Sfinția Sa, n-au întunecat și n-au șters nimic din portretul său riguros și amabil de atunci. Avea pe atunci vârsta de aproape 50 de ani.
Înalt, sprinten, energic, privire pătrunzătoare, părul și barba rase, voce clară și autoritară. Pe cât era de sever și de autoritar, pe atât era de prietenos, bun, milos, înțelegător, apropiat de cei săraci și umili și necruțător cu cei mândri, desfrânați și necinstiți. La sărbătorile mari, găsea o zi în care lua masa cu cei umili din preajma lui: vizitiul, șoferul, bucătăreasa, administratorul de la gospodărie, cei doi ucenici din casa arhierească. Când mai trăia mama sa, și ea era la aceeași masă de familie. Dormea puțin. Mânca puțin. Seara nu mânca nimic. Îi plăcea însă să întrețină plăcut pe cei invitați la masă. Aproape totdeauna avea invitați la masă, mai ales persoane de care avea nevoie în diverse probleme episcopale.
Era un om sincer, deschis, nu-i plăceau compromisurile și nici vicleșugurile.
Era un om activ, înzestrat cu un admirabil dar gospodăresc.

Umbla prin eparhie, în vizite canonice, îndemnând preoții să-și întrețină frumos bisericile și cimitirele, să restaureze biserici bătrâne sau să facă altele noi.
La centrul episcopal din orașul Bălți, a construit o mare catedrală aproape de centrul orașului, care între timp a fost pictată. În marginea orașului Bălți a cumpărat un teren, l-a înconjurat cu gard, a sădit vie și livadă, a construit un palat - Palatul Episcopal, conceput cu etaj, dar n-a realizat decât parterul, întrucât a fost invitat ca mitropolit la Cernăuți. În curtea palatului a construit o biserică, având hramul Sfintei Paraschiva, după modelul bisericii meșterului Manole de la Curtea de Argeș.
Plecând de la episcopia din Bălți, ca mitropolit la Cernăuți, n-am mai putut urmări activitatea sa de acolo.
În timpul războiului II-lea mondial, fiind delegat ca șef al misiunii creștine în Transnistria, a avut și acolo o activitate foarte bogată.
După întoarcerea din Transnistria, a plecat în străinătate, în Franța, unde deasemenea nu-i cunosc activitatea și unde și-a încheiat zbuciumata sa viață, - totuși creatoare, în vârsta de 85 ani.
Doamne, odihnește cu drepții, pe adormitul robul Tău, Visarion Mitropolitul.

The handwritten notes of St. Sofian for the chapter
The Spiritual Portrait of a Vladika.

gând statornice învățătura cea dreaptă că icoanele
nu sunt idoli ci semne vii de bine cuvântare dumnezeiască
în viață și în casa noastră de creștini.

www.ingramcontent.com/pod-product-compliance
Lightning Source LLC
LaVergne TN
LVHW091120080826
845145LV00008B/1987

* 9 7 8 1 9 6 0 6 1 3 1 5 8 *